THE ILLUSTRATED ENCYCLOPEDIA OF

PREDATORS

THE ILLUSTRATED ENCYCLOPEDIA OF
PREDATORS

ANDROMEDA

THE ILLUSTRATED ENCYCLOPEDIA
OF PREDATORS

Consultant Editor: Andrew Branson
Managing Editor: Lionel Bender
Art Editor: Ben White
Designers: Malcolm Smythe, Ben White
Text Editors: Miles Litvinoff, Madeleine
    Samuel, Barbara Taylor-Cork
Production: Clive Sparling

Media conversion and typesetting:
Robert and Peter MacDonald,
    Una Macnamara

Planned and produced by:
Andromeda Oxford Ltd
11–15 The Vineyard, Abingdon,
Oxfordshire OX14 3PX

Copyright © Andromeda Oxford Ltd 1993

Copyright © Priscilla Barrett 1984

ISBN 1 871869 15 3

Published in Great Britain by
Andromeda Oxford Ltd
This edition specially produced for
Selectabook Ltd

Origination by Alpha Reprographics Ltd,
England

Printed in Hong Kong by Dai Nippon Ltd

Authors:
Jill Bailey
Martyn Bramwell
Robin Kerrod
Christopher O'Toole
John Stidworthy

CONTENTS

INTRODUCTION

The Illustrated Encyclopedia of Predators provides an ideal introduction to animals that hunt in order to survive. Many of these animals may seem to be fierce and frightening. But some, for example the dolphins, seem remarkably gentle and affectionate towards people and even use a system of communication that parallels our own speech. This encyclopedia contains examples from the main groups of animals: simple animals, insects and spiders, fish, reptiles, birds and mammals.

It is often forgotten that animals such as Sea anemones and Corals are predators. Such animals are referred to as "simple animals" in this encyclopedia because their basic body plan and organization are often not as intricate or highly developed as those of other animals. Simple animals are all animals without backbones (invertebrates) that live in the sea, fresh water or moist land habitats. The Illustrated Encyclopedia of Predators explains how simple animals are able to attract and then capture their prey without needing to move.

The encyclopedia also includes entries on insects and spiders. The most important characteristic of all these animals is that they have an external skeleton (exoskeleton), or cuticle. This has enabled them to live in almost every habitat. They are also all jointed-limbed creatures without backbones (invertebrates). Some of these, such as the scorpion, are known to us as predators. Others seem almost defenceless, but the dragonfly, for example, can fly to speeds of 22kph and is capable of capturing a frog.

Perhaps best-known among birds that hunt are the so-called birds of prey, or raptors (from the Latin meaning plunderers). The encyclopedia explains how some of these birds, such as falcons, buzzards and eagles, capture their prey. Each of these birds share the same specialization for finding food and for holding and tearing apart the bodies of other animals: acute vision, strong legs and feet mostly equipped with sharp curved claws, and a hooked beak.

While birds of prey eat fish, mammals, reptiles and other large prey – either dead or alive – many aerial hunters feed mainly on insects. These include the nightjar and hoopoe. During the day, the nightjar rests on the forest floor, or perched on branches, or among the stones and dry scrub of a savannah or desert region. It begins to hunt during the night, and remains in flight all the time it is hunting. It is capable of swallowing a cloud of mosquitoes or a huge tropical moth in one go. Some of the larger species will snap up a small night-flying bird if the chance comes along.

The Illustrated Encyclopedia of Predators also includes entries on fish. Fish are found in almost every watery habitat, from lakes in mud and underground to the oceans. In this encyclopedia, the reader can discover the different ways in which fish can hunt their prey. For the predatory fish, meals are a rare occurrence, but they have ways of making the most of any opportunity. Many have large eyes adapted for seeing in dim light. Some have huge gaping jaws that can seize prey as large as themselves. Others rely on luring their prey to them. Since attractive colours are of little use in semi-darkness, the fish use luminous (glowing) lures instead. The encyclopedia explains how viperfish have mouths armed with long sharp teeth: the front teeth stab the victim, teeth in the throat help to grip it and push it gradually down the throat to the stomach.

Scientists call meat-eating animals "carnivores". Most carnivorous mammals that live on land belong to a group called the Carnivora, which includes cats, dogs, bears, weasels and hyenas. Carnivores that hunt in the sea fall into two groups. First, the seals, sea lions and walrus, which spend much of their time at sea catching fish and other animals. These are called the Pinnipedia. The second group is the so-called Toothed whales (dolphins, porpoises, Sperm whales), which hunt fish and other large prey. The lifestyles of most of these species are explained in the encyclopedia.

Many species of animal are threatened with extinction as a result of human activities. In this encyclopedia the following terms are used to show the status of a species as defined by the International Union for the Conservation of Nature and Natural Resources:

Endangered – in danger of extinction unless their habitat is destroyed and they are not hunted by people.

Vulnerable – likely to become endangered in the near future.

Rare – exist in small numbers but neither endangered nor vulnerable at present.

Each article in this encyclopedia is devoted to an individual species or group of closely related species. The text starts with a short scene-setting story that highlights one or more of the animal's unique features. It then continues with details of the most interesting aspects of the animal's physical features and abilities, diet and feeding behaviour, and general life-style. It also covers conservation and the animal's relationships with people.

Fact Panel

The "Fact Panel" (opposite) consists of the various symbols that appear throughout the book. These symbols summarize key characteristics of a species or a group of species. A black circle, for example, indicates an animal or group of animals that is active primarily at night, such as foxes, whereas a red circle indicates an animal or group of animals that is active during the day, hawks for example. Other symbols describe such characteristics as "Group size", "Conservation status", "Habitat", "Diet" and "Breeding". Range maps indicate where the particular animals dwell.

Some of the symbols used are relevant only to a particular species. "Mouthparts", for example, refers only to those entries on insects and spiders. Here, you can discover whether insects bite their prey or suck blood from them. A comparison of the similarities between young and adults is made only for simple animals.

These symbols and maps give readers an immediate grasp of the key elements of an animal's behaviour and its chances of surviving in today's world. One can tell at a glance whether to expect a particular species to appear in a swamp or on a mountain top, in a forest or in an open field, in daylight or in darkness, alone or in thousands. The "Fact Panel" symbols are a form of naturalist shorthand. The symbols are a way of organizing animals by their habitats and, in terms of their relationship to the world's environment, by their probable fate.

Fact Box

Each entry contains a "Fact Box" which uses the symbols that appear in the "Fact Panel" in the front of the book. The symbols denoting habitat, activity time and diet, for example, appear in the "Fact Box" which also includes a range map.

The "Fact Box" also includes a list of the common and scientific (Latin) names of species mentioned in the main text and photo captions. For species illustrated in major artwork panels but not described elsewhere, the names are given in the caption accompanying the artwork. In such illustrations, animals are shown to scale unless otherwise stated; actual dimensions may be found in the text.

Comparison Silhouettes

In addition to the descriptive symbols in the "Fact Panel", in many cases the encyclopedia suggests the relative size of animals by comparing them to an average-size human being, or a part thereof. It is difficult to imagine how big an eagle is, or a leopard, or a sperm whale. But when you look at a picture of a frog sitting next to a human foot, you can tell immediately how big it is. Comparison silhouettes appear in the upper right hand corner of many pages in this encyclopedia.

FACT PANEL: Key to symbols denoting general features of animals

SYMBOLS WITH NO WORDS

Activity time

● Nocturnal

◓ Daytime

◒ Dawn/Dusk

○ All the time

Group size

◪ Solitary

▦ Pairs

◨ Small groups (up to 10)

■ Herds/Flocks

◸ Variable

Adults (insects)

Ⓦ Winged

Ⓦ Wingless

Metamorphosis (insects)

◫ Incomplete (young like adults)

◫ Complete (young unlike adults)

Mouthparts (insects)

⬜ Biting

⬜ Piercing and Sucking

⬜ Sucking

⬜ Biting and Sucking

Young/adult comparison (simple animals)

◻ Young like adults

◻ Young unlike adults

◹ Likeness of young to adults varies with species

Conservation status

☠ All species threatened

☠ Some species threatened

No species threatened (no symbol)

SYMBOLS NEXT TO HEADINGS

Habitat

◤ General

◢ Mountain/Moorland

◿ Desert

〜 Sea

■ Amphibious

◢ Tundra

◣ Forest/Woodland

● Grassland

≋ Freshwater

⌄ Fresh and/or Sea water

◉ Parasitic

Diet

■ Other animals

■ Plants

◪ Animals and Plants

Breeding

◯ Seasonal (at fixed times)

◯ Non-seasonal (at any time)

Relationship with man (insects)

☒ Harmful

☑ Beneficial

☒ Disease vectors

☒ Crop disease vectors

⊗ Crop pests

SEA ANEMONES, JELLYFISH

It is a sunny day in summer and the sea is deep blue. Children paddling watch a dinner-plate sized transparent jellyfish as it slowly pulsates near the surface. Once their eyes have become used to looking in the water, they notice that there is not one, but a whole swarm of, Common jellyfish. In each circular body, four horseshoe-shaped purple blobs mark the animal's reproductive organs.

The jellyfish is basically a bell-shaped animal with a mouth in the middle underneath. The fringe of the bell carries stinging tentacles. The mouth opens into a space inside the body where food is digested. The body has two skin-like layers of cells with jelly in between.

A sea anemone is built to a similar plan, but is upside down compared to a jellyfish. It spends most of its time anchored to the seabed, and is tubular rather than bell-shaped. Again, it has a mouth surrounded by stinging tentacles, leading into the hollow body. The sea anemone type of body is known as a polyp.

SEA ANEMONES, JELLYFISH Phylum Cnidaria
(about 5,400 species)

Habitat: seas, free-swimming or bottom-dwelling, from tidal zone to ocean depths; small number of freshwater species.

Diet: capture other animals up to size of fish; some filter particles of food from the water.

Breeding: very varied, but both sexual and asexual. Some species alternate between two forms in their life history – free swimming sexual jellyfish (medusa) and sedentary asexual polyp.

Distribution: worldwide.

Size: from about 1mm to 3m across, with tentacles up to 20m long.

Colour: very varied, from transparent to dull to brilliant.

Species mentioned in text:
Beadlet anemone (*Actinia equina*)
Blue cyanea jellyfish (*Cyanea lamarcki*)
Common jellyfish (*Aurelia aurita*)
Compass jellyfish (*Chrysaora hyoscella*)
Hydra (e.g. *Hydra viridissima*)
Portuguese man-o'-war (*Physalia physalis*)

Most of the animals of the jellyfish and anemone group (Cnidaria) live in the sea, but a few species are found in fresh water, including the small anemone-like *Hydra*, which is very common in canals, ponds and lakes.

SIMPLE, BUT COMPLICATED
Although the cnidarian body plan is a simple one, there are many variations in the animals' shapes, and also in their life histories. Some kinds have a

jellyfish stage which reproduces sexually, giving a larva that settles on the seabed to become a polyp. The polyp reproduces asexually, dividing to form little jellyfish. These break off and swim away to an independent life, and start the cycle again.

In large species of jellyfish, the polyp stage lasts only a short while. In sea anemones, the jellyfish stage has disappeared. They can reproduce sexually, or by budding.

LIVING TOGETHER
Many polyps live together in colonies. Their mouths and tentacles are separate, but their bodies are joined by strips of tissue at the base. Colonies may be tiny, like those of some of the sea firs to be found on the shore. Or they can be very large, especially in those cnidarians known as corals (see pages 14-17).

Confusingly, some of the animals that at first sight seem to be jellyfish turn out, when examined closely, to

◄Sea anemones rest attached to the seabed waiting for food. They are often well camouflaged against being found by large prey.

▲ Green, as here, red or strawberry coloured, the Beadlet anemone, 7cm tall, is common on European coasts.

▼ The Compass jellyfish can have a bell 30cm across. It has 24 stinging tentacles, and 4 long mouth "arms".

be colonies of polyps. An example is the Portuguese man-o'-war. It has an air-filled jelly float on the surface which allows it to be carried by the wind. Below this are many polyps. Some are tentacle-like and sting for food and defence. Others act as mouths for the colony. Several polyps are specialized for reproduction.

STINGS

A special characteristic of animals of the jellyfish and sea anemone group are the arrays of stinging cells on their tentacles. Inside each cell is a barbed thread coiled up. When prey or an enemy touches the tentacle, it triggers the cells to fire out their threads. This punctures and holds the prey, and injects venom.

Other cells on the tentacles shoot out threads which entangle prey. A person touching the tentacles of small anemones on the shore can feel these threads grip. Some species of jellyfish and anemone can capture and paralyse large fish. Many species, though, feed on small particles of food in the water, which they capture on sticky mucus on the tentacles.

SWIMMING AND DRIFTING

Many jellyfish are active swimmers. Repeatedly, they relax muscles in the bell, then contract them, shooting out bursts of water for a kind of jet propulsion. But often the jellyfish is not strong enough to swim against the currents in the ocean's surface, and gets carried along by them.

To help keep their muscles moving together, jellyfish have a ring of nerves around the bell. They also have simple sense organs. The Common jellyfish has eight notches round its rim. In each is a pigment spot which is sensitive to light. There is also a small hard pellet in a special body cavity. As the bell tips, the pellet presses against the top or bottom of the cavity. Using this information the jellyfish can keep on an even keel.

Most jellyfish are only a few centimetres across, but some can grow very large. The Blue cyanea is generally about 20cm in diameter, but individuals have been seen more than 3m across, trailing tentacles many metres long. A large Portuguese man-o'-war may have tentacles 18m long trailing behind. Although they are simple animals such giants are among the biggest of the animals without backbones (invertebrates). Also, the stings of both these species can be dangerous to humans.

STANDING AND WAITING

Sea anemones are usually fixed to the seabed and play a waiting game. They wait for small animals to blunder into their tentacles or to be carried there by water currents. Then they trap them and the tentacles fold over to push the victims into the mouth.

Many kinds of anemone live on the shore. If they are uncovered by the tide, they fold in their tentacles and become rounded blobs. Once covered by water again, they emerge, spreading their tentacles wide to give the maximum chance of catching food. Other kinds live deeper in the sea, stretching wide to catch food falling from above. Some burrowing anemones live in sand with only the tentacles around the mouth exposed.

NEIGHBOURLY FIGHTS

Although sea anemones usually stay in one place, some of them can move about slowly. They may glide on their bases. Some even move by somersaulting. Beadlet anemones have even been seen to fight one another, one bending over slowly – this may take 10 minutes – to give a sting to the other. Usually the biggest wins. Such fights may help clear a good feeding space for an anemone.

◄▼Mediterranean and North Atlantic sea anemones and jellyfish The 20cm-across *Cyanea lamarcki* (**1**) has a powerful sting. Common jellyfish (**2**), up to 25cm across. Portuguese man-o'-war (**3**), extends to 30cm long. Beadlet anemone (**4**). Plumose anemone (*Metridium senile*) (**5**), to 8cm or more. *Obelia geniculata* (**6**), a colony, up to 4cm tall. *Sertularia operculata* (**7**), a colony, to 45cm high. *Eunicella verrucosa* (**8**), a sea fan, colony to 30cm high. *Peachia hastata* (**9**), a burrowing anemone 10cm long. Jewel anemone (*Corynactis viridis*) (**10**), about 0.5cm across. Dead man's fingers (*Alcyonium digitatum*) (**11**), colony height 20cm.

3

4

5

9

11

10

CORALS

From an orbiting space station, the astronauts look down at the Earth. As they pass over Australia they see a line running down the east coast where the sea is a different colour. They are looking at a structure 1,900km long, the biggest ever built by living creatures. It is the Great Barrier Reef, built by millions of coral polyps over millions of years.

Corals are colonies of sea anemone-like creatures (see pages 10-13), to which they are related. The polyps make skeletons of some kind and are given the name coral, but the type that build huge reefs are those known as stony corals. These are found only in areas of sea close to the shore in the tropics where the water is clear, as mud and silt can soon bury and kill corals. There are corals in cooler climates. For example, there are many solitary corals living off European coasts. But the greatest abundance and development of coral is in warm seas.

DEPENDENT ON LODGERS

Reef-building corals are dependent on single-celled algae that live inside them. The algae make food by using sunlight, so they must be near enough

to the surface for light to reach them. In especially clear water, this may be possible to depths of 75m. They also need a temperature of 21°C to do well. The algae help get the lime out of seawater that the corals use for their skeletons and provide some oxygen.

SKELETONS

The skeleton of a coral polyp is secreted by the animal's base. When a polyp separates (buds off) from its parent, the two organisms remain connected to one another by strips of

▲ Dead corals provide a support for other organisms. Here polyps grow on the dead skeleton of a coral colony.

▶ A coral reef in the Red Sea containing many different species. The reef is home to fish and other animals.

tissue that extend sideways. As new polyps secrete skeleton around their bases, so the lime builds up more and more. The living polyps may form a skin on an enormous block of coral which is full of holes, the little sockets marking where their ancestors lived.

Different species of coral bud and grow in different patterns. There are brain corals and staghorn corals, their names reflecting the shapes they grow into. Sometimes one area of reef will be made up of a single type of coral. More often corals of all shapes and sizes will be growing together.

DAY AND NIGHT

Some corals are active most of the time, but during the day on a coral reef it is often just the hard, rough coral skeletons that are readily visible. Their owners are withdrawn into their sockets. By night, the reef looks very different. The millions of tiny polyps

---

CORALS Class Anthozoa
(*about 4,000 species*))

 Habitat: seas, particularly warm shallow waters.

Diet: tiny animals, which are trapped using tentacles.

Breeding: mainly by budding; also reproduce sexually, producing a tiny larva which becomes a polyp.

Distribution: over much of the world; reef-building corals only in tropics.

Colour: very varied; many extremely colourful.

Species mentioned in text:
Black corals (e.g. *Antipathes subpinnata*)
Brain corals (e.g. *Diploria strigosa*)
Mushroom coral (genus *Fungia*)
Organ-pipe coral (genus *Tubipora*)
Precious red coral (*Corallium rubrum*)
Sea fans (*Gorgonia* species)
Sea whips (*Leptogorgia* species)
Staghorn corals (*Acropora* species)
Stony or hard corals (e.g. *Madrepora* species)

emerge to clothe the skeletons in soft bodies and waving tentacles, giving an altogether softer outline to the reef. Small planktonic animals come nearer to the sea's surface in the darkness to feed on planktonic plants. The polyps catch them with their tentacles, bring them to the mouth, then eat them.

OTHER FORMS AND LIFE-STYLES

The black corals are a group that do not build reefs. Instead they form slender plant-like colonies with a horny skeleton. The polyps surround this and cannot be retracted. The skeleton has many thorns.

The gorgonians, or horny corals, make branching colonies looking a little like trees. They are called sea fans and sea whips. Because their skeleton is horny they sway in the sea currents. Some of them are brilliantly coloured. Precious red coral, used in jewellery, belongs to this group. It has become rare in many places as a result of being collected by people in too great a number. This coral strengthens its body with lime particles. In the middle of the colony these fuse into a hard block. It is this which is cut out and shaped for ornament.

The Organ-pipe coral of tropical waters has yet another growth form, with the polyps in vertical tubes connected by evenly spaced horizontal cross-bars. The stony skeleton of the mushroom corals looks like the gills of a huge upturned mushroom.

▲ This coral has used its stinging cells to paralyse a worm. Between the main polyps are smaller budded polyps.

KINDS OF REEF

In 1842 the English biologist Charles Darwin noticed that there are three main ways in which reefs grow. Some form close to the shore on rocky coastlines. These are called fringing reefs. Others are separated from the shore by lagoons or channels. They are known as barrier reefs. They have formed as the seabed subsided.

The third sort of reef is the atoll, a circle of coral, with or without an island in the middle. An atoll forms where an undersea volcano pushes out from the water to form an island,

and then slowly sinks. A coral reef forms on its fringes, growing upwards to keep pace with the sinking land. In some places coral reefs have been growing upward at the rate of about 1cm a year for thousands of years.

EVERYTHING IN ITS PLACE

Different parts of a coral reef are home to different species. On the side of the reef exposed to wind and waves, the reef-building corals and seaweeds grow well. Lower down in the water, below 50m, these do not grow so well. There, conditions suit solitary corals and the waving sea fans.

The crests of reefs suit yet other species, such as the staghorn corals, which provide shelter for many small fish. Some corals grow happily over a range of depths, but others change their skeleton shape according to the conditions – lumpy if they live near the surface, delicately branched if they are at depth. In some shallow-water forms, the polyps are open most of the time, but the same species may open only at night in deeper water.

LARVAL SEARCH

Although most corals reproduce by budding, the polyps may sometimes reproduce sexually. The result is a tiny flattened swimming larva. This searches for a well-lit empty patch of reef on which to settle. Many never find a suitable site and die. Those that do, change into polyps. Only a few of these thrive, but those that succeed will split many times to produce the typical reef-building coral with its millions of polyps and huge skeleton.

▲ ▼ In some corals, such as the brain corals, a new polyp may not completely separate from its parent. This results in a group of joined polyps, separated from others by a ridge. Such a group can be seen above. The result is the ridged mound (brain-shaped) skeleton below.

LOBSTERS, CRAYFISH

A lobster pot sits on the seabed, with a bait of pieces of fish inside. From behind a rock the dark shape of a lobster moves towards the pot. But another larger one arrives. The two rivals for the food size up one another. The larger lobster moves towards the other with its huge pincers at the ready. After a brief struggle, the small lobster flees. The large lobster squeezes into the pot and feeds. However, when it tries to leave, it is trapped.

LOBSTERS, CRAYFISH Infraorders
Astacidea, Palinura (*more than 1,500 species*)

 Habitat: seas and fresh water, on the bottom.

 Diet: mainly meat, often obtained by scavenging, but also hunting prey.

Breeding: sexes separate; female keeps fertilized eggs under her abdomen. Some produce larvae, others young resembling parents.

Distribution: worldwide.

Size: length 10-60cm.

Colour: very varied; dull browns to bright reds, blues.

Species mentioned in text:
American lobster (*Homarus americanus*)
American spiny lobster (*Panulirus argus*)
European common lobster (*Homarus gammarus*)
European crayfish (*Astacus astacus*)
European spiny lobster (*Palinurus vulgaris*)
Red crayfish (*Astacus fluviatilis*)
Scampi (*Nephrops norvegicus*)

The lobster group includes some of the largest and longest-lived of the crustaceans. Some may live for 100 years or more if they escape the lobster fisherman. The American lobster can be 60cm long, and weigh 22kg.

There are two main types of lobster, typical and spiny. Typical lobsters, and crayfish, walk on just four of their five pairs of "walking legs". The front pair have been converted into large pincers, and the next two pairs of legs also have tiny pincers at the end. In the spiny lobsters, also known as rock lobsters and crawfish, there are no pincers. Often the body is very spiny, as the name suggests, and the spines can cause damage to human hands.

Lobsters have long, well-developed abdomens, but the "swimming legs" are too small to propel such large animals, and have other uses.

WEAPONS AND PROTECTION
A large typical lobster, such as the American lobster, can give a powerful nip with its large pincers. It uses them for fighting other lobsters, or for catching and tearing apart prey. The lobsters can catch fish, and break the shells of molluscs to get at the soft parts within. But much of the time, they do not hunt prey and instead feast on the remains of dead animals that fall to the bottom of the sea.

In fact, the pincers on each side are not identical in size and form, except in small lobsters, where they are both thin and toothed. As the lobster goes through successive moults, the pincer on one side becomes larger than the other. Its teeth grow rounded and it is used for crushing.

A lobster's skin is toughened by calcium salts, so it can be very hard and thick, giving good protection as well as acting as a skeleton for the animal. Like other crustaceans, a lobster has to shed its skin (moult) to grow, and even a large individual is in danger for a short time before the new skin hardens.

Lobsters chew their food well, using their pincers (if present), and the mouthparts around the mouth, to shred it. The food is then swallowed into the gizzard, which is a type of stomach with a tough lining where muscles help grind it more.

AN ARRAY OF SENSES
Lobsters have a pair of eyes, and two pairs of antennae. These are all prominent. Not quite so obvious are the thousands of tiny bristles over the body that work as sense organs. These detect chemicals and give a good sense of touch.

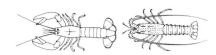

►The American spiny lobster takes part in spectacular mass migrations in the autumn. Lobsters follow one behind the other in chains which may be up to 60 individuals long, keeping in touch with their antennae. As many as 100,000 may travel together, by both day and night, and they may cover 15km in 24 hours.

▼ *Jasus novaehollandiae* is a rock lobster from southern Australia. Like others of this group it has no pincers, but has a very spiny shell.

► This crayfish, *Astacus pallipes*, hides under stones or in burrows in the river bank during the day. At night it emerges and feeds on snails, worms and grubs.

▼► The European spiny lobster (1) grows to 50cm long. It is found in rocky crevices and stony places down to a depth of 70m. *Scyllarides latus* (2) is a flattened lobster about 35cm long with short legs. It lives on rocks, stones and sand. A European lobster, *Homarus gammarus* (3), in an aggressive pose. It lives among rocks and in crevices.

1

Although a lobster's eyesight is reasonable, many species live in dark places and they tend to be most active at night. It is likely that their other senses are more important to them. In the bases of the first antennae are balancing organs that help the lobster determine whether it is level in the water, upside-down and so on.

A STICKY BEGINNING

When lobsters mate, the male places sperm on the female's body near where her eggs will emerge – at the bases of the third legs. As the eggs are laid, they are fertilized. They then stick to the swimming legs on the female's abdomen, and stay there until they hatch. Each larva that emerges swims and feeds in the plankton and goes through many stages of development before it settles on the seabed to start its adult life.

DIVERSE HABITATS

Lobsters live offshore along most of the world's coasts, and some inhabit deep ocean waters down to 4,000m.

There are also about 500 species found in fresh water, and these are known as crayfish. They are mostly around 10cm long. Because they need calcium for their shells, they are most common in water with a high lime content. The European crayfish and the Red crayfish introduced to North America are typical, living concealed during the day and hunting at night. Sometimes they sit in burrows with just their antennae and claws protruding, waiting to grab prey.

In most respects, crayfish are very similar to sea lobsters, but they differ slightly in their breeding. They mate in autumn, and the female carries the eggs stuck under her tail through the winter. In late spring they hatch, not as larvae, but as tiny fully formed crayfish. It may be several years before they mature.

WANDERING MASSES

Spiny, or rock lobsters, live up to both of their names. They hide in dens between rocks, coming out to hunt. An individual may use several dens, hundreds of metres apart, that are within the area where it wanders as

◀This delicate transparent floating larva (head pointing up) will turn into the spiny lobster shown opposite (1).

it hunts on the seabed. After a few weeks, the spiny lobster may move several kilometres to a new area.

Some spiny lobsters also migrate with the seasons. When the temperature drops in autumn, American spiny lobsters move south to a warmer area 50km or more away.

COLOUR CHANGE

Some species of lobster are naturally orange or red. These colours are often produced by pigments called carotenoids that are similar to those found in plants such as carrots. But many species of lobster, in life, are darker colours, such as the blue-black of the European lobster. Its colour is due to the combination of a carotenoid pigment with a protein. When the lobster is cooked for eating, it turns red because the protein part of the colour is broken down, leaving just the pure carotenoid showing.

LOBSTERS AS FOOD

People usually catch lobsters in traps, where they are drawn by a bait into a tunnel. This opens into a larger chamber from which they find it difficult to escape. The part of the lobster eaten is mainly the white meat of the large claw muscles and the other legs, and also the muscle of the abdomen.

The European common lobster and the American lobster are both caught in large numbers in cool waters. In warmer waters, many of the lobsters that are harvested commercially are spiny species. Freshwater crayfish are also good to eat, and are caught in several parts of the world. Scampi, which has become a popular seafood in recent years, is a kind of lobster. It is about 15cm long, and it burrows in bottom mud. It is collected by dragging nets along the seabed (trawling).

OCTOPUS, SQUID, CUTTLEFISH

A shape emerges from a crevice between two rocks. It flows across the seabed, changing the whole time, with sometimes a suckered arm reaching out in front. It is an octopus hunting. It has seen a crab. It moves stealthily towards it. As the octopus approaches its meal, it suddenly changes colour from a drab greenish-brown to dark red. It gathers itself in. Then the crab moves, and it pounces. It folds the crab in its arms and bites it with its beak.

Octopuses, together with cuttlefish, squids and their relations make up the group of animals called cephalopods ("head-feet"). They are molluscs, but look very different from the static clams or slow-moving snails. Cephalopods are active hunters. Some of them are among the fastest of all creatures in the sea over short distances. They also include the biggest of the invertebrates, and those with probably the most efficient sense organs and brains.

ARM AND SHELL VARIATIONS
The great majority of cephalopods are squids of various kinds. Most are highly active, torpedo-shaped and built for fast swimming. Many travel in shoals, and they move too quickly to be easily caught in nets. They have ten long arms.

Cuttlefish also have ten arms, but these are usually rather small and flattened. They often live close to, or buried in, the sea floor. They have an internal shell, the cuttlebone, which when they die washes up on to beaches and is used by bird-keepers to provide calcium for their pets. Many squids have an internal shell too, but it is often just a small horny stiffening bar.

Octopuses, as the name indicates, have eight legs. They usually stay near the seabed, and are the least active of cephalopods, hiding among rocks and catching slow-moving prey. They have no shell.

The pearly nautiluses are the only living cephalopods with a hard outer shell. They are the most ancient of cephalopods, and have existed for hundreds of millions of years.

ARMS ON ITS FOOT
In cephalopods, the muscular foot of other molluscs such as the snails has become a ring of tentacles, the arms, around the mouth. The arms have

►A prey's eye view of a Pacific octopus (*Octopus dofleini*) off the coast of Oregon. This animal is usually mottled brown or greyish-yellow, but when it is excited it flushes red.

OCTOPUS, SQUID, CUTTLEFISH Class
Cephalopoda (*650 species*)

 Habitat: sea, often near surface.

 Diet: fish, shellfish.

Breeding: internal fertilization; lay eggs; emerging young resemble parents.

Distribution: worldwide.

Size: length from about 5cm to 20m.

Colour: very varied; browns, reds, white. Some capable of much colour change.

Species mentioned in text:
Blue-ringed octopus (*Hapalochlaena maculosa*)
Common cuttlefish (*Sepia officinalis*)
Common octopus (*Octopus vulgaris*)
Common pearly nautilus (*Nautilus pompilius*)
Giant squid (*Architeuthis harveyi*)
Lesser octopus (*Eledone cirrhosa*)
Little cuttlefish (*Sepiola atlantica*)

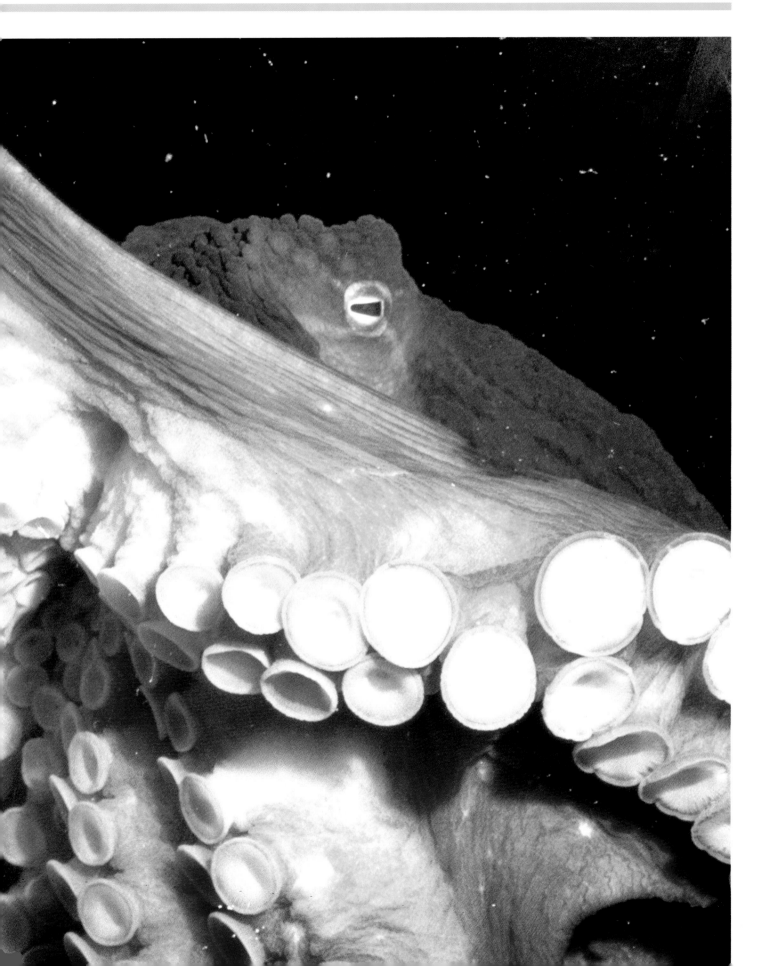

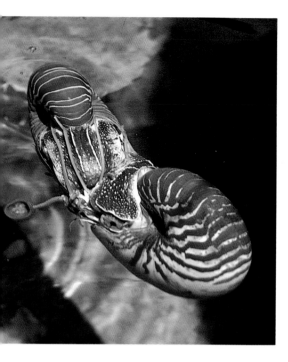

▲ The pearly nautiluses live in the tropical waters of the Indian and Pacific Oceans. Here a pair are mating.

▼ The Little cuttle grows to only 5cm long. It swims using a bird-like flapping of its short, wide, side fins. Sometimes it burrows in the sand.

suckers on them that can grasp prey. In some species of squid the suckers have sharp claws to help in the task. At the entrance to the mouth is a hard horny beak. This can bite into hard prey, for example crabs. Many cephalopods can inject poison as they bite, and kill prey such as crustaceans even quicker. The Blue-ringed octopus, a small tropical species, has a bite that can kill a person.

As well as the mouth, the head bears two large eyes. Like humans, cephalopods seem to be creatures that rely mainly on eyesight. They also have a very large (for an invertebrate) brain, which may have protecting gristle around it.

Behind the head is the body region, which contains the digestive system and reproductive organs. As in other molluscs, it is covered by a mantle. In the mantle cavity are large gills. The lower edge of the mantle cavity is drawn out into a funnel. This plays an important part in cephalopod life. When the mantle cavity walls relax, water is drawn in. When the walls contract, water can be ejected quickly through the funnel. This gives the useful option of jet propulsion when the animal needs to travel fast.

CATCHING A MEAL

Squid often rely on their speed to catch food, and can take fast-moving fish like mackerel. Two of the ten arms are specially developed for prey capture. They can be folded back to the head, then suddenly shot out to grasp food and bring it to the mouth.

Cuttlefish search for prey such as shrimps on the seabed, blowing water out of their funnels to uncover buried individuals. A cuttlefish may have to back off to get its prey-catching arms to the right distance to be shot out.

Octopuses have no special arms for capturing animals, and they "jump" on to their victims. The Common octopus can be a greedy feeder. In captivity it may eat 20 to 30 crabs a day.

AN ARRAY OF SENSES

The eyes of the primitive nautiluses are little more than poor pin-hole cameras, but an octopus's eyes are strikingly like ours in their build. Each has a lens and very sensitive retina. Tests show that an octopus is capable of seeing extremely well and can detect some types of light, such as polarized light, that we cannot. The pupil of an octopus's eye is slit-shaped, and the animal keeps the slit horizontal, no matter what angle its body is at.

Below each eye, near the entrance to the mantle cavity, is a pit containing a chemical sense organ that can sample the water which enters. Each cephalopod also has organs that can detect which way up the animal is in the water. Octopuses seem to have chemical sense cells over much of their surface, so can put out an arm to "taste" something. They also have a good sense of touch, and can distinguish between different textures and types of surface. They are good at picking up and manipulating objects.

▲▶ **Two species of cephalopod** The Common octopus (1) lives in the Mediterranean area and north to the English Channel. It grows to a maximum of 1m long overall, but is often smaller. The Common pearly nautilus (2) grows about 20cm long. Over 30 tentacles protrude from the protective shell when the nautilus is active.

CHANGEABLE COLOUR

A cephalopod's skin is thin and sensitive. It is also amazingly good at changing colour. An octopus can alter instantaneously from one colour to another, and colour patterns, even the texture of the skin, are changeable. Often the colours are good for camouflage, blending with the tones of the background. But they may also show mood. An octopus about to pounce flushes dark. One that is frightened becomes light coloured and flattens itself against rocks. Sometimes waves of colour may pass across the skin.

The Common cuttlefish, too, has a dazzling colour range. It can be sandy to match the sea bottom, almost colourless, or various shades and patterns, culminating in the zebra stripes of a courting male. Animals like these with good vision can use colour signalling with good effect.

Colour change is under the control of the brain. The colours exist in the skin in special pigment cells. Each cell has little muscles attached, so it may be spread wide or become just a pinhead. Pigment cells may have black, reddish, orange, yellow, silvery or other pigments, giving a huge range of possible colour combinations.

INVISIBLE WITH INK

Another visual trick can be played by these molluscs. Opening into the mantle cavity is a gland that produces a dark pigment. A quantity of this can be shot out in a little cloud when the animal is alarmed. The cloud is about the same size as the animal itself. As it ejects the pigment, the cuttlefish changes colour and shoots away by jet propulsion. An enemy is left looking at the puff of ink, as it is called, while the cuttlefish escapes unnoticed.

Most cephalopods are able to produce ink. In the case of the Common cuttle it quite literally is ink, for the dried glands of these animals used to be ground up and used as writing-ink.

MAKING LIGHT

Many ocean-dwelling squid can produce their own light. They have special light-producing organs, often in bands or patches along the body. Each species has its own patterns and colours. The little squid *Lycoteuthis* has a set of blue, white and red "lights". These probably allow the squids to recognize and signal to one another, and in some cases help camouflage them or lure prey.

FLYING SQUAD

Most of the squids that live near the surface have bodies just slightly denser than sea water. Their movement and the action of their fins keeps them up. They ripple the fins along the sides of the body and use jet propulsion for movement. A number of species can get up such a speed that they can shoot several metres out of the water to escape enemies. A few can "fly" above the surface for 45m.

Some cephalopods have special ways of making themselves buoyant. The Common pearly nautilus dives to 600m, but can rise or fall by changing the amount of gas in the chambers of its shell. Cuttlefish can perform a similar buoyancy trick with the gases in their spongy shell.

GIANTS

Generally, cephalopods are small. The majority of squids are less than 30cm in length. Most octopuses are about 1m long and are certainly not man-eaters, but there are some giants. One Pacific octopus can grow to 9m across with arms spread.

The real giant, though, is the Giant squid, which lives in the sea depths. This can grow to a total length of 20m to the end of its arms. Such monsters have suckers on the arms that are 30cm or more across. Little is known about their habits, but Sperm whales sometimes bear scars that were obviously made by the suckers and beak of Giant squids they tried to eat.

The most buoyant parts of a Giant squid are the arms. This monster of the deep may hang motionless in the water like an upside-down umbrella, waiting for prey.

MATING AT ARM'S LENGTH

In most cephalopods the male is larger than the female, but the reverse is true in all species of octopus. The male cephalopod develops its third arm as an organ for placing a packet of sperm into the female's mantle cavity.

Among octopuses, the two partners mate at arm's length. After this, the eggs are fertilized internally and then shed into the water.

Cephalopod eggs are relatively large and yolky. In the Common cuttlefish, the eggs are laid singly. In the Common squid, they are laid in strings, and all the females in a shoal may lay their eggs close to one another's.

In the Common octopus, up to 150,000 eggs are laid in bunches over a period of about a week, often under the roof of the female's lair. She stays guarding them, washing them with jets of water from her funnel, for some 6 weeks. The eggs hatch as minute octopuses, and the female soon dies. In many cephalopods, both adults die shortly after breeding.

◀ Here it is mating time for a group of squid (*Loligo* species) off the coast of California. A male transfers a packet of sperm with a special arm.

▶ The Lesser octopus grows 50cm long, and has a single row of suckers down each arm. Here an individual has caught a crab, one of its favourite foods.

DRAGONFLIES, DAMSELFLIES

Dragonflies hawk and dart up and down a slow-moving, weed-filled river. Their aerial acrobatics catch the eye, for these wingborne hunters are brightly coloured. Fluttering among the waterside weeds are their more delicate relatives, blue and red damselflies. They, too, hunt various insect prey on the wing.

The body plan of dragonflies and damselflies has remained virtually unchanged since the Carboniferous period, 345-280 million years ago. But no modern species can match some giants of the Carboniferous, which had wingspans of up to 75cm. Today, the largest species is one of the Giant damselflies of South America, with a wingspan of about 18cm.

Dragonflies and damselflies have long, thin bodies and large mobile heads with enormous eyes and very powerful jaws. There are two pairs of wings each with a complex network of veins.

Dragonflies are usually larger, faster and more powerful fliers than damselflies. When at rest, they hold their wings outspread, while damselflies fold their wings over their bodies.

HUNTING ON THE WING

Dragonflies and damselflies prey on other flying insects, especially small flies, but also bees and flying beetles. Everything about them is geared to hunting on the wing. They have good vision, with some species being able to detect the slightest movement from a distance of 18m. They can accelerate quickly in the air, and some have been recorded flying at 22kph. As well as rapid turns of speed, they can hover, fly backwards or even loop-the-loop.

The insects' hunched-up thorax contains the powerful flight muscles; the six spiny legs hang forward in a grasping fashion and act as a kind of aerial trawl for catching insects. Large dragonflies, like the Brown hawker, may grab small frogs from the ground, and damselflies often pluck up aphids and beetle larvae from plants.

WHEELS AND TANDEMS

In many species of dragonfly each male adopts and patrols a territory around a pond or along a river bank. The territory usually contains suitable egg-laying sites for the females. A territorial male defends his patch

▶A female Broad-bodied darter dragonfly rests on a waterside plant. Her wing veins are very prominent.

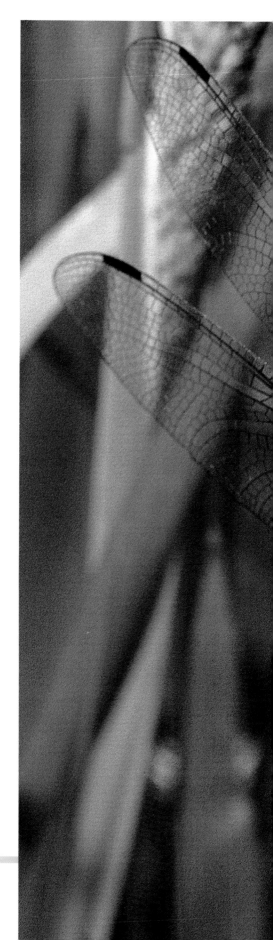

DRAGONFLIES, DAMSELFLIES
Order Odonata (*about 5,000 species*)

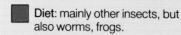 **Habitat:** larvae aquatic; adults aerial, usually near water, but often migrate some distance away.

Diet: mainly other insects, but also worms, frogs.

Relationship with people: beneficial – eat some plant pests.

Distribution: worldwide.

Size: length 1.8-15cm, wingspan 2.5-17.5cm.

Colour: drab browns to bright blue, green, yellow, red, often metallic.

Species mentioned in text:
Banded demoiselle (*Calopteryx splendens*)
Broad-bodied darter dragonfly (*Libellula depressa*)
Brown hawker dragonfly (*Aeshna grandis*)
Giant damselflies (*Megalopropus* species)

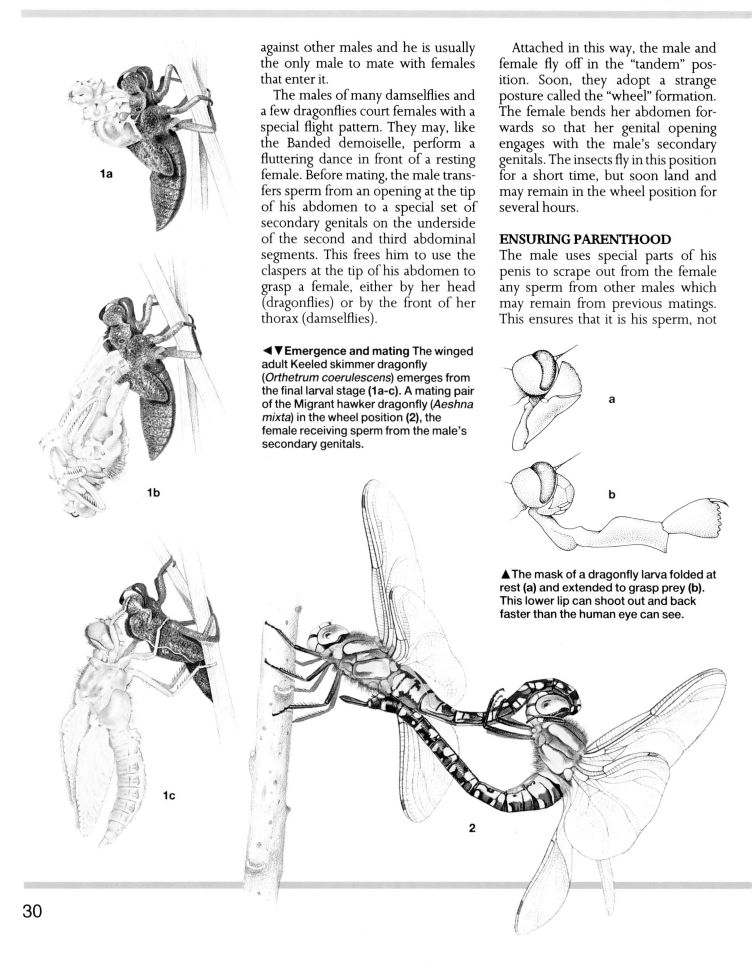

against other males and he is usually the only male to mate with females that enter it.

The males of many damselflies and a few dragonflies court females with a special flight pattern. They may, like the Banded demoiselle, perform a fluttering dance in front of a resting female. Before mating, the male transfers sperm from an opening at the tip of his abdomen to a special set of secondary genitals on the underside of the second and third abdominal segments. This frees him to use the claspers at the tip of his abdomen to grasp a female, either by her head (dragonflies) or by the front of her thorax (damselflies).

◀▼**Emergence and mating** The winged adult Keeled skimmer dragonfly (*Orthetrum coerulescens*) emerges from the final larval stage **(1a-c)**. A mating pair of the Migrant hawker dragonfly (*Aeshna mixta*) in the wheel position **(2)**, the female receiving sperm from the male's secondary genitals.

Attached in this way, the male and female fly off in the "tandem" position. Soon, they adopt a strange posture called the "wheel" formation. The female bends her abdomen forwards so that her genital opening engages with the male's secondary genitals. The insects fly in this position for a short time, but soon land and may remain in the wheel position for several hours.

ENSURING PARENTHOOD
The male uses special parts of his penis to scrape out from the female any sperm from other males which may remain from previous matings. This ensures that it is his sperm, not

▲The mask of a dragonfly larva folded at rest **(a)** and extended to grasp prey **(b)**. This lower lip can shoot out and back faster than the human eye can see.

those of a rival, which fertilize the eggs of his mate. The males of several species remain in tandem with their mates while they lay eggs.

UNDERWATER DRAGONS

The larvae of dragonflies and damselflies live and grow in and around water. Many are found in still ponds, others in fast-flowing streams, while a few live among the damp leaf litter of forests.

The larvae are drab, brownish-grey, mottled creatures. Their ugliness gives no hint of the adult beauty to come. They creep about on the muddy bottoms of ponds and rivers, or among water weeds.

Damselfly larvae are slender, and each has three leaf-shaped gills at the tip of the abdomen. These absorb oxygen from the water and allow waste carbon dioxide to pass out of the insects. The larvae swim with a side-to-side motion and the gills help by acting like paddles.

Dragonfly larvae have internal gills hidden in a chamber at the end of the gut. They breathe by sucking water into the chamber and then squirting it out. This enables the larvae to dart forward in a kind of jet propulsion and is a means of escape from such enemies as fish.

Larval dragonflies and damselflies prey on many small water creatures, including worms, snails, water fleas, other insect larvae, tadpoles and small fish. They catch prey using their lower lip, or labium, which is highly modified and hinged, forming a structure called the mask. Two hooks at the end of the mask spear the victim and bring it within reach of the jaws.

When fully grown, the larvae climb up the stem of a water plant into the air and shed their skin for the final time to reveal the adult dragonfly or damselfly. The final body colours may take several days to develop. Meanwhile, the young adult feeds and improves its flying skills.

▲Egg-laying and hatching Without the help of her mate, a female Golden-ringed dragonfly (*Cordulegaster boltonii*) (1) uses her ovipositor specially modified for laying eggs in gravelly streams. A male Azure damselfly (*Coenagrion puella*) (2) helping a female to lay her eggs. On her own, this female Southern hawker dragonfly (*Aeshna cyanea*) (3) lays an egg in a water-logged stump. An adult Azure damselfly (4) hatches.

MANTIDS

In East Africa, a hoverfly lands on a flower in search of sweet nectar. The unsuspecting fly fails to notice that part of the flower is in fact a mantid. It pays with its life, for suddenly, the "flower" erupts, and the fly is trapped in the vice-like grip of two spiny legs. Once again, the mantid's resemblance to a flower has paid off.

MANTIDS Order Mantodea
(*about 1,800 species*)

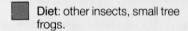

■ **Habitat:** mainly trees and shrubs in warmer countries, especially the tropics. A few ground-dwellers.

■ **Diet:** other insects, small tree frogs.

☑ **Relationship with people:** on balance beneficial, for they kill some pest insects.

Distribution: found in all the warmer parts of the world.

Size: length 1-15cm.

Colour: mostly drab green, grey or brown, resembling plant background; a few brightly coloured flower mimics.

Species mentioned in text:
African flower mantid
  (*Pseudocreobotra ocellata*)
Common European mantid (*Mantis religiosa*)
Crinkled leaf mantid (*Acanthops falcata*)
Grass mantids (*Polyspilota* species)
Mottled-green mantids (*Acontista* species)
Smaller leaf mantids (*Tithrone* species)
Stone-mimicking mantids
  (*Eremiaphila* species)

Mantids are insect masters of the ambush attack. Their front legs are an armoury of spines and hooks and they act like a hinged (gin) trap. They grab any insect that wanders within their reach, and bring the prey to their powerful toothed jaws.

IN PRAYING POSITION

Lightning attack requires excellent eyesight, and mantids have large eyes set on the top of a triangular-shaped head. The eyes are sensitive to the slightest movement and the head is very mobile and swivels freely as the mantid's gaze follows a moving insect.

When a mantid waits for prey, it usually sits with its front legs raised, as if in prayer. This gave rise to the the popular name of Praying mantis for the Common mantid, which is found in Europe and North Africa.

A LIFE OF STEALTH

Most mantid species live on trees and shrubs, while a number are found on the ground. Success as an ambush predator depends on not being seen by potential prey, and the mantids have many disguises.

The African flower mantid is pink, with fleshy outgrowths to the body that resemble the petals of flowers on which it sits. Several species are green and resemble a leaf in shape. The Crinkled leaf mantid of South America looks almost exactly like a crinkled leaf. It swings gently from side to side, as though blown by a gentle breeze.

While these disguises enable mantids to excel as surprise-attack hunters, they also protect mantids from falling prey themselves to lizards, birds and insect-eating mammals. If threatened, some species strike out with their spined forelegs to inflict a painful jab.

▼A stone-mimicking mantid takes advantage of its remarkable resemblance to a stone and seeks prey in the stony desert of the Arava Valley, southern Israel.

▲ Poised for attack, a mottled-green mantid awaits prey on a flower in Trinidad. With the grasp of its front legs it can entrap an unwary insect in an instant.

▼ A female grass mantid eats the head of a male while he continues to mate with her. A second male sits on her back while she continues her grisly meal.

DEADLIER THAN THE MALE

Most people believe that a female mantid always eats her mate during copulation. But this is only partly true. In the smaller leaf mantids of South America, for example, cannibalism of this sort is never seen. In other species, it occurs in some instances.

Scientists now think that if a male mantid courts a female correctly, he is safe. If his courtship ritual is defective in some way, the female mistakes him for a prey species and eats him. By only mating with males that have courted her in the proper manner, and eating those which do not, a female mantid may ensure that her sons inherit the correct courtship behaviour and therefore live to father many offspring of their own.

The males of many mantid species avoid being eaten by approaching the female carefully from behind and then leaping on to her back, out of reach of her front legs. Being smaller than the female, he is harder to grab in this position.

Female mantids lay between 10 and 400 eggs in a frothy mass called an ootheca, which soon hardens and dries in the air. It is usually attached to a stem, tree trunk or rock. Despite the protection of the ootheca, many mantid eggs are destroyed by the larvae of parasitic wasps.

WASPS

Black and yellow wasps are unwelcome visitors to a garden picnic. They are after sugary foods like jam. Nearby other members of the insect raiding party are at work. Some are stripping wood fibres from an old fence post, while others are preying on flies.

These wasps are the "yellow-jackets" familiar to everyone. They are social insects and live in colonies. But the majority of wasps have solitary lifestyles. Most of these species have larvae that all develop as parasites of other insects. The females of some solitary wasps are nest-builders and hunt insect prey as the sole source of food for their larvae.

SAWFLIES AND WOOD WASPS

The most primitive wasps are the sawflies, so called because the females have an egg-laying tube, or ovipositor, which has serrated blades like a saw. The female uses this to insert eggs into the tissues of plants.

The larvae of most sawflies resemble caterpillars and have a similar way of life to theirs, eating leaves and stems. Many are specialists on one, or a group of closely related, host plants. Some larvae are pests, such as those of the European pine sawfly, which can seriously damage young trees by stripping them of their needles.

Allied to the sawflies are the horntails and wood wasps. Larvae of the Giant wood wasp bore through and eat the solid timber of spruce trunks. They transmit a fungus disease which may eventually kill the trees.

WINGS AND WAISTLINE

All wasps have two pairs of wings. In sawflies and wood wasps, these have a complex network of veins. When in flight, the wasp's front wings are

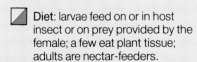

WASPS Order Hymenoptera *(at least 200,000 species)*

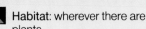

Habitat: wherever there are plants.

Diet: larvae feed on or in host insect or on prey provided by the female; a few eat plant tissue; adults are nectar-feeders.

✓ **Relationship with people:** mainly beneficial as killers of pest insects.

Distribution: almost worldwide.

Size: length 0.2mm-5cm.

Colour: varied, from all black to patterns of yellow and/or red and black, metallic green, blue, bronze.

Species mentioned in text:
Alder wood wasp (*Xiphydria camelus*)
Cabbage braconid (*Apanteles glomeratus*)
European pine sawfly (*Neodiprion sertifer*)
Giant wood wasp (*Urocerus gigas*)
Hornet (*Vespa* species)
Ichneumon wasp (e.g. *Pseudorhyssa, Rhysella* species)
Yellow-footed braconid (*Apanteles flavipes*)

coupled to the hind wings by a row of little hooks on the leading edge of each hind wing. The hooks latch on to a fold on the rear edge of the forewing.

In primitive wasps, the abdomen is broadly attached to the thorax. In all other species there is a narrow "wasp waist" between the thorax and abdomen. The waist is the result of a narrowing between the first and the second abdominal segments.

PARASITIC WASPS

Almost all kinds of insect are attacked by parasitic wasps. There are even tiny wasps called chalcids which lay their eggs in the eggs of other insects. Some chalcids lay their eggs in the larvae of other parasitic wasps.

▼Workers of a European hornet tend larvae in their six-sided cells. The paper nest is made from chewed wood fibres.

▲More than 50 parasitic braconid wasp larvae have fed inside this dying caterpillar and have burst out to spin cocoons and pupate.

◄A female ichneumon wasp drills with her ovipositor to lay an egg in a hidden Alder wood wasp larva. The wasp behind – a different species – will lay her egg in the same hole and her larva will eat those of the ichneumon and wood wasps.

A SLOW DEATH FOR THE HOST

Many parasitic wasps attack only one species of insect. Others lay their eggs in any exposed insect larva or pupa.

Female parasitic wasps often have long ovipositors for laying their eggs in host larvae hidden deep in wood. Many deposit the eggs in or on the caterpillars of butterflies and moths. Each wasp larva eats the insides of the host, which eventually dies. After several moults, the larva spins a cocoon inside the host's body or on its surface before changing to an adult.

35

Because many parasitic wasps attack only one host, some have been used as natural control agents for pests. In Barbados, the Yellow braconid wasp is used to keep down the numbers of the Sugarcane stem borer, a moth caterpillar. Farmers and gardeners in Europe and North America have an ally in the Cabbage apanteles, a wasp whose larvae kill caterpillars of the Cabbage white butterfly.

HUNTING SPECIES

Hunting wasps differ from parasitic wasps in two important ways. First, they do not use the ovipositor as an egg-laying tube. Instead, it has become a sting for injecting poison into insect prey. Second, they provide a safe place, the nest, in which the prey is stored for their larvae to feed on.

Having a nest requires that the wasp can find its way home after a hunting trip. Wasps (and bees) do this by memorizing both near and distant landmarks around the nest on special "orientation flights" just after the nest is completed. They also use the position of the Sun in the sky as an additional guide.

According to species, the nest may be a simple or branching burrow in the ground or soft, dead wood. Some hunting wasps use the old burrows of wood-boring beetles. A few collect mud which they use to build exposed nests on stones.

Whatever the nest type, each contains a number of special chambers called cells. A single larva develops in each one, feeding on stung and paralyzed insects caught by the mother wasp. Each wasp species specializes on a particular kind of prey, such as caterpillars, flies, beetles or spiders.

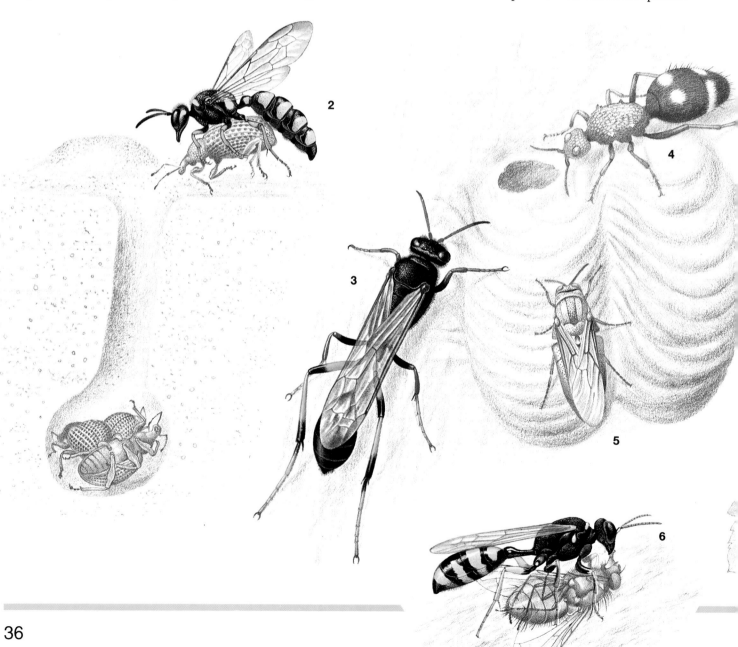

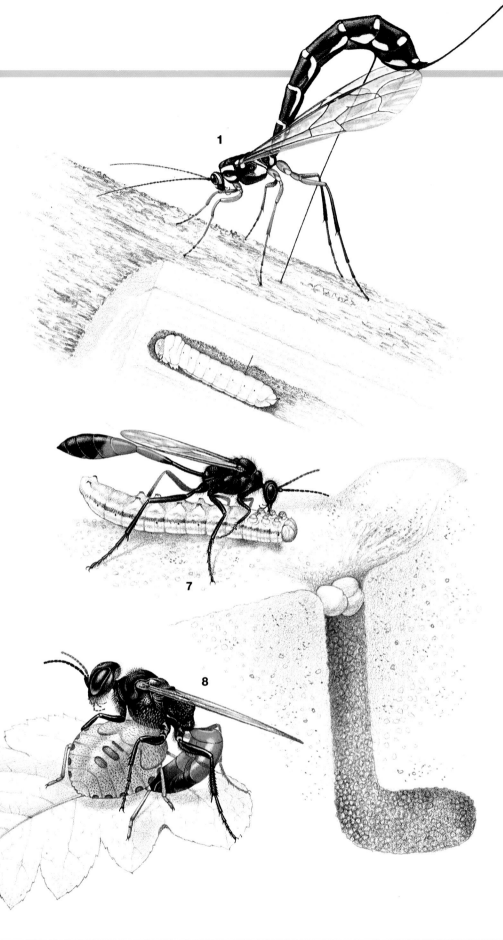

SOCIAL WASPS

Almost all the social, or colonial, wasps are paper-making species like the yellow-jackets and hornets. These belong to the family Vespidae.

Each colony consists of one or a few egg-laying females called queens, and a larger number, often thousands, of sterile females which are known as workers. The colony is founded by one or more mated queens. These build the first few cells in the nest using a tough paper that they make from wood fibres stripped off trees and old posts. Nests may be built hanging from branches or the eaves of houses. Some species always build their nests underground.

The first generation of offspring of the queen consists of only female workers. These take over the duties of catching insect prey and extending and repairing the nest, while the queen concentrates on egg-laying. In all the vespid wasps, the eggs are laid in the cells before any food is provided. The workers supply the nest with chewed insect prey rather than whole insects. Some vespines are pests of beehives, but on balance they are beneficial as they kill a wide range of pest species for their larval food.

Eventually new queens and males are reared. These mate and the colony dies out. Only mated queens survive the winter in hibernation. They start the colony cycle again next spring.

◄Wasps at work A female ichneumon, *Rhyssa* species (1), uses her long ovipositor to lay an egg in a wood wasp larva. A weevil-hunting wasp, *Cerceris arenaria* (2), returns to her nest with prey. A spider-hunting wasp, *Sceliphron spirifex* (3), at her mud nest, watched by two parasitic wasps, a wingless female "velvet ant", *Dolichomutilla guineensis* (4), and a female jewel wasp, *Stilbum cyanurum* (5). A fly-hunter, *Mellinus arvensis* (6), with prey. An American thread-waisted wasp (*Ammophila aberti*) (7), returning with prey. A female solitary wasp, *Astata boops* (8), stings her prey, a shieldbug larva.

ANTS

On a hot, summer afternoon, the air is full of flying ants. They pour out of nests in their thousands and take to the air. These are males and females on their once-in-a-lifetime mating flights. In the air, they are not alone. Swifts and swallows swoop and glide, making the most of this flying food bonanza.

Ants are everywhere. Nevertheless, in temperate areas, most people only notice them on the few days in the year when the winged males and females stage their spectacular mating flights. In the tropics, things are different. There are thousands of species, some of them very large, and no-one can fail to notice them. They get everywhere in their search for food.

FOOD-GATHERERS, EGG-LAYERS
Ants are a special group of wasps (see pages 34-37). All ant species are social and live in colonies. Each colony has one or more egg-laying females called queens, and hundreds, thousands or even millions of workers. The workers are sterile, wingless females which, under normal circumstances, do not lay eggs. Their role is to forage for food, rear the young and defend the nest. For almost all of their lives, the queens are nothing but stay-at-home egg-laying machines.

FOUNDING THE COLONY
After mating, a male ant soon dies. The female returns to the ground and sheds her wings. She has no need for them any more. Shortly after her flight muscles will break down to release nutrients for making eggs.

In the Common black and Common yellow ants, which live in Europe

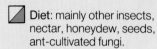

ANTS Order Hymenoptera: Formicidae (*about 14,000 species*)

Habitat: varied, most species in forests and grasslands.

Diet: mainly other insects, nectar, honeydew, seeds, ant-cultivated fungi.

Relationship with people: mainly beneficial, as killers of pests.

Distribution: worldwide except polar regions and high mountain tops.

Size: length 1mm-3.5cm.

Colour: mainly reddish or black.

Species mentioned in text:
Army ant (*Eciton burchelli*)
Carpenter ants (*Campanotus* species)
Common black ant (*Lasius niger*)
Common yellow ant (*Lasius flavus*)
Driver ant (*Dorylus nigricans*)
Harvester ants (*Messor* species)
Leaf-cutter ants (*Atta* species)
Long-footed ant (*Anoplolepis longipes*)
Red ants (*Myrmica* species)
Slave-maker ant (*Polyergus rufescens*)
Slow ants (*Leptothorax* species)
Weaver ants (*Oecophylla* species)
Wood ants (*Formica* species)

and North America, what happens next is typical. The queen finds a crack in the soil or a space under a log or stone and excavates a little chamber or cell. There, she lays her first batch of eggs. She does not feed, but lives off her flight muscles and body fat.

The queen guards the eggs and the larvae that hatch from them, licking them with her tongue to keep off dirt and fungal spores. She continues to lay more and more eggs, but does not collect food for the larvae. Instead, the larvae feed on the eggs constantly produced by the queen.

JOBS IN THE HOME

After moulting their skins three or four times, each larva spins a papery silk cocoon and pupates inside it. Eventually, the first generation of workers emerges. These ants extend the nest by digging out additional chambers and galleries, and they forage for food. Ants are tidy, and one of the workers' tasks is to remove droppings and other debris, and place it outside in their own rubbish dump.

The workers also defend the nest against raiders from other colonies, which may try to enter and steal eggs and larvae as food. Each colony has its own characteristic smell and intruders are recognized immediately.

Many ants, such as the common red species, are all armed with a sting and use this in defence. Others, like the Common black ant and the wood ants, have no sting. But they are not defenceless. They squirt out an irritating spray of formic acid from glands in their rear ends.

The Slave-maker ant raids the nests of other ant species and steals their pupae, taking them back to its own nest. It eats some of the pupae, but most hatch out and the new workers live as slaves in the colony.

NESTS AND MOUNDS

Underground ant nests can be up to several metres deep, with tunnels and chambers on many levels. The workers tend to keep eggs and larvae in clumps of individuals of similar age. In hot weather, they move the eggs close to the soil surface to benefit from the warmth. At night and in cold weather, they take the eggs deep into the nest.

Many ant species, for example the Common yellow, make protective mounds of earth above their underground nests. Wood ants make their surface mounds out of pine needles. Carpenter ants are so-called because they excavate their nests in the trunks of trees. Weaver ants make their nests by weaving living leaves together. Many large workers fold over the edges of a leaf, gripping them with their jaws. At the same time smaller workers, each with a larva in its jaws, weave the leaf edges together with jets of silk squirted out by the larvae.

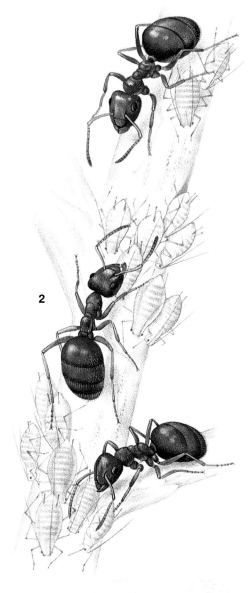

◄▶Ants at work Wingless workers of the Australian bulldog ant (*Myrmecia gulosa*) **(1)**, tend their eggs, larvae and pupae, which are simply scattered around the nest chamber. The winged female has smaller jaws than the workers. The workers forage singly and use their powerful stings to quell insect prey. Workers of the Common black ant **(2)**, tend aphids for sweet honeydew. "Honeypot" workers of a *Myrmecocystus* species **(3)** from North America never leave the nest. Other workers feed them masses of nectar.

ANTS ON THE MOVE

Worker ants leave the nest to forage for food. Many species are opportunists and scavenge on freshly dead insects or kill their own insect prey. If a worker has found a good source of food, it leaves a scent trail on its way back to the nest. Other workers follow this along the ground and soon appear at the feeding site.

A scent trail may attract aggressive ants and therefore some species, such as the slow ants, do not leave a trail. In these, an ant returning to a good food supply is closely followed by a second nest mate. This doubling may continue until there are as many ants on the move as in trail-laying species.

Ants on the move are a spectacular sight in tropical South America. Here, huge colonies of the Army ant are permanently travelling. Each one may have as many as 700,000 members. They march in columns, carrying their eggs and larvae with them. At night, they rest in a temporary bivouac under a rock or in a hollow tree.

HUNTING PARTIES

An Army ant colony sends out swarm raids to hunt insects and other small animals in the leaflitter. The raiding column can be 105m long and 8m wide, with the leaders fanning out in front to scout for prey. It is amazing to realize that the workers are all blind; they rely entirely on scent trails laid down by the scouts. A special soldier class of workers with large jaws stands either side of the column, facing outwards, on guard.

In Africa, Driver ants have a similar way of life, but they stay longer in their resting places and often dig deep into the soil to make their nests. Their raiding columns can catch and kill prey as large as lizards and snakes.

THE SWEET LIFE

Ants are very attracted to sweet, sugary liquids and the foragers can always be seen attending colonies of most

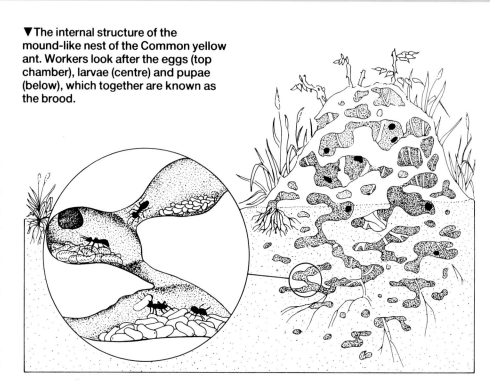

▼The internal structure of the mound-like nest of the Common yellow ant. Workers look after the eggs (top chamber), larvae (centre) and pupae (below), which together are known as the brood.

▶Leaf-cutter ants return to their nest with pieces of leaf. They use these to make a compost for a fungus they eat. Like all ants, this species is capable of great feats of strength. As here, it can lift and carry pieces of leaf more than 10 times its own weight and size.

sap-sucking aphids (greenfly, blackfly), where they eat the honeydew excreted from the aphids' rear ends. They may stroke the aphids with their antennae to induce them to produce more honeydew. Ants often guard aphids from other, predatory, insects.

Back at the nest, the forager ants regurgitate liquid food for the queen and larvae. Solid food is chewed up before being passed on. Returning foragers also feed workers which look after the eggs and larvae.

The caterpillars of many of the blue butterflies produce a sweet liquid which attracts ants. Some ant species take the caterpillars into their nests. The caterpillars eat the ant larvae, but the ants seem not to mind because all the caterpillars continue to provide the liquid from glands on their backs.

▲A raiding party of Army ants returns to its bivouac with a centipede it has caught. The larger workers are soldiers.

▶ Workers of the Long-footed ant kill a Cocoa weevil in Papua New Guinea.

ANTS AND PLANTS

Harvester ants forage for seeds, which they take back and store in their nests. In this way, the seeds get dispersed and some survive to grow into plants.

Violets have seeds adapted to take advantage of foraging ants, although these are species which do not normally harvest seeds. The ants cannot eat the seeds as they have hard, smooth coats. Instead, they eat little edible outgrowths from each seed. When the ants have finished eating them, they discard the seeds on their rubbish dump, where they germinate.

In Central and South America, leaf-cutter ants cut out pieces of leaf which they take back to their nests. There, they chew the leaves to a pulp, which they use as a compost. On this they grow a kind of fungus that only lives in their nests and on which they feed.

SCORPIONS

As the sands of the Arizona desert cool down at dusk, a night shift of small creatures emerges. From under stones and out of burrows they come – mice, centipedes and beetles. And among them a female scorpion scuttles in search of insect prey. Soon, she finds a grasshopper. In an instant, the scorpion grasps the insect in her claws. She quells its struggles with a killing stab from the sting in her tail.

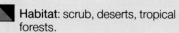
The reputation of true scorpions as killers is only partly deserved. For although they all have a venomous sting, very few pose a threat to humans. At worst, a typical sting is no more painful or dangerous than that of a wasp or hornet. Nevertheless, the habit of inspecting one's shoes each morning when in scorpion country may prevent a painful surprise.

There are some species, though, which can inflict a fatal sting. The Durango scorpion from Mexico can kill a person, and the Austral scorpion of North Africa has a venom as powerful as that of a cobra. Its sting will kill a dog as large as an Alsatian in 7 minutes and an adult human after 6 or 7 hours.

KILLING MACHINES

Scorpions have had at least 345 million years in which to perfect this killing power. The oldest of all arthropod fossils is a scorpion and they were possibly the very first arthropods to conquer the land.

Scorpions, like their arachnid relatives the spiders, have eight legs. They appear in fact to have 10 legs, but the front pair of "legs", which bear a pair of grasping pincers, are really massively enlarged pedipalps.

The body of a scorpion has two main sections, the prosoma and the abdomen. There is no distinct head

▲ Lurking on a branch, this scorpion awaits unsuspecting prey with pincers poised. The sting is at the tip of the tail.

region, and the prosoma, which bears the mouth, is covered with a horny carapace. Just in front of the mouth is a pair of three-segmented biting jaws called chelicerae.

Scorpions have a pair of simple eyes in the middle of the carapace, and between 2 and 5 pairs of small eyes near its front edge. The sex organs and genital opening are in the underside of the first abdominal segment.

Directly behind the single genital opening are tiny structures unique to scorpions, the pectines. These are a pair of comb-like structures which touch the ground as the scorpion walks. They detect vibrations caused by prey, and are very sensitive. Desert scorpions can detect a burrowing cockroach from a distance of 50cm. It is possible that the pectines also allow the scorpion to assess the texture of the ground.

The scorpion uses its pincers to grab and hold on to prey while it arches its tail forward to inject venom. The venom is a nerve poison and it has an instant effect on insects, which are the main prey of scorpions.

Scorpions have a very thick, tough cuticle. This protects the soft tissues and is almost completely waterproof. In desert-dwelling scorpions, it prevents the loss of too much body fluid. In extreme heat, species such as the Arizona scorpion burrow in the sand as far down as 85cm to keep cool.

Not all scorpions are desert animals. Many species like damp conditions and live in rain forests. Close relatives of scorpions, the harvestmen, are common in temperate regions.

▲A relative of true scorpions, this sun or wind spider crushes to death insects and small lizards with its huge chelicerae. It lacks poison glands.

▼This large harvestman stalks prey on a leaf in Venezuela. It uses its large fang-like chelicerae to seize insects. Harvestmen have just two eyes, not the four pairs of most sighted arachnids.

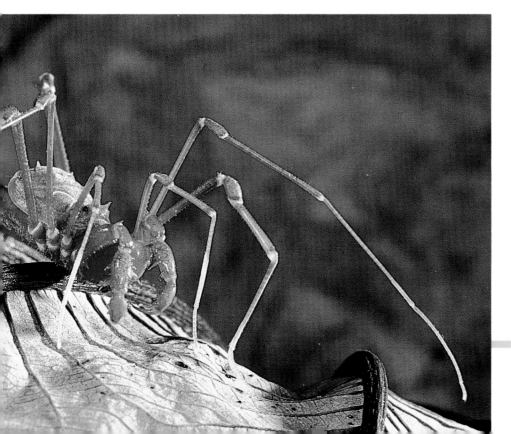

MATING AND MATERNAL CARE

Before mating, scorpions have a long courtship. The pair face each other with tails uplifted and circle around. The male then seizes the female with his pincers and they walk backwards and forwards together for hours.

Eventually, the male deposits a sperm package, or spermatophore, on the ground. He then manoeuvres his mate so that her genital opening is just over the spermatophore and she can take the sperm into her body.

Female scorpions lay between 1 and 95 eggs. The eggs soon hatch and the young scorpions climb on to their mother's back, where they stay until after their first moult.

WHIP SCORPIONS

The relatives of scorpions include sun or wind spiders (subclass Solifugae), harvestmen (Opiliones) and the whip scorpions. The latter are mainly tropical and have no sting in their whip-like tails. Whip scorpions like the Giant American species are often called vinegaroons because when disturbed, they spray their enemies with acetic acid. They walk on only three pairs of legs. The front pair are long and thin and used as "feelers".

SPIDERS

A young spider stands on tiptoe at the top of a grass stem. With its abdomen tilted upwards, it releases a fine silk thread into the breeze. The silk rises in the warm air and soon exerts a strong pull on the animal. The spiderling lets go and drifts up into the air, carried aloft by its thread.

The spider's action is usually known as ballooning and it is a good way of travelling far without using much energy. Ballooning is the reason why spiders are among the earliest colonizers of new islands which have arisen out of the sea because of volcanic action. Indeed, spiders are the most successful of the non-insect arthropods. They have invaded almost all parts of the world and live in almost all habitats.

Spiders all catch and eat living prey comprising mainly insects. However, birds, frogs, and even fish, form part of the diet of some species.

BUILT FOR SUCCESS

The body of a spider has two main parts: the cephalothorax and the abdomen. The cephalothorax consists of a combined head and thorax region covered with a hardened shield called a carapace. It bears four pairs of legs. The mouth is at the front of the underside and is flanked by a pair of fangs called chelicerae. These are used in feeding, defence and, sometimes, for digging. A poison gland opens into the the tip of each chelicera. When feeding, the spider uses its fangs to inject a killing poison into prey. It then injects digestive juices, which reduce the prey's tissues to a liquid on which the spider feeds.

▶A lynx spider eats a termite in Kenya. Most of these spiders are green and sit motionless on leaves until an unwary insect wanders by. Lynx spiders are skilled at leaping from leaf to leaf.

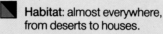

SPIDERS Subclass Araneae (*at least 30,000 species*)

Habitat: almost everywhere, from deserts to houses.

Diet: mainly insects; a few species eat fish, small lizards, birds.

✓ **Relationship with people:** a few dangerous species, but most are beneficial because they kill insect pests.

Distribution: worldwide, except Antarctica.

Size: body length 0.7mm-9cm, legspan up to 26cm.

Colour: varied, from black, mottled greys and browns, to red, green.

Species mentioned in text:
Baboon spiders (*Harpactira* species)
Black widow spider (*Latrodectus mactans*)
Bolas spiders (*Mastophora* species)
Brown recluse spider (*Loxosceles reclusa*)
Common garden spider (*Araneus diadematus*)
Dark garden wolf spider (*Pardosa pullata*)
Large house spider (*Tegenaria gigantea*)
Lynx spiders (*Peucetia* species)
Orb spiders (*Argiope* species)
Raft spider (*Dolomedes fimbriatus*)
Spitting spider (*Scytodes thoracica*)
Sydney funnel-web spider (*Atrax robustus*)

The chelicerae are flanked by a pair of pedipalps, which are appendages sensitive to touch and taste. Spiders use these in the same way as insects use their antennae. Male spiders use their pedipalps as a sperm store and for introducing sperm into the body of the female during mating.

Spiders have usually eight simple eyes on the front of their cephalothorax. The jumping spiders and the net-casting spiders all have excellent sight, better than in any other land invertebrates. The abdomen contains the heart, gut, respiratory system, sex organs and the silk glands.

SILK

Silk is very important in the lives of all spiders, even in those species that do not spin the familiar thread webs.

Silk is a special kind of protein. Spiders make it in glands near the tip of the abdomen. They use their legs to draw out the silk from the spinnerets, which are hollow finger-like projections at the tip of the abdomen. The liquid silk hardens as it is drawn out. The threads are stronger than steel threads of the same diameter, and can be stretched for up to one third of their length without breaking. This is amazing considering that the finest silk threads are less than 0.00005mm across and the thickest are only four times greater than this!

Most spiders start life surrounded by silk. The female encloses her batch of eggs in a protective sac of silk. Many species hide their egg sacs in crevices and never see their offspring. Some, though, like the Dark garden wolf

▲A baboon spider from South Africa. Although one of the so-called bird-eating spiders, large insects and small lizards are the more usual prey of this species.

▼An orb spider straddles its web. The web is conspicuous to birds so that they avoid blundering into, and damaging, it.

spider, carry their egg sacs around with them, attached to the spinnerets. Each female will defend her egg sac to the death. When the 40 or so eggs hatch, the spiderlings climb on her back and remain there until their first moult. After this they leave their mother and fend for themselves.

CAUGHT IN A WEB

Spiders usually show their presence by their webs, which they use to trap insect prey. The cobwebs found in houses are usually the sheet webs of the Large house spider. This is the hairy, mottled grey species which so often ends up in the bath.

The Garden spider is responsible for the beautiful orb (disc-like) webs that fill the spaces between plants in late summer and autumn. Webs of this type are covered with sticky droplets that help to trap any insects that blunder into them. The vibrations caused by the struggling insect alert the spider, which runs across the web and kills the prey.

OTHER FEEDING METHODS

The bolas spiders of North America catch insects in a very unusual way. Each spider hangs horizontally from a silk thread slung underneath a twig. It draws out a 5cm-length of silk and

attaches a bead-sized droplet of sticky gum at the end. Somehow, the spider can sense the presence of, say, an approaching moth and swings the silk line in its direction. The spider's aim is such that the sticky droplet of gum hits the moth, which is then pulled to within reach of the deadly fangs.

The Spitting spider of Europe and North America catches insect prey by spitting out two thin streams of sticky gum through its chelicerae. These streams move from side-to-side, so the insect is stuck down firmly by two zig-zag lines of sticky thread.

Apart from the egg sac, wolf spiders have little use for silk. They do not

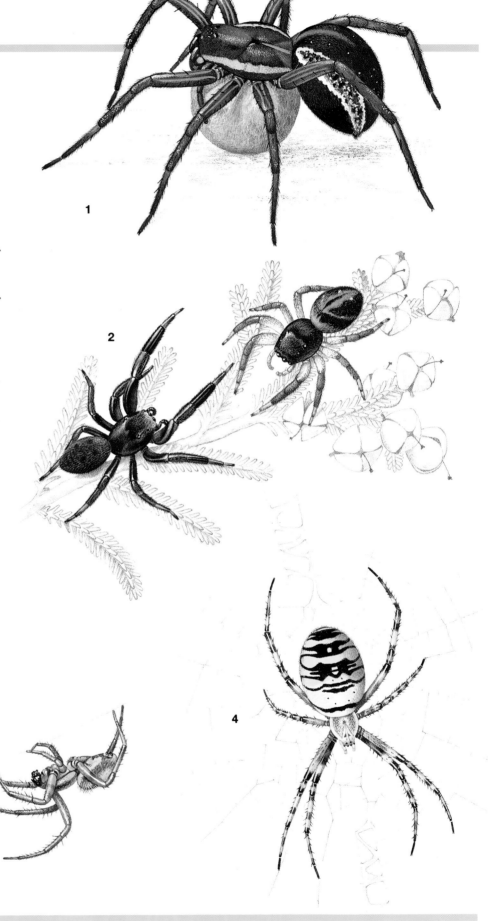

spin a web in which to trap prey. Instead, they roam over the ground and actively hunt small insects.

DANGEROUS SPECIES

Many people have an instinctive fear of spiders, but this is hardly justified. Only a very few of the 30,000 species pose any threat. The Black widow is one of them and is found in most warm countries. Its bite causes great pain and paralysis of the muscles. If the muscles involved in breathing are affected, the bitten person may die.

The poison of the Brown recluse of North America kills tissues around the bite. The effect can spread to become a gaping black wound 15cm across, which takes a long time to heal.

A bite from the notorious Sydney funnel web spider of south-eastern Australia can also be fatal. It results in a massive build-up of fluid in the lungs, leading eventually to coma and death. As with the Black widow's bite, an antipoison is available.

◄By dangling its front feet as bait into the water from a leaf raft, this Raft spider has caught a minnow.

►Typical spider behaviour A female Raft spider (1) carries her egg sac. A male jumping spider, *Evarcha arcuata* (2), courts a female, right, with movements of his front legs. A male orb spider, *Araneus quadratus* (3), right, vibrates the female's web in such a way that she recognizes him as a mate not prey. A warningly coloured orb spider, *Argiope bruennichi* (4), sits in the middle of her web.

SHARKS, RAYS, SKATES

A coral reef glows in the shafts of sunlight filtering through the deep blue water. Red and orange corals sway in the current, and small shoals of brightly coloured fish dart in and out among them in search of food. Suddenly, a shadow falls on the reef as a Reef shark glides past, its fins scarcely moving, the water undisturbed by it passage. It sees a diver and swerves, revealing its pale underparts and the curve of its huge mouth.

Scientists group sharks and their close relatives, the rays, skates and chimaeras, separately from other fish. This is because their skeletons are made of cartilage instead of bone. Their slit-like gill openings and rough bumpy scales distinguish them from all other classes of fish. Sharks (Subclass Selachii), which are dealt with first here, include some of the largest fish in the world. The biggest of all, the Whale shark, reaches a record length of 12.65m and weighs up to 15 tonnes.

HUNTERS AND GENTLE GIANTS

Sharks are found in oceans all over the world, but are most common in the tropics and sub-tropics. Only the sleeper sharks live permanently in cold Arctic waters, where they feed on other fish and seals. Many species migrate from the tropics to temperate waters in summer. A few even invade rivers: the Bull shark has been found up to 1,600km inland in the Zambesi and Mississippi rivers.

Most sharks have more or less torpedo-shaped, streamlined bodies, with two prominent dorsal fins on their backs, and a forked tail. When swimming near the surface, the largest dorsal fin often breaks the surface, warning human swimmers of the danger below. The most streamlined sharks are fast swimmers and fierce predators, feeding mainly on other fish and squid. Several of the largest sharks, such as the Basking and Whale sharks, are harmless and feed mainly on tiny animals and plants called plankton. The Basking shark grows to 9m long and can weigh 5 tonnes.

ON THE SEABED

Some sharks spend most of their time on the seabed, feeding on shellfish (crustaceans and molluscs). They have flattened bodies and are quite sluggish swimmers. The cat, nurse, and carpet sharks use their pectoral fins to "walk" on the ocean floor. The angel sharks and the wobbegong of Australia are so flattened that they look more like rays than sharks. They usually have a camouflage colouring in the form of mottled browns and greys to conceal them as they lie in wait for their prey.

MYSTERIOUS SHAPES

A few species of shark have strange shapes the purpose of which is still unknown. Each sawshark has a long narrow snout with a row of saw-like

---

SHARKS, RAYS, SKATES Class Chondrichthyes
(*about 440 species*)

Habitat: mainly sea water but some in fresh water.

Diet: fish, molluscs and other shellfish. Some large sharks also take dolphins and seals, others filter feed on plankton.

Distribution: worldwide.

Breeding: internal fertilization; 2-80 eggs. Some lay eggs in horny cases, others retain eggs inside the female until after hatching; in live-bearers, up to 40 young may be born at a time.

Size: length 60cm-12.65m.

Colour: shades of brown, grey and blue, often with camouflage markings.

Species mentioned in text:
Basking shark (*Cetorhinus maximus*)
Blue shark (*Prionace glauca*)
Blue-spotted stingray (*Taeniura lymma*)
Bull shark (*Carcharhinus leucas*)
Common skate (*Raja batis*)
Dogfish (*Scyliorhinus scyliorhinus*)
Great white shark (*Carcharodon carcharias*)
Grey sharks (*Carcharhinus* species)
Hammerhead sharks (*Sphyrna* species)
Little skate (*Raja erinacea*)
Luminous shark (*Isistius brasiliensis*)
Mako shark (*Isurus oxyrhinchus*)
Pacific manta ray (*Manta hamiltoni*)
Porbeagle shark (*Lamna nasus*)
Reef shark (*Carcharhinus menisorrah*)
Sand tiger sharks (*Odontaspis* species)
Sawfish (*Pristis pristis*)
Sleeper sharks (*Somniosus* species)
Soupfin shark (*Galeorhinus zyopterus*)
Tiger shark (*Galeocerdo cuvier*)
Torpedo rays (*Torpedo* species)
Whale shark (*Rhincodon typus*)
Wobbegong (*Orectolobus maculatus*)

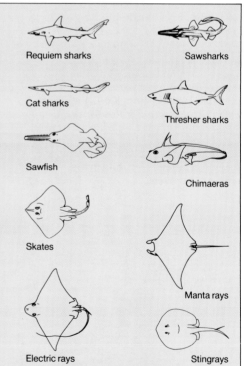

Requiem sharks

Sawsharks

Cat sharks

Thresher sharks

Sawfish

Chimaeras

Skates

Manta rays

Electric rays

Stingrays

teeth along each side. Since the shark feeds on shellfish, the saw cannot be much use for hunting, and is probably used in defence. Even stranger are the huge hammerhead sharks. Scientists now think their large heads contain organs for detecting faint pulses of electricity coming from their prey.

ROWS AND ROWS OF TEETH
In most parts of the world, sharks are feared for their savage bites. Although made of cartilage, their jaws are very strong – the Great white shark can bite through a man's arm or leg in one go. Its bite is 300 times more powerful than a human's.

In most sharks, all of the teeth are triangular in shape, and razor-sharp. A shark has many rows of teeth in its mouth. It can grow new teeth every few days if necessary. As those in front wear down, others move forward from the row behind to take their place, so that the shark always has a set of good sharp teeth. At any one time, a shark may have up to 3,000 teeth in its mouth, arranged in 6 to 20 rows. It may use over 20,000 during its life-time. Usually only the first two rows are used for feeding. As the shark grows larger, its teeth get bigger too. A Great white shark 6.4m long may have teeth 5cm long.

▲ The Great white shark is a formidable predator, attacking dolphins, porpoises and seals as well as other fish and, rarely, people.

Some sharks have teeth specialized for a particular diet. Fish-eaters have very long thin teeth to grip their slippery prey. Species that feed mainly on hard-shelled crustaceans and mol-luscs often have flat teeth for grinding and crushing shells.

GARBAGE COLLECTORS
Sharks will eat almost anything. An astonishing collection of items has been found in the stomachs of some

Tiger sharks – old boots, cans of paint, car licence plates, dead dogs, and human arms and legs. In 1799, an American rebel ship was chased by a British man-o'-war. The Yankee captain threw overboard his ship's papers in order to avoid being identified. The papers were later recovered from the stomach of a recently caught shark, and the captain was sent to prison.

MAN-EATERS
There are many accounts of sharks attacking people, often fatally injuring them. However, the chances of being attacked by a shark are far less than the chance of being struck by lightning. Each year humans kill tens of thousands of sharks, yet fewer than 100 humans are attacked by these fish.

Only about 10 per cent of shark species attack humans. These include the Mako, Tiger and hammerhead sharks. The most feared is the Great white shark. This reaches a length of 12m and a weight of 1,135kg. Attacks are most common in warm waters, especially off the Australian coast.

Sharks are not particularly attracted to humans – their smell is unfamiliar. Most probably the shark mistakes the flailing legs and arms of swimmer for the flippers of a seal or the fins of a large fish. Sharks are attracted to blood, however, and an injured swimmer is in serious danger. So is an angler who trails fish bait behind his or her boat in shallow water, and a spear fisherman who carries his wounded catch with him in a net.

FINDING FOOD
Many sharks have poor eyesight, but they have an excellent sense of smell. A shark can detect one part of blood in a million parts of water – equivalent to 1 drop diluted in 115 litres. They are also very sensitive to vibrations in the water, which might be caused by the movements of potential prey.

Sharks usually kill their prey by taking large jagged bites out of them,

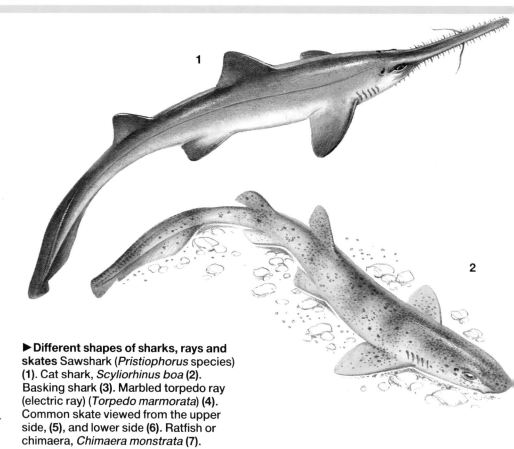

▶ **Different shapes of sharks, rays and skates** Sawshark (*Pristiophorus* species) **(1)**. Cat shark, *Scyliorhinus boa* **(2)**. Basking shark **(3)**. Marbled torpedo ray (electric ray) (*Torpedo marmorata*) **(4)**. Common skate viewed from the upper side, **(5)**, and lower side **(6)**. Ratfish or chimaera, *Chimaera monstrata* **(7)**.

then waiting while the victim bleeds to death. Thresher sharks, however, first stun their prey with blows from their very long powerful tails. Several threshers work together to drive fish into shallow water, lashing their tails to concentrate the fish into a group.

SILENT SWIMMERS
Sharks are skilful swimmers. They are propelled by their powerful tails, and glide through the water with no tell-tale ripples or bubbles to give away their approach. They use their large pectoral fins for tilting down or up, twisting and turning, and braking. Sharks have no air-filled swimbladders, so they must keep swimming to avoid sinking. But they do have oily livers. Oil is lighter than water, and helps to make the fish buoyant. The Basking shark used to be hunted for its oil, which was used in lamps. The liver of a medium-sized Basking shark can yield up to 900 litres of oil.

▲ A dogfish in its egg capsule, ready to emerge. The female dogfish lays 18 to 29 eggs, each measuring about 5cm wide and 11cm long. The curly tendrils anchor the egg-case to rocks or seaweeds. The young fish hatches after about 9 months.

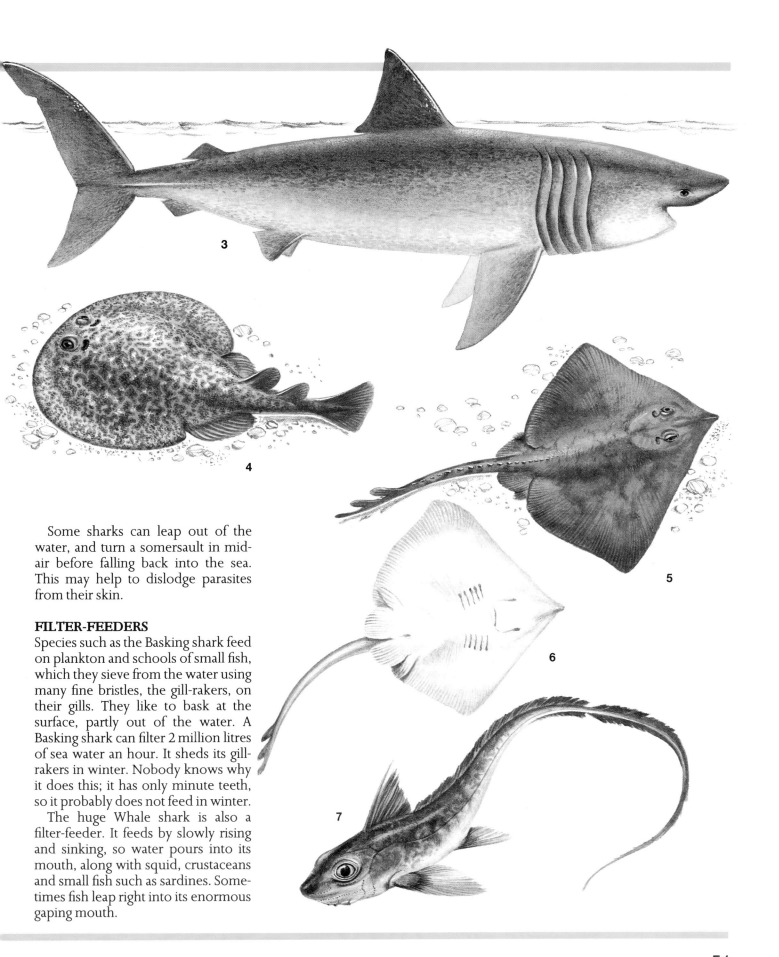

Some sharks can leap out of the water, and turn a somersault in mid-air before falling back into the sea. This may help to dislodge parasites from their skin.

FILTER-FEEDERS

Species such as the Basking shark feed on plankton and schools of small fish, which they sieve from the water using many fine bristles, the gill-rakers, on their gills. They like to bask at the surface, partly out of the water. A Basking shark can filter 2 million litres of sea water an hour. It sheds its gill-rakers in winter. Nobody knows why it does this; it has only minute teeth, so it probably does not feed in winter.

The huge Whale shark is also a filter-feeder. It feeds by slowly rising and sinking, so water pours into its mouth, along with squid, crustaceans and small fish such as sardines. Sometimes fish leap right into its enormous gaping mouth.

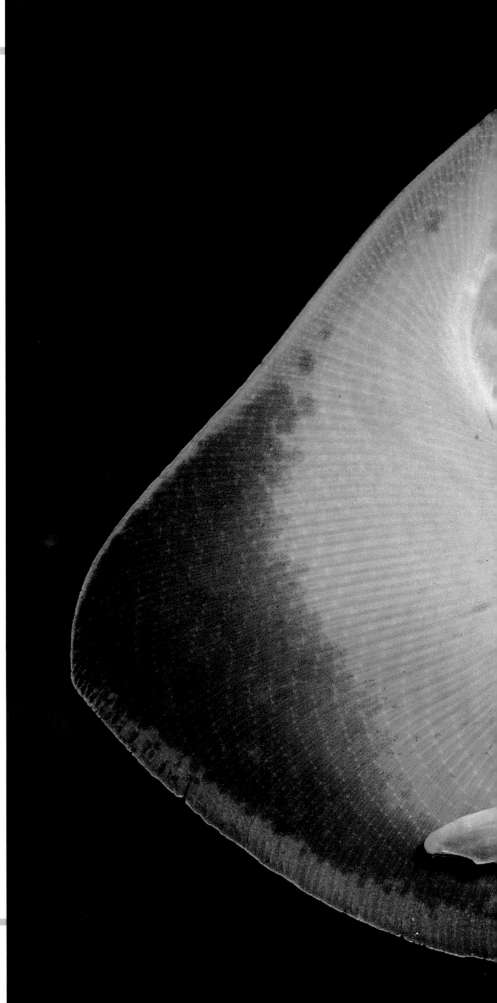

DIAMOND-SHAPED DESIGNS

Rays and skates (Order Batiformes, about 320 species) are very flattened fish that live on the sand and mud at the bottom of seas and rivers. There they prey on molluscs, crustaceans and other fish. They also feed on dead animal remains, and help to keep the seabed clean. Most species lie in wait for their quarry, but the manta rays feed by sifting plankton and small fish from the water. Electric rays stun fish with electric shocks, while eagle rays get at shellfish by squirting water from their mouths to blast away the sand. They can excavate holes 30cm deep.

Rays and skates have no anal fin. The pectoral fins are fused to the sides of the head well in front of the gill slits. Many species have both a longish snout – giving them a diamond shape – and a long narrow tail. In some, the tail is armed with poisonous spines for defence. The mouth and gill slits are on the underside of the body. Water enters the gills through a large opening, the spiracle, on the top of the head behind the eyes. When resting, skates may raise their heads just above the seabed and take in water through the mouth too.

FLYING UNDERWATER

Rays and skates are found in most parts of the oceans. A few species live as deep as 6,000m, while some South American species live in rivers. They range in size from the Little skate, which grows to 50cm long, to the 7m-wide, 1,360kg Pacific manta ray.

The huge pectoral fins of rays and skates are often referred to as wings. When swimming, manta rays and eagle rays flap these up and down. Skates and stingrays "fly" through the water using a wave-like movement of their pectoral fins from front to rear.

▶The underside of a Common skate showing the large mouth, the nostrils (looking rather like eyes), the gill slits, and the rather muscular pelvic fins.

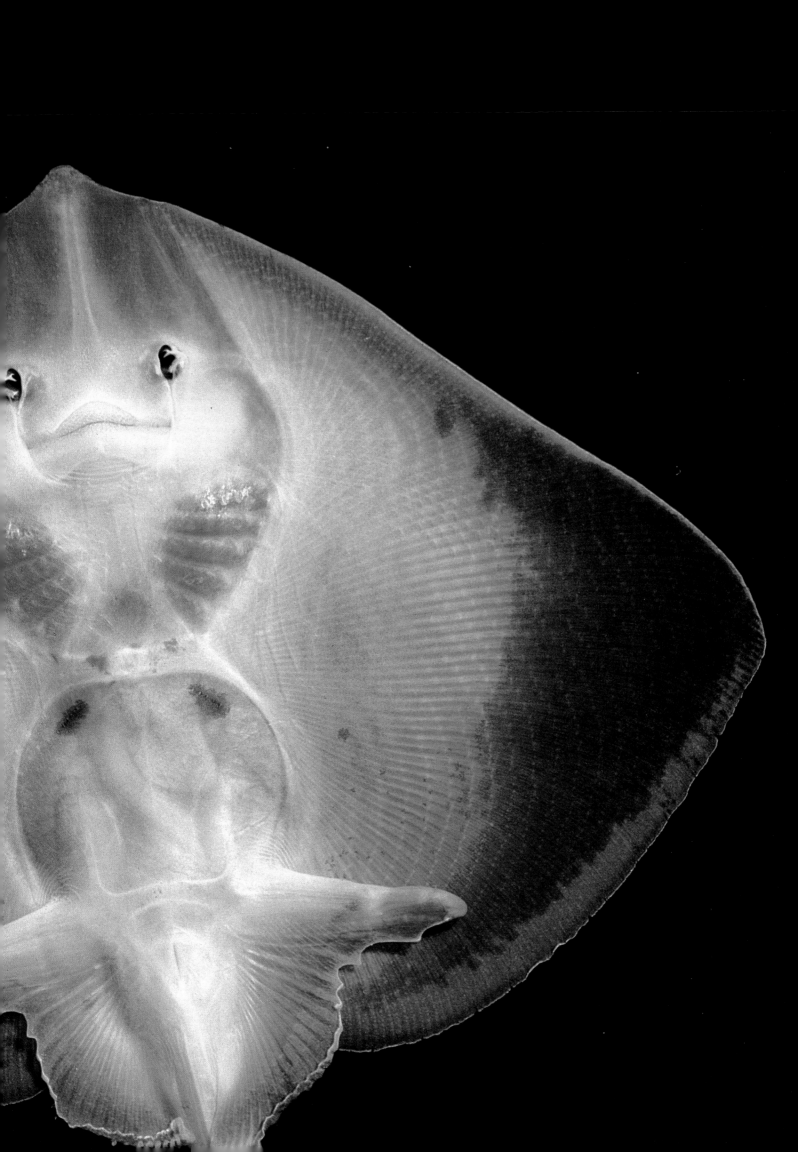

OCEAN DEVIL

The Pacific manta ray may have a "wingspan" over 6m. Two fins project from its head rather like horns, hence its common name of devil fish. It is one of the few rays to live in the open water. It feeds on crustaceans and small fish, and will often chase shoals of fish into the shallows to force them into its mouth. Manta rays make leaps out of the water, crashing back to the surface with a loud slap.

SHOCK TACTICS

Most sharks and rays have organs on their heads, near their eyes, which can detect faint pulses of electricity. As a

▲ Spread like a butterfly, this eagle ray, *Aetobatus narinari*, inhabits tropical and sub-tropical waters.

fish moves in water, it sets up a weak electric field, which the shark can detect. These are the most sensitive electric organs known in nature. Electric rays and torpedo rays can also produce electricity, and use it to stun their prey. They can give quite powerful shocks of up to 60 volts.

SAWS, SPINES AND BEAKS

The sawfish, up to 6m long, looks more like a shark than a ray, with large dorsal fins and small pectoral fins. Its

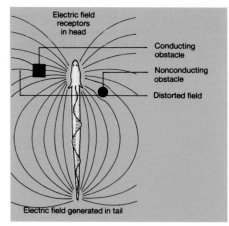

▲ An electric fish produces an electric field around itself, which is disturbed by objects in the water.

amazing snout is armed with 12 to 30 pairs of saw-like teeth, and has many uses. It can slash at shoals of fish, stunning or killing them. It can impale several fish at a time, which are later scraped off on the seabed and eaten. The saw is also used to dig in the mud for shellfish. It is a valuable defence, too, and can inflict lethal wounds on enemies many times larger than the sawfish, such as some whales.

The ratfish (Subclass Holocephali, about 23 species), often called rabbit-fish or chimaeras, are relatives of sharks that live in cold water down to depths of 2,400m. They feed on the seabed, propping themselves up on the tips of their fins. They have blunt heads with large metallic blue-green eyes, and very prominent lateral line systems on the head and sides. The large dorsal fin is tipped with poisonous spines. Their teeth are fused together to form a bird-like beak which the fish use to crush the shells of molluscs and crustaceans. Male ratfish have an extra pair of claspers on their heads, which may be used to grip the female during mating.

BABY IN A BAG
Sharks and rays have some very unusual methods of reproduction. They all perform internal fertilization; the male's pelvic fins possess a pair of claspers on their inner edges, which form a tube down which sperm is passed into the female during mating. They produce relatively few eggs, but the young are well-developed when they hatch or are born.

Skates and some sharks lay each of their eggs in a horny case, called a sea purse or mermaid's purse. Safe inside, the embryo feeds on the yolk and reaches a good size before hatching. The empty purses can often be found washed up on the seashore.

In many sharks, stingrays and the sawfish the eggs remain safe inside the female until they hatch. In some species the newly hatched fish then feed on the yolks of any remaining unfertilized eggs before escaping to the water outside. In the sand tiger sharks, from six to eight embryos are formed, which then eat one another until only two are left.

In a few sharks, such as the grey, Blue and hammerhead species, a kind of placenta (fleshy growth containing blood vessels) develops to link the young shark embryo to the mother's blood vessels to bring food to it, rather like mammal embryos are fed. This ensures that the young sharks are well-developed and able to hunt well soon after they are born.

LUMINOUS SHARKS
The Luminous shark, which lives in tropical and sub-tropical waters, gives off a bright green light from the underside of its body. Some spiny dogfish that live in deep water also have light-producing organs along the sides of their bodies. The light may serve to attract prey – mostly squid – or it may be a kind of camouflage, hiding the dogfish's dark silhouette from predators lurking below.

FOR FOOD AND SPORT
Only a few sharks, for example the spiny dogfish and the Soupfin shark, are fished in large numbers for food. But some, such as the thresher, Mako and Porbeagle sharks, are popular sport fish because they put up such a good fight when hooked. Other sharks and rays are a nuisance to fishermen, taking bites out of fish caught in nets or on hooks.

EELS, TARPONS

In the warm, shallow waters off the Red Sea coast, patches of sunlight dancing across the pale coral sand illuminate a strange garden. Speckled tendrils sway in the current, bending towards the oncoming water. But these are not plants. As the shadow of a large fish falls over the sand, the garden eels vanish into their burrows. When the Sun once more touches their burrows, the eels emerge.

Eels are the most snake-like of all fish, with long cylindrical bodies and long, narrow fins that seem scarcely to interrupt their body outline. These fins do not have stiff supporting rays, but are soft and flexible. While most fish have about 30 spinal bones, some freshwater eels have as many as 260.

Eels are ideally shaped for sliding in and out of crevices, or burrowing into soft sand or mud. This is their main defence. Also, eels all appear to be almost naked – the scales of most species are tiny – and a thick slime covers the skin, making them hard to grasp and often distasteful to eat.

WIDESPREAD AND VARIED
Eels are found all over the world in oceans and seas, from the coast to the cold dark depths several kilometres beneath the surface. A few species also live in fresh water, but these return to the sea to breed.

Most eels are predators, preying on other fish, crustaceans, molluscs and worms. A few are parasitic as adults, feeding on other fish – mainly the sick or dying. The teeth of eels vary according to their diet. Those that feed on very small water animals have teeth like fine brushes, while larger predators have vicious fangs. Eels that specialize in eating shellfish have flat teeth for crushing and chewing.

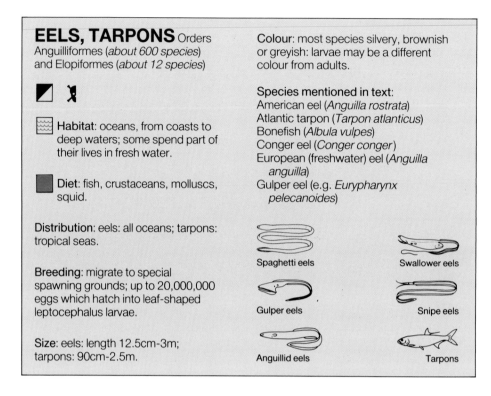

EELS, TARPONS Orders
Anguilliformes (*about 600 species*) and Elopiformes (*about 12 species*)

Habitat: oceans, from coasts to deep waters; some spend part of their lives in fresh water.

Diet: fish, crustaceans, molluscs, squid.

Distribution: eels: all oceans; tarpons: tropical seas.

Breeding: migrate to special spawning grounds; up to 20,000,000 eggs which hatch into leaf-shaped leptocephalus larvae.

Size: eels: length 12.5cm-3m; tarpons: 90cm-2.5m.

Colour: most species silvery, brownish or greyish: larvae may be a different colour from adults.

Species mentioned in text:
American eel (*Anguilla rostrata*)
Atlantic tarpon (*Tarpon atlanticus*)
Bonefish (*Albula vulpes*)
Conger eel (*Conger conger*)
European (freshwater) eel (*Anguilla anguilla*)
Gulper eel (e.g. *Eurypharynx pelecanoides*)

Spaghetti eels

Gulper eels

Anguillid eels

Swallower eels

Snipe eels

Tarpons

BLOODHOUNDS OF THE SEA
Eels have the best sense of smell of all fish. Large nasal chambers lined with smell detectors stretch from the nostrils at the tip of the snout almost to the eyes. The European freshwater eel can detect 1 part of chemical in 1 million million million parts of water, the equivalent of detecting a molecule of scent in each nasal chamber.

MENACING MORAYS
Moray eels include some of the largest – up to 3m long – and most dangerous eels. Like the equally large Conger eel, they live on rocky coasts and on coral reefs in tropical and sub-tropical regions. By day they hide in crevices and underwater caves, where they lie partly concealed, watching the ocean world go by. Moray eels have thick leathery skin, and often have brilliant colours and markings. When open, their huge mouths extend back behind their eyes. They have a pair of conspicuous tubular nostrils near the front of the snout, and another smaller pair near the eyes.

▶ Moray eels spend most of the day guarding the entrance to their favourite crevices and looking out for passing prey. Their thick skin extends over the fins, making them difficult to distinguish.

Moray eels are very bad-tempered fish, and can inflict nasty bites on divers that approach too close. The wounds are deep, and easily become infected. Despite their evil reputation, moray eels do not feed on large prey. Their attacks on divers are usually the result of surprise or provocation. They hunt at night for fish and all types of shellfish.

In the ancient Roman world, moray eels were a sign of wealth. They were kept in captivity, and displayed by the hundred at banquets. The family of the moray eels, Muraenidae, is named after a wealthy Roman, Licinius Muraena, who lived in the second century BC and was famous for his captive morays. These eels are good to eat, and are caught for food in the Far East and the Mediterranean region.

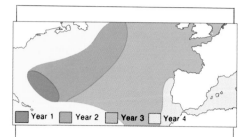

▲ European eels hatch from eggs laid in the Sargasso Sea, then drift as leptocephali on the Gulf Stream until they reach the coasts and rivers of Europe.

▼ Most eels have transparent leaf-like larvae called leptocephali. In some species these grow very large: those of the deep-sea spiny eels grow up to 183cm long before shrinking and changing into adults.

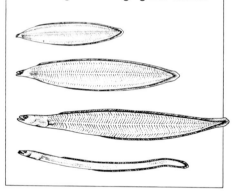

▼ A European freshwater eel, stranded by receding flood waters, wriggles overland in search of water.

GIANT EARTHWORMS?

Freshwater eels are found along the coasts and in the rivers and lakes of most continents, except for the west coasts of America and along the south Atlantic coasts. They hide by day and come out to feed at night.

Until the last century, no juvenile freshwater eels had ever been found, and there were many theories as to how the fish reproduced. The ancient Greek philosopher Aristotle thought that the eels were born from earthworms that were created in the mud. Later, scientists believed they were born from a small fish, which in German is still called Aalmutter – the eel-mother. Then in 1777 an Italian, Mondini, found eel eggs.

TRANSPARENT YOUNG

By the early 1800s everyone believed that freshwater eels mate and spawn (lay eggs), but they had not found where the fish met to do this. Then, strange transparent leaf-like fish called leptocephali (meaning thin heads) were caught off the coasts of Europe. When these fish were kept in an aquarium, they slowly changed into eels. The leptocephali were the larvae of freshwater eels.

MYSTERIES OF MIGRATION

Early this century, the Danish scientist Johannes Schmidt tracked leptocephali back across the Atlantic Ocean, looking for smaller and yet smaller (younger) larvae. On reaching the Sargasso Sea, just to the north of the Caribbean islands, he found newly hatched larvae. Thus the spawning grounds of the European freshwater eel were discovered and its amazing life story was revealed.

In spring, the adult eels spawn at depths of about 400m in the Sargasso Sea and then they die. The tiny larvae, called glass fish, drift eastwards almost 5,000km on the Gulf Stream currents until they reach the rivers of Europe. The journey takes them up to 3 years.

How they navigate is a mystery, but they may be well be able to follow the Earth's magnetic field.

Nobody knows exactly how the leptocephali feed and grow on this journey. They have strange forward-pointing teeth on the outside of their jaws, and no food has ever been found in their stomachs. Perhaps they absorb through their skin vital nutrients and minerals from the sea water.

The life cycle of the American eel is similar. It breeds in the western part of the Sargasso and its leptocephali take only 1 or 2 years to reach fresh waters.

Why the eels should have evolved such a long migration is a mystery. It may be that the spawning and feeding grounds became established millions of years ago, before the continents of the Americas and Europe drifted apart, and the route has lengthened as the continents have moved.

FROM GLASS TO GOLD

Once the leptocephali enter coastal waters, they change shape, develop pectoral fins and scales, and change into "elvers". The elvers migrate up-river in their thousands. On one day in 1886, 3 tonnes of elvers were caught in a single English river. These small fish can climb weirs and even struggle overland if the ground is wet enough.

Gradually the elvers develop an olive-brown colouring and yellow bellies, and become yellow eels. Their bodies are now adapted for living in fresh water, and they feed and grow in the rivers for several years. Female eels travel much further up rivers than males, which tend to stay around the river mouth. The males stop growing after about 5 years, but the females can grow for up to 15 years, and get bigger.

▶ Garden eels lean into the water current to feed. Carefully spaced about 50cm apart, each eel is just out of reach of its neighbour. Garden eels seldom leave their burrows.

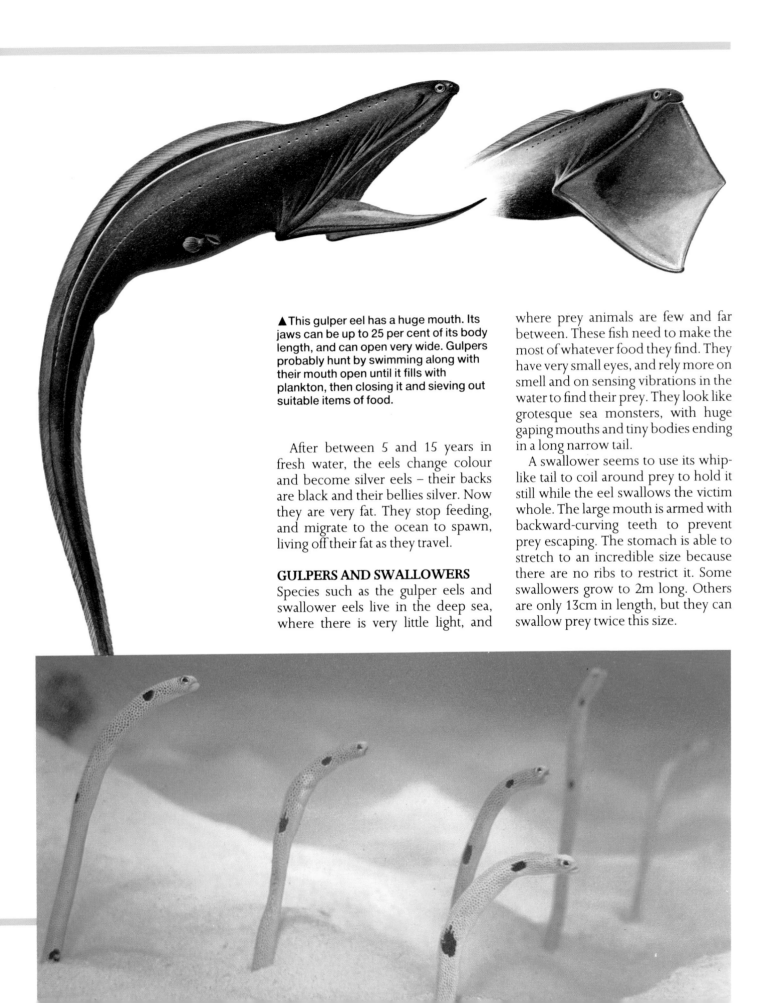

▲This gulper eel has a huge mouth. Its jaws can be up to 25 per cent of its body length, and can open very wide. Gulpers probably hunt by swimming along with their mouth open until it fills with plankton, then closing it and sieving out suitable items of food.

After between 5 and 15 years in fresh water, the eels change colour and become silver eels – their backs are black and their bellies silver. Now they are very fat. They stop feeding, and migrate to the ocean to spawn, living off their fat as they travel.

GULPERS AND SWALLOWERS
Species such as the gulper eels and swallower eels live in the deep sea, where there is very little light, and where prey animals are few and far between. These fish need to make the most of whatever food they find. They have very small eyes, and rely more on smell and on sensing vibrations in the water to find their prey. They look like grotesque sea monsters, with huge gaping mouths and tiny bodies ending in a long narrow tail.

A swallower seems to use its whip-like tail to coil around prey to hold it still while the eel swallows the victim whole. The large mouth is armed with backward-curving teeth to prevent prey escaping. The stomach is able to stretch to an incredible size because there are no ribs to restrict it. Some swallowers grow to 2m long. Others are only 13cm in length, but they can swallow prey twice this size.

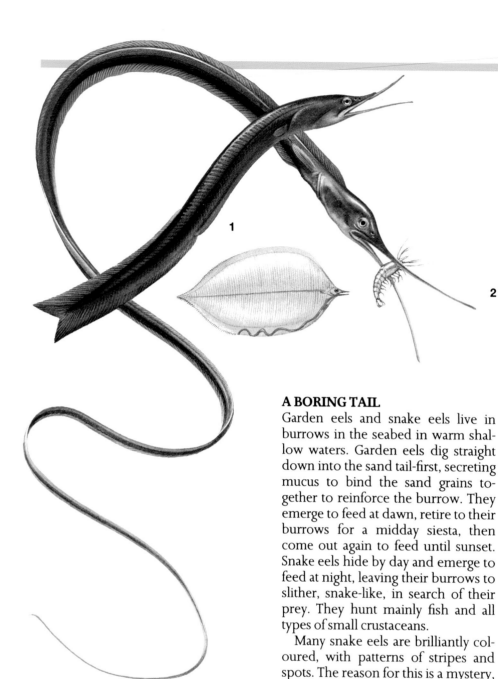

1

2

▲ **Two species of snipe eel** A Curtailed snipe eel (*Cyema atrum*), almost 15cm long, and its leptocephalus larva, 8cm long (**1**). A snipe eel with its prey (**2**). These strange deep-sea eels have long spreading jaws that cannot meet. They spend a lot of time hanging vertically in the water, mouth down. They feed on shrimps, which have long thin legs and long antennae that probably get entangled on the eels' fine teeth.

A BORING TAIL

Garden eels and snake eels live in burrows in the seabed in warm shallow waters. Garden eels dig straight down into the sand tail-first, secreting mucus to bind the sand grains together to reinforce the burrow. They emerge to feed at dawn, retire to their burrows for a midday siesta, then come out again to feed until sunset. Snake eels hide by day and emerge to feed at night, leaving their burrows to slither, snake-like, in search of their prey. They hunt mainly fish and all types of small crustaceans.

Many snake eels are brilliantly coloured, with patterns of stripes and spots. The reason for this is a mystery, since they move around only at night, when their colours cannot be appreciated. Snake eels use their stiff, sharp tails to bore into the sand or mud. This way, they can remain on guard as they burrow, ready to defend themselves with their vicious teeth.

LIVING SPAGHETTI

Some of the thinnest burrowing eels are the spaghetti, or worm, eels. These have slender, apparently scaleless and finless, bodies. They are very unusual among eels in burrowing head-first into the sand or mud, where they

remain during the day. At maturity they leave their burrows and become shimmering, long-finned eels.

PRIMITIVE TARPONS

Tarpons and their close relative, the bonefish, are primitive fish, and look remarkably similar to the ancestors of today's bony fish.

Today, these species live in tropical seas, where they feed on other fish and squid. They have teeth on the roof of the mouth and on the tongue, as well as on the jaws. Tarpons are skilful swimmers, and rely on speed to get them out of trouble. Nicknamed "silver kings", their large silvery scales reflect light as if they are made of polished metal. The Atlantic tarpon grows up to 2.5m long and can weigh more than 130kg. The bonefish rarely grows to a weight of more than 9kg. It has a wedge-shaped snout, which it uses to dig in the mud for shellfish.

Like the eels, tarpons and the bonefish produce leptocephalus larvae. The adults migrate to the ocean to spawn, and the larvae migrate back to the coasts, where they metamorphose and grow in warm lagoons and mangrove swamps. Sadly, these nursery grounds are increasingly at risk from drainage and pollution. Their waters are often low in oxygen, but the tarpons use their swimbladders like lungs, and take oxygen from the air.

LEAPING SILVER

Tarpons are famous for making huge leaps out of the water. Since they have few predators, the reason for these leaps is not known. Tarpons are very popular with anglers as they can be caught close to the shore, and put up a fierce fight, twisting and turning and leaping into the air. They are not edible, so most catches are released.

▶ A shoal of tarpons feeds around a rocky outcrop. The tarpons' gleaming scales are sometimes made into items of jewellery.

PIKE, SALMON, TROUT

As the water tumbles in a rush of white foam, thundering on to the rocks below, a gleaming Atlantic salmon leaps out of the water, squirming as it tries to gain enough power to clear the waterfall. The rushing water beats it back, but it tries again and again with dogged persistence until it reaches the calmer water above.

Many species of the salmon family are famous for their great migrations across oceans and up fast-flowing rivers. Together with pike and trout, they include several common fish, some of which are prized by anglers while others are important as food.

Most members of this group of fish have a small fleshy fin on their back, directly above the anal fin. They are long narrow-bodied fish, and their paired fins are set especially far back on the body. Pike, salmon and trout are carnivores – they feed on other animals. Large species feed mainly on other fish, while smaller ones eat insects, molluscs, worms and many other small invertebrates.

DANGER IN THE SHADOWS

Pike are fierce predators that lie in wait for other fish. Their bodies are long and narrow and their snouts are elongated and flattened. They have a formidable set of sharp teeth, not only on their jaws, but on the roof of their mouth as well. Their skin is greenish in colour and they have a pattern of yellowish spots that helps to conceal their outline as they skulk among the waterweeds. The dorsal, pelvic and anal fins are set far back on the body, and help to propel the fish forward rapidly once it sights its prey.

Pike live and hunt alone. Some live for many years and reach a considerable size. The largest species is the muskellunge of North America. This may be over 1.5m long and can weigh up to 30kg. It is said to catch ducks and muskrats as well as fish. Pickerel are small relatives of the pike. They seldom grow to more than 30cm long.

SLEEPING THROUGH DROUGHT

Mudminnows are tiny cousins of the pike, rarely reaching more than 15cm in length. They live in slow-flowing streams, bogs and ditches, where they lie in wait for small crustaceans and young fish. During periods of low rainfall, when their homes dry up, they burrow into the mud and sleep.

MANY GUISES, MANY NAMES

The Brown trout is a very common European fish, and has been introduced to many parts of the world for food and sport. Different populations can look and behave differently, and

►Large pike are often cannibals and readily make a meal of a smaller pike.

PIKE, SALMON, TROUT Order Salmoniformes
(over 300 species)

Habitat: rivers, streams, lakes, oceans at all depths; many species move from freshwater to the sea or vice versa at certain stages of their lives.

Diet: mainly invertebrates, fish.

Distribution: most cool fresh waters; oceans almost worldwide.

Breeding: usually seasonal; many species migrate to special spawning grounds. Many thousands of eggs laid in a season.

Size: length 3cm-1.5m.

Colour: mostly green, brown, grey.

Species mentioned in text:
Atlantic salmon (*Salmo salar*)
Ayu (*Plecoglossus altivelis*)
Barrel-eyes (*Opisthoproctus grimaldii*)
Brown trout (*Salmo trutta*)
Capelin (*Mallotus villosus*)
European or Northern pike (*Esox lucius*)
Muskellunge (*E. masquinongy*)
Pacific salmon (*Oncorhynchus* species)
Rainbow trout (*Salmo gairdneri*)
Sockeye salmon (*Oncorhynchus nerka*)

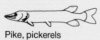
Pike, pickerels

Slickheads

Salmon, trout

Ayu

Argentines

Mudminnows

the trout also changes its appearance as it grows older. This has given rise to many names for the same species. Some trout remain in lakes throughout their lives and are called Lake trout. River trout live in rivers, and can change their colours to match the river bed. Some migrate to the sea to feed and become very silvery, thereafter being called Sea trout. These grow so well on the plentiful food in the sea that large individuals are referred to as Salmon trout.

▼Silvery shoals of Atlantic salmon were once common in the rivers of western Europe and eastern North America, but their numbers have declined as a result of overfishing and river pollution.

THE GREAT MIGRATIONS

Many salmon and trout travel to a special place to spawn. Some simply move to a shallower part of the river or lake, or even migrate from lakes to streams. Other species spend their adult lives at sea, but return to the coast or to the rivers to spawn.

The small, silvery capelin is caught in many thousands as it gathers at its favourite spawning sites in shallow coastal waters. Its close relatives, the smelts, head for the rivers. Smelts are very fatty fish. The natives of British Columbia used to catch so many migrating smelts that surplus fish, full of oils, were used as natural candles.

The greatest migrations, though, are undertaken by the salmon. Adult Pacific salmon often travel hundreds of kilometres to the mainland to breed. After this journey, they used to migrate more than 1,600km up the rivers of British Columbia to spawn, but today their way is often blocked by dams for irrigation and hydro-electric power. In some parts of the world, special fish ladders are built alongside dams to enable salmon to reach their spawning grounds. The salmon may travel 115km a day.

FATAL ATTRACTIONS

When the adult salmon reach their spawning grounds, males and females pair up. Since they left the ocean, the

▲Salmon can leap waterfalls 3m or more high, using a flick of their powerful tail.

◀▼At the spawning ground, a female Sockeye salmon (opposite) makes a nest in the gravel of the river bed. The large yolky eggs (second photo) are hidden in the gravel to conceal them from predators. The newly hatched salmon fry (third photo) feed on the remains of the yolk. When the yolk sac is almost exhausted (bottom photo), the fry start to feed on small invertebrates.

Male and female salmon (below) lie side by side as they spawn. The eggs and milt are shed into a hollow in the river bed dug out by the female.

males have lost their silvery shine, and have developed bright colours. Male Atlantic salmon develop blotches of red or purple, while male Pacific salmon may turn dark red. The male's jaws have become long and hooked, so they meet only at the tip. This does not matter, since the adult salmon do not feed while they are in fresh water.

The spawning grounds usually have clear water and a gravelly bed. The female salmon lays her eggs in a hollow in the gravel, known as a redd. The male sheds his sperm over them in a milky liquid called milt. Then the female moves upstream and digs another redd. As she does so, she flicks gravel over the eggs in the previous redd. This hides them from the eyes of predators and prevents them being washed away. The salmon may go on spawning for a fortnight. During this time, a female Pacific salmon may lay up to 5,000 eggs.

After spawning, Pacific salmon die. The Atlantic salmon survive to spawn again, but they are exhausted and have lost up to 40 per cent of their body weight. Many succumb to disease, and do not complete the long journey back to the sea. No salmon are known to survive more than four spawnings.

FINDING THEIR WAY

Salmon always return to the rivers of their birth to spawn, usually in the autumn. How they find their way is a mystery. They may use the position of the Sun to navigate, and perhaps the direction of the Earth's magnetic field. Ocean currents set up faint electrical fields, and the salmon may be able to detect these.

As they get nearer to home, the fish can identify the smell and taste of their home river. Each river carries its own special chemicals, washing in from the soil around it, from the underwater plants, and from fish and other animals living in the river. The salmon may even recognize the faint smell of young relatives still in the river.

▲ The Rainbow trout from North America gets its name from a band of shimmering colour that runs along its flanks. It has been introduced to other continents.

▼ A fisherman has caught a giant Pacific salmon as it journeyed to its spawning grounds. Some individuals weigh more than 45kg.

GROWN-UP NAMES

Salmon and trout go through many different stages as they grow up, and each stage has been given a name. A newly hatched salmon is called a fry or alevin. It is a tiny transparent fish only about 2cm long. By the time it has grown to about 13cm long, it has developed dark oval blotches, known as parrs, on its sides and is called a parr. These markings help camouflage the fish as it hunts.

After from 1 to 3 years, a silvery sheen develops over the parr markings, and the young salmon, now known as a smolt, is ready to migrate to the sea. Once in the sea, it grows rapidly, and after 2 years or more it is ready to return to the river to spawn.

SEEING IN THE DARK

Some relatives of salmon and trout live and breed in the deep sea. Argentines get their name from their silvery sides (argentum is Latin for silver). They are small fish with large eyes for seeing in the dark. Some deep-sea smelts have even larger forward-looking eyes which are set in tubes, rather like pairs of headlights. Others have tubular eyes that point upwards. They have names like spookfish or barrel-eyes.

Several of these fish have light-producing organs that glow in the dark. Bacteria in these organs perform chemical reactions that produce light. The spookfish has a flattened belly which acts as a reflector for the light it produces. The light beamed down from its belly helps to camouflage the fish when seen by predators below, which are looking up towards the brighter surface waters.

The deep-sea searsids have a novel defence. They produce a cloud of luminous particles that flash for a few seconds, giving the fish time to disappear into the darkness.

A CHANGE OF TEETH

The ayu is a strange fish that lives in the Far East. Unlike the salmon, the ayu lives as an adult in fresh water, and migrates to the sea in order to breed.

When the young fish enter the rivers, their teeth change drastically. At sea, the ayu uses cone-shaped teeth to feed on small invertebrates. In fresh water, it sheds these teeth and grows a series of comb-teeth on each jaw. Each comb has 20 to 30 fine teeth that form a kind of sieve. Inside the mouth is a group of conical teeth, which are thought to be used to scrape algae off the rocks and into the fish's mouth. The fish then closes its mouth and the water is forced out, leaving the very nutritious algae behind.

UNHELPFUL PARENTS

Unlike salmon and trout, pike do not make nest hollows. They simply shed their eggs and milt in shallow water and leave the young to fend for themselves. The eggs are quite large – 2.5-3cm across – and a big pike may lay several hundred thousand eggs a year. The pike fry start to hunt from the day they hatch.

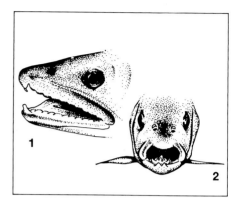

▲The remarkable teeth of the ayu. The comb teeth (1) meet when the jaws are closed, forming a sieve. Conical teeth at the front of the mouth (2) may be used to scrape algae off rocks.

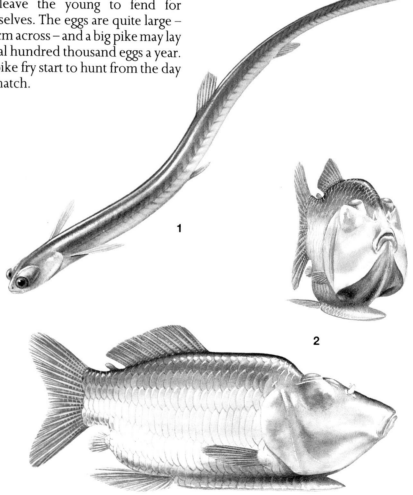

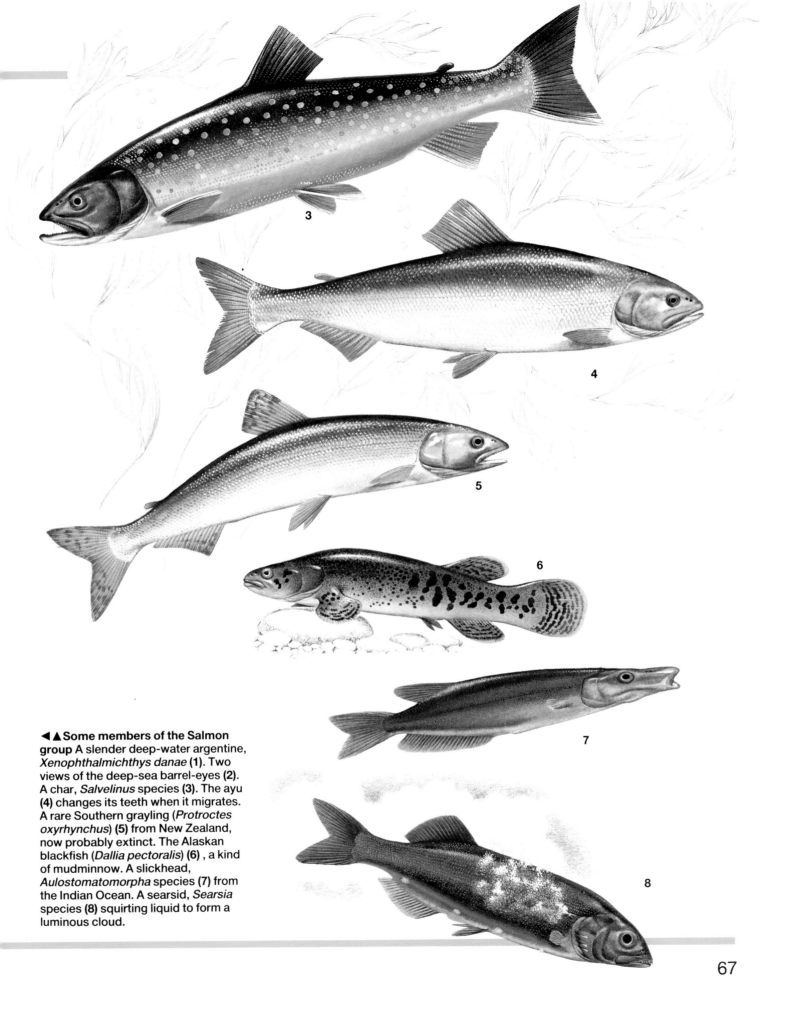

◀▲ **Some members of the Salmon group** A slender deep-water argentine, *Xenophthalmichthys danae* (1). Two views of the deep-sea barrel-eyes (2). A char, *Salvelinus* species (3). The ayu (4) changes its teeth when it migrates. A rare Southern grayling (*Protroctes oxyrhynchus*) (5) from New Zealand, now probably extinct. The Alaskan blackfish (*Dallia pectoralis*) (6), a kind of mudminnow. A slickhead, *Aulostomatomorpha* species (7) from the Indian Ocean. A searsid, *Searsia* species (8) squirting liquid to form a luminous cloud.

SCORPIONFISH, GURNARDS

SCORPIONFISH, GURNARDS Order

Scorpaeniformes (*over 1,000 species*)

 Habitat: mostly marine, some fresh water.

Diet: fish, invertebrates.

Distribution: worldwide.

Breeding: seasonal; some species migrate to special spawning grounds. Most lay up to 200,000 eggs on sea bed or rocks; sculpin eggs float to surface; bullheads make nest depression. Other species are live-bearers.

Size: length up to 2m.

Colour: some highly camouflaged in brown, dark red, green, with mottled pattern; others are brilliant orange or pink, or have warning stripes of red and white.

Species mentioned in text:
Bullhead or Miller's thumb (*Cottus gobio*)
Flying gurnard (e.g. *Dactylopterus volitans*)
Lionfish (*Pterois* species)
Oilfish (*Ruvettus pretiosus*)
Sea robins (*Prionotus* and *Trigla* species)
Sculpins (*Cottus* species)
Stone fish (e.g. *Synanceia horrida*)
Zebrafish (*Pterois* species)

Stonefish

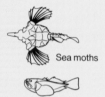
Sea moths

Gurnard

Lionfish

A small fish hovers over the reef, dipping its head to feed on the tiny fronds of seaweed coating the rock. Suddenly, a huge eye in the rock blinks, a gaping chasm opens up, and the fish is sucked inside. The rock was the grotesque head of a scorpionfish, covered in red flaps of seaweed-like skin. The fish was its breakfast.

Scorpionfish and their numerous and varied relatives are all designed for defence, with different combinations of armour-plating, venom and disguise. Scorpionfish and gurnards have a bony ridge reinforcing the cheek just below the eye. Many have bony plates in the skin, especially on the head, and often spines on the gill covers and the dorsal fin. The pectoral fins are large, with wide bases.

MULTI-PURPOSE FINS

The five species of flying gurnard have very large, brightly coloured pectoral fins, used as a display to frighten off predators. The pectoral fins are occasionally spread for gliding above the water surface in brief "flights". The pelvic fins of the true gurnards have another use. They have stiff spines, used like little legs for walking slowly over the seabed or for propping up the fish as it rests on the bottom.

The sea robins use their pectoral fins for both swimming and walking. These fins are in two parts. The upper part has soft rays and is spread and flapped like wings when swimming. By contrast, the lower part has stiff separated rays and is used for walking, and for probing the bottom for food. A sea robin can even turn over rocks with its pectoral fins.

◄Despite its lurid colours, the strange outline of this stone fish is not easily recognizable as that of a fish.

SAFE WITH FATHER

Members of the scorpionfish group reproduce in various ways. Some have internal fertilization and give birth to baby fish. Oilfish females give birth to up to 3,000 young at a time. Most species, though, lay eggs, often in large numbers. These may be laid in rock crevices or on the seabed.

Gurnard eggs float in the plankton, at risk from many dangers, but most sculpin fathers guard their eggs until they hatch. The bullhead, which lives in European streams, makes a kind of nest. The male digs out a hole under a stone, and the female lays the eggs on the roof of this little cave. The stones prevent them being washed away.

◄This lionfish from the Atlantic Ocean has bright colours to warn of the danger from its poison-tipped spines.

▼A deep-water gurnard from Australia (*Lepidotrigla mulhalli*) flashes its pectoral fins in a defensive display. The sudden burst of colour can startle a predator.

DANGEROUS FISH

Zebrafish and lionfish are some of the most spectacular fish of rocky areas and reefs. The rays of the dorsal and pectoral fins are separated and spiny, and the fish often swim with them widely spread. Venom glands at the base of the fin spines deliver poison along a groove in each spine. The fish drift slowly through the water, as if daring other creatures to approach. They will attack other fish that come too close. They sometimes use their large pectoral fins like a net to drive other species into corners of the reef.

MASTERS OF DISGUISE

Several scorpionfish and stone fish are so well camouflaged that it is easy to mistake them for pieces of rock. Their outlines are knobbly; their colours blend well with those of their background – brown or grey, mottled with black and other colours. Tiny flaps of skin resemble the growth of algae on rocks and add to the effect. A few species can even change colour if they move to another background. Some reef-dwelling kinds are brilliantly coloured in pink, orange or red, resembling the brightly coloured sponges and sea squirts that grow over the nearby rocks.

Scorpionfish and stone fish usually stay in much the same area, defending their home ground against other fish. They lie in wait for small fish, crabs and other invertebrates, either leaping out when prey comes within reach, or sucking it in by suddenly opening their huge mouths.

Stone fish are by far the most poisonous fish in the world. They lie in wait to ambush their prey on the seabed or on corals, perfectly camouflaged. Their fin spines inject a poison that can kill a person in 2 hours.

◄This scorpionfish's disguise ideally suits it to a life spent lying in wait for prey. The seaweed-like flaps of skin on its chin and flanks disguise its shape.

CICHLIDS, GOURAMIS

Two male Siamese fighting fish are exploring their new aquarium. Their long fins trail gracefully through the water as they weave among the weeds. Suddenly, they come face to face. There is a furious confrontation. Whirling and twisting, they strike out at each other, biting out large chunks of fins and flesh.

▼ An archerfish shoots down an insect by spitting droplets of water at it.

CICHLIDS, GOURAMIS Order
Perciformes (*about 8,000 species*)

▨ ✗

⌇ Habitat: mostly fresh water.

◼ Diet: mostly fish, invertebrates.

Distribution: worldwide.

Breeding: eggs laid in hollow in mud or sand, or in bubble nest. Some species are mouth-brooders.

Size: length 4-50cm.

Colour: most colours occur.

Species mentioned in text:
Archerfish (e.g. *Toxotes jaculatrix*)
Angelfish (*Pterophyllum scalara*)
Discus fish (e.g. *Symphysodon aequifasciata*)
Siamese fighting fish (*Betta splendens*)

Cichlids

Gouramis

Cichlids and gouramis are small to medium-sized freshwater fish, many of which are popular aquarium fish. They have a wide variety of diets, but are mostly meat-eaters. The plant-eaters often have chisel-like teeth in the front of the mouth for cutting weeds or scraping algae off rocks. A few have comb-like teeth for filtering plankton from the water.

Fish-eating types have many sharp pointed teeth for gripping their slippery prey, while the mollusc-eaters all have strong blunt throat teeth used for grinding up the mollusc shells.

A few cichlids are specialists. Some feed on the eggs and young of other mouth-brooding cichlids. They force the parents to literally cough up their offspring. Another group of cichlids feed only on fish scales.

GRACEFUL ANGELS
Cichlids and gouramis have a single dorsal fin, which in some species can be large and beautiful. The pelvic fins are often thin and trailing.

The South American angelfish has a very flat body, and both dorsal and anal fins are very large, so that its body is almost circular. The tips of all the fins trail off into thin filaments. As the fish swims slowly among the weeds, it has a dreamy appearance. This has made it popular in aquaria. Angelfish grow up to 30cm long in the wild.

AIMING FOR INSECTS

Archerfish live in the river estuaries and mangrove swamps of South-east Asia. They all have flattened bodies, large eyes and an upward-directed mouth that looks as if it is pouting. They catch insects by spitting a stream of water droplets at them and knocking them into the water. The drops are formed in a tube made by pressing a fleshy part of the tongue against a groove in the roof of the mouth. If the insect is near the water, an archerfish may leap out of the water and seize the insect in its jaws instead.

FIGHTING FISH

Male cichlids and gouramis become markedly aggressive in the breeding season. The males set up territories in which to court the females and bring up their families. They defend these areas against other males. First, they will try a threat display: both fish raise their dorsal fins, and move slowly towards each other, lashing their tails to slap water against their rival. If this does not work, the fighting starts, and they start mouth-pulling. Eventually, one of the fish, usually the smaller one, tires and swims away.

BLOWING BUBBLES

Numerous gouramis and fighting fish make bubble nests at the surface of the water. The male blows bubbles through a sticky mucus. The female sheds her heavy eggs into the water, and the male has to get them up to the nest. A male fighting fish will turn the female upside down as he sheds his sperm. The eggs are fertilized as soon as they are produced, and the male catches them in his mouth and sticks them to the bubble nest.

A MOUTHFUL OF BABIES

Most cichlids take good care of their eggs and young. Both mother and father keep an eye on the fry: if they stray too far, their parents pick them up in their mouths and move them to a safe place. Some cichlids guard their eggs in their mouths, too.

Tilapias, African cichlids that are often reared as food fish, start by making a nest for the eggs. The male makes the nest and guards it against other males. He displays to attract females to lay their eggs in it, usually about 20 at a time. As soon as he has shed his sperm over them, the female takes both eggs and sperm into her mouth. The eggs are fertilized here and remain safe until they hatch, as their mother, unable to feed, hides in a sheltered place.

After the eggs hatch, the young fish swarm around their mother, apparently attracted by the dark colour of her mouth and eyes. Later they will follow her around in a tight shoal.

STICKING TO MUM AND DAD

The discus fish of the Amazon basin in South America also keep their eggs in their mouths. After hatching the fry become attached to plants and rocks by tiny threads while they use up the yolk in their yolk sacs. When they are old enough to swim around, they make for their parents' bodies. There, for several days, they feed on a special mucus secreted by the adults' skin.

▲Two male gouramis press their lips together, but not for love. They are threatening each other, each trying to push the other away.

▼A female mouth-brooder cichlid keeps her eggs safely in her mouth until they hatch. The newly hatched fry return to their mother's mouth if danger threatens.

DRAGONFISH, LANTERNFISH

In the dimly-lit depths of the Atlantic Ocean, a fierce hunter with staring silver-rimmed eyes is stalking a small fish. A wiggling lure with a luminous red tip draws the unsuspecting fish towards the dragonfish's gaping mouth, there to be impaled on the curving dagger-sharp teeth.

The deep sea is a rather ghostly world where the only light comes from a dim gleam in the direction of the water surface, and the coloured points of light on the bodies of luminous fish. The fish are few and far between at this depth, but altogether they make up an incredibly large number. This is because a large volume of the ocean is deep water. In fact, the average depth of the oceans is 3,790m.

For the predatory fish, meals are a rare and unpredictable occurrence, but they have ways of making the

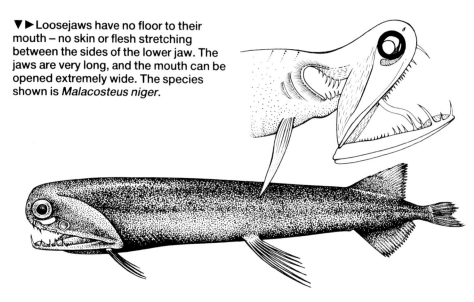

▼▶Loosejaws have no floor to their mouth – no skin or flesh stretching between the sides of the lower jaw. The jaws are very long, and the mouth can be opened extremely wide. The species shown is *Malacosteus niger*.

most of any opportunity. Many have large eyes adapted for seeing in dim light. Some have huge gaping jaws that can seize prey as large as themselves. Others rely on luring their prey to them. Since attractive colours are of little use in semi-darkness, the fish use luminous (glowing) lures instead.

Some equally bizarre adaptations help to protect the smaller predators from the larger ones. Silver sides that mirror the blackness of the ocean and patterns of many luminous spots that confuse their outlines are among the disguises used.

FEARSOME PREDATORS

Viperfish are some of the fiercest predators of the oceans. Their mouths are armed with long sharp teeth that curve backwards so that their prey cannot escape. The front teeth of the upper jaw point forwards and are used to stab their victims. Still more flexible teeth in the throat help to grip the prey and push it gradually down the throat to the stomach.

Many viperfish are less than 30cm long, but some reach a length of 60cm or more. However, a viperfish is able to swallow a fish of its own size or larger. Its powerful jaws can be separated to make a large mouth. Also, the bones of the neck are made of flexible cartilage so that it can throw its head back to open the jaws yet more.

As the fish opens its mouth to seize its prey, it draws its heart and gills deeper into its body, safely out of the way of the struggling prey. Its stomach is extremely elastic, and can stretch around large prey.

DRAGONFISH, LANTERNFISH

Dragonfish: Order Stomiiformes (*about 250 species*); lanternfish: Order Myctophiformes (*about 250-300 species*); Lizardfish: Order Aulopiformes (*about 190 species*).

 Habitat: Dragonfish and lanternfish oceans, mid to deep water; Lizardfish oceans, all depths.

 Diet: fish, crustaceans and other invertebrates.

Distribution: all oceans.

Breeding: little is known. Males often much smaller than females. Larvae may look very different from adults.

Size: length 2.5cm-2m.

Colour: deep sea species mostly dark brown or black, or silvery with mirror sides; most have light organs. Lizardfish grey, green, red, yellow or orange and white with mottled pattern.

Species mentioned in text:
Bristlemouths (e.g. *Valenciennellus tripunctatus*)
Deep-sea viperfish (*Chauliodus sloani*)
Dragonfish (e.g. *Grammatostomias, Stomias* species)
Lanternfish (e.g. *Myctophum* species)
Lizardfish (e.g. *Saundia gracilis*)
Stalk-eye dragonfish (*Idiacanthus fasciola*)
Tripodfish (genus *Bathypterois*)

Stomiatidae

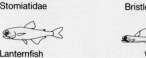
Lanternfish

Lizardfish

Bristlemouths

Viperfish

Hatchetfish

These fish stay in deep water from 1,500 to 2,500m down by day, and move up to about 450m to hunt at night. Their large silver-rimmed eyes are up to 30 times more sensitive to dim light than human eyes. Rows of tiny light-producing organs pick out the viperfish's shape, giving off a strange blue-green light.

TELESCOPIC EYES

The deep-sea hatchetfish has bulging tubular eyes with yellow lenses that are directed upwards. They act rather like binoculars, giving the fish good vision in the dim light. The hatchetfish, which is only about 8cm long, feeds on small crustaceans. It can see their silhouettes outlined against the

◄The head of a viperfish, a vicious deep-sea predator with sharply pointed teeth. The silvery background to its eye is a reflector which helps it to see in dim light. Organs that produce light inside its mouth help to lure fish to their death.

▼This deep-sea hatchetfish, genus *Argyropelecus*, looks fat from the side, but thin when seen from in front.

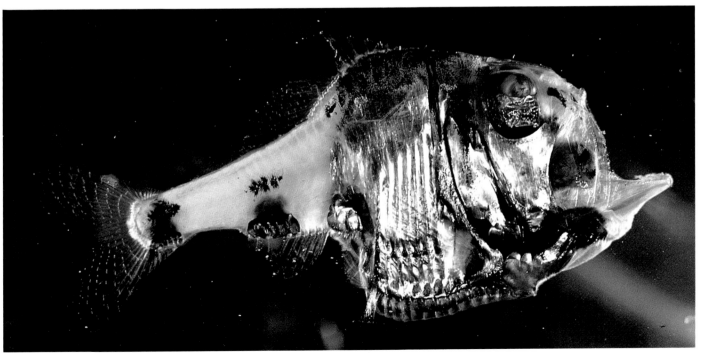

faint glow of light coming down from the surface. To prevent its own predators detecting it in the same way, it has some light-producing organs on its belly which conceal its shadow. Its mirror-like sides reflect the colour of the dark water around it, so it is almost invisible when viewed from the side.

DRAGONS OF THE DEEP
Although they rarely grow longer than 30cm, deep-sea dragonfish are fierce predators. They have slender dark bodies covered in large scales, and a large head armed with long curved teeth. Their mouths open so wide that they probably cannot be closed completely. To catch its prey, the dragonfish has a long lure on its chin, with a swollen luminous tip. In some species of dragonfish, the lure may be five times longer than the fish itself. Nobody knows how it is used.

BRISTLEMOUTHS
Bristlemouths probably comprise the world's most numerous fish – they occur in even greater numbers than herrings. They live in fairly deep water in all the world's oceans, and tens of thousands can be caught at a time in trawl nets.

Bristlemouths get their name from their fine bristle-like teeth. They are tiny fish – many are no more than 6cm long – and they feed on small crustaceans and other invertebrates. Many larger fish depend upon them as their most important food, and they could one day supply the human population as well, in the form of protein-rich fish paste.

◄With its large teeth and glowing (luminous) chin lures, this deep-sea hunter displays the typical features of scaled dragonfish.

▼Decorated with lights – a deep-sea viperfish photographed under ultraviolet light shows a brilliant pattern of organs that produce light. Its widely spread (gaping) mouth and long teeth show it to be a fierce predator.

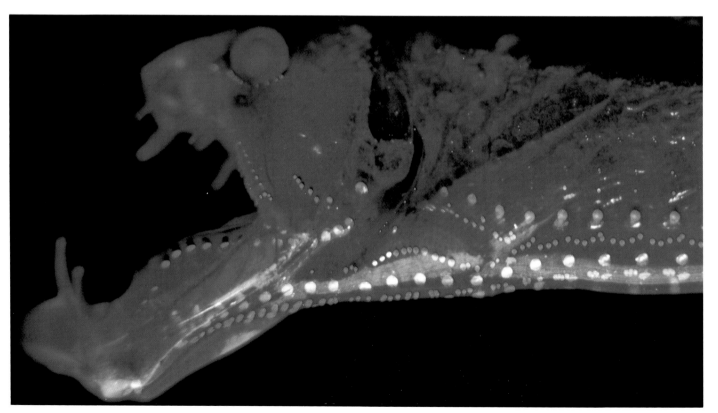

GIANT TAILS

Giant tails, or giganturids, are strange eel-like fish. They have smooth scaleless skin, a large mouth, savage teeth, and a tail fin that is drawn out into a long thin filament. Giant tails have extraordinary forward-pointing tubular eyes at the sides of their heads, rather like the headlamps of some racing cars. This gives them very good vision for hunting their prey. Many of the fish they catch are luminous, so the giganturid's mouth and stomach have a thick black lining to hide the light emitted from its last meal.

LIVING LANTERNS

Many deep-sea fish have light organs – tiny patches of skin that give off light, usually in the form of a bluish-green glow. Sometimes the scales overlying the light organs form lenses to concentrate the light. There may also be silvery reflectors behind the light organs or coloured skin in front for further effect. The light is produced by special chemical reactions. Often the light organs are arranged in long, parallel rows along the fish's body, like pearly buttons.

In many fish the amount of light given off is controlled by the fish's nervous system. In several deep-sea fish, each eye can detect how much light is reaching it from the surface waters, and adjust the fish's own light output to match.

OCEAN CAMOUFLAGE

In these dimly lit waters, there is still a faint glow of light coming down from the surface, so each fish casts a shadow on the water below. This gives away its presence to any predator lurking

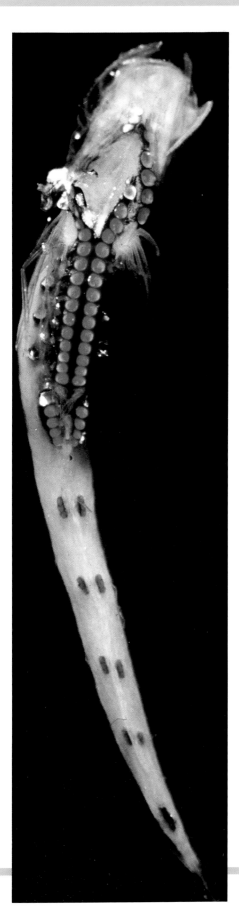

► The string of beads on the underside of this bristlemouth are its light organs. Each species has its own distinctive pattern, and males and females often have slightly different patterns, too.

below. There is not enough light for pale colours to be of any use in camouflaging the shadow, but light organs serve the same purpose.

Silvery mirror sides reflect the exact colour and brightness of the water around, so giving perfect camouflage at any time of day.

LIGHTS FOR SHOW

Not all light organs are for camouflage. In many dragonfish and viperfish, tiny light organs occur in distinct patterns along the fish's outline – on its upper and lower edges and fins. These may be used by the fish to recognize members of their own species, or to find mates. They could also be used by the fish to space themselves out, so that they are not hunting too close to each other. Some deep-sea fish have large bright light organs under their eyes. These may be used like headlamps to find their prey.

BRAVE DECOY

Male lanternfish have a very bright light organ on their back close to the tail. Females do not have this light. One of the main enemies of lanternfish are tunas. Tuna fishermen in the Pacific were puzzled because when they examined the tuna they caught, the tunas' stomachs contained mainly male lanternfish. Most of the lanternfish they caught in their nets, though, were females.

It may be that when they are set upon by tunas, the male lanternfish dart away, flashing the tail lights and diverting the attention of the tuna from the females. The females stay put and in theory should escape the tuna. However, instead they get trapped in the fishermen's nets. Thus the male lanternfish's sacrifice is wasted.

LURED BY THE LIGHT

Some deep-sea fish use lights to lure their prey. Dragonfish have fleshy luminous growths on their chins and these may act as a lure. If another fish

77

comes close to the lure, they start viciously snapping and biting at it. The lure may also be used to sense vibrations in the water to warn the fish of approaching prey. The viperfish has a lure on the tip of its dorsal fin instead. It can swing it round in front of the mouth when necessary.

Animals that use lures to entice their prey risk having the lure damaged by hungry prey. The viperfish has light organs inside its mouth as well, so its prey is led closer and closer to its unsuspected and certain death.

SEA LIZARDS
In warm shallow seas the world over live small lizard-like fish that waddle over the seabed, using their pelvic fins like stubby little legs. Lizardfish are often overlooked because they are usually well camouflaged. They spend much of their time propped up on their fins, waiting for small fish and shrimps to swim within reach. Then they dart out very quickly, just as lizards dart after their prey. Their speed is due to their tail fins, and as they move they spread their pectoral fins rather like wings. The lizardfish leap on their prey and swallow them whole. The most famous lizardfish is a species of Bombay duck from the delta of the River Ganges, which is eaten dried and salted as a delicacy.

LIVING TRIPODS
The tripodfish are kinds of lizardfish that live on the floor of the deep sea, sometimes as deep as 6,000m. Their tail fins have a long stiff lower lobe and the pelvic fins are also stiff, so the fish have a natural tripod to prop them up on the bottom. This enables them to search for food in the clearer water above the muddy seabed.

Sometimes tripodfish walk on these stilts. At other times they leap along rather like little frogs, using the tripod to land on. The pectoral fins are also very long and fine, and these may be used to sense vibrations in the water.

Tripodfish's eyes are very small, and the water where they live is very dark, so they need to use other senses to find their food.

REPRODUCTION AT DEPTH
Very little detail is known about the reproduction of many of these deep-sea fish. Bristlemouth eggs have been found floating in the ocean, and they hatched into tiny larvae rather like sardines. The luminous organs did not appear until after the larvae had changed into adults.

MINIATURE MALES
One of the strangest of stories is that of the Stalk-eye dragonfish. This has weird larvae with eyes on very long stalks (up to one-third of the body length) at the side of the head. The eyes can swivel to look in different directions. They also have transparent bodies, and their intestines are so long that the rear part of them hangs out of the body. As the larvae grow, the eye-stalks gradually become shorter, and so do their intestines.

Male and female of the Stalk-eye dragonfish develop rather differently. The female becomes black, and grows pelvic fins, rows of light organs, and luminous chin lures and powerful jaws with curved teeth. The male, however, is brown, and has no pelvic fins, lure or teeth. Instead, he has a large light organ just below his eye. He does not feed or grow once he becomes adult, so he remains less than 5cm long. The female, though, is an active predator, and may reach a length of over 30cm.

▼ This is not a lizard hiding among heather, but a lizardfish, genus *Synodus*, among corals on the Great Barrier Reef of Australia.

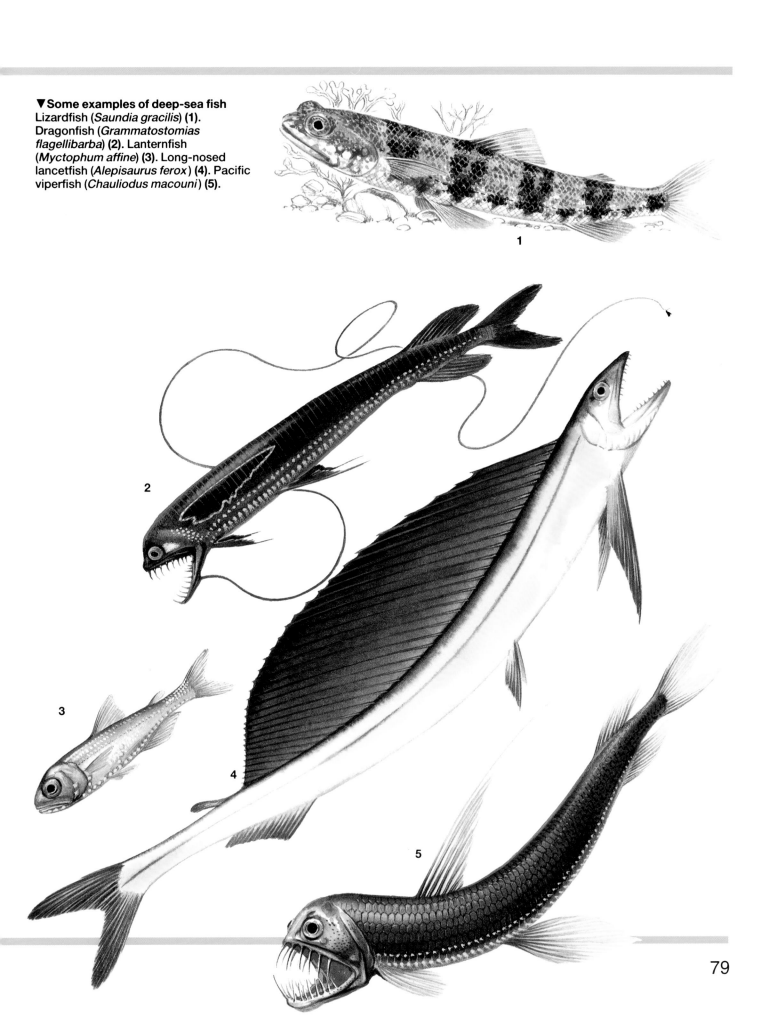

▼**Some examples of deep-sea fish**
Lizardfish (*Saundia gracilis*) **(1)**.
Dragonfish (*Grammatostomias flagellibarba*) **(2)**. Lanternfish (*Myctophum affine*) **(3)**. Long-nosed lancetfish (*Alepisaurus ferox*) **(4)**. Pacific viperfish (*Chauliodus macouni*) **(5)**.

TOADFISH, ANGLERFISH

A small fish hovers over the coral reef, searching for food. As it passes a seaweed-covered rock, it spots a fleshy worm that wriggles enticingly. The fish draws closer to investigate, unaware that it is being watched by a pair of eyes in the "rock". As the fish prepares to take the bait, the anglerfish suddenly opens its huge mouth and the little fish is sucked in.

Toadfish, frogfish and anglerfish are some of the laziest predators in the oceans. They are well camouflaged; some are even covered in little flaps of skin to look like a rock coated in small pieces of seaweed. Some of the anglerfish that live on coral reefs may be brilliantly coloured, but they are easily mistaken for sponges or sea squirts. They wait for their prey to come within reach, then open their huge mouths. Water rushes in, and the prey is swept in with it. Other anglerfish go one step further than this. A fleshy lure or "bait" is wiggled in front of the mouth to draw the prey closer.

FISH THAT CROAK

Toadfish live at the bottom of clear temperate and tropical seas, buried in the sand or hidden among seaweeds. They have broad toad-like heads with bulging eyes, very large mouths and lots of small sharp teeth. Their pelvic fins are stiff and muscular, like stubby little legs, and toadfish can hop across the sea floor in much the same way that toads move. When its prey – a small fish or shrimp – comes within reach, a toadfish will leap on it, snapping its huge jaws tight shut.

The resemblance to toads does not stop here: toadfish can actually croak. They each have a heart-shaped swim-bladder that is used to amplify the sound. The resulting sounds are loud enough to be heard out of water. Underwater they can be deafening – from 60cm away the volume can be 100 decibels, equivalent to the sound of a railway train. As well as these loud blasts, each toadfish also produces quieter grunts and growls.

The sounds are probably used by the toadfish to defend its territory. It guards fiercely the area of the seabed in which it hunts. If another fish approaches, this will provoke a whole series of grunts and blasts, accompanied by threatening postures. After mating, male toadfish are left to guard the eggs. They will croak loudly if their eggs are threatened.

TROUBLE WITH TOADS

The toadfish's disguise can prove a problem to divers and swimmers. It is easy to step on a toadfish by accident. This can be an unpleasant experience, because the toadfish has sharp hollow spines on its dorsal fin and gill covers, which inject venom when touched. The wound is extremely painful, but is not known to be fatal.

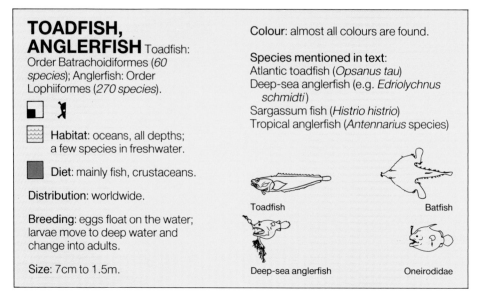

TOADFISH, ANGLERFISH Toadfish: Order Batrachoidiformes (*60 species*); Anglerfish: Order Lophiiformes (*270 species*).

Habitat: oceans, all depths; a few species in freshwater.

Diet: mainly fish, crustaceans.

Distribution: worldwide.

Breeding: eggs float on the water; larvae move to deep water and change into adults.

Size: 7cm to 1.5m.

Colour: almost all colours are found.

Species mentioned in text:
Atlantic toadfish (*Opsanus tau*)
Deep-sea anglerfish (e.g. *Edriolychnus schmidti*)
Sargassum fish (*Histrio histrio*)
Tropical anglerfish (*Antennarius* species)

Toadfish

Batfish

Deep-sea anglerfish

Oneirodidae

► Toadfish are sluggish predators that rely on their camouflage in catching their prey. This species, from the Atlantic Ocean, has a voice like a foghorn.

◄A tropical anglerfish wiggles its fleshy lure to attract small fish to come within reach of its large mouth. When it opens its mouth, the prey will be sucked in.

SKILFUL FISHERMEN

In most anglerfish, the first dorsal fin ray has become a long flexible lure for attracting prey. This ray is often separated from the rest of the fin and set well forward on the snout, so as to lure the prey towards the angler's large mouth. A small flap of skin at the tip of the lure can look very like a small fish when it is wiggled rapidly.

Some anglerfish can bend their lure down almost in front of their mouths as the prey comes closer. They must be sure to open their mouths quickly and suck in the prey before it has time to take a bite at the lure.

A WORLD OF CAMOUFLAGE

Far out in the Atlantic Ocean is the Sargasso Sea, named after the many large clumps of a floating seaweed called sargassum weed. Many of the creatures that live in the sargassum weed are camouflaged to match it. Crabs, shrimps, sea slugs and fish are all coloured greenish-brown, mottled with yellow like the weed. Survival is a tricky business where both predator and prey are camouflaged.

The master of camouflage is the Sargassum fish, a small frogfish. Not only does its colour match the sargassum weed, but its body shape looks like the irregular outlines of the seaweed. The rays of its fins sometimes end in round swellings that resemble the air bladders of sargassum weed. The fish's pectoral and pelvic fins are muscular, like little legs. It climbs about in the weed, creeping up on its prey, mainly crustaceans and small fish, including other Sargassum fish.

DANGER IN THE DEEP

Deep-sea anglerfish all look much like miniature sea monsters, with gaping mouths, long curving fangs and weird

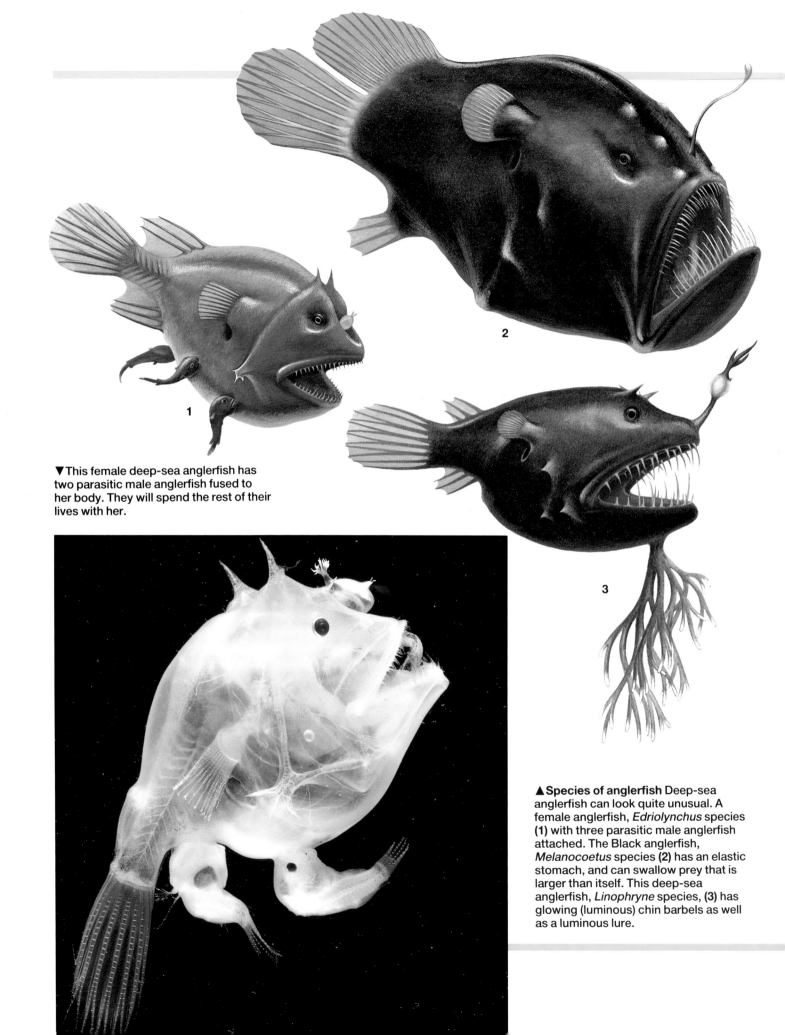

▼This female deep-sea anglerfish has two parasitic male anglerfish fused to her body. They will spend the rest of their lives with her.

▲Species of anglerfish Deep-sea anglerfish can look quite unusual. A female anglerfish, *Edriolynchus* species **(1)** with three parasitic male anglerfish attached. The Black anglerfish, *Melanocoetus* species **(2)** has an elastic stomach, and can swallow prey that is larger than itself. This deep-sea anglerfish, *Linophryne* species, **(3)** has glowing (luminous) chin barbels as well as a luminous lure.

shapes. Most have very smooth dark brown or black bodies, with no scales, but some have bony lumps or spines in their skins.

In deep water, very little light penetrates, so ordinary lures would be no real use. The lures of many deep-sea anglers have luminous tips. Often the tip of the lure is swollen, and contains bacteria that produce light by various chemical reactions. The lures flash yellowish-green or blue as the angler-fish hunts. Certain deep-sea species have very long lures than can be held out a long way in front of the mouth. These are slowly drawn in as the prey comes closer.

FISHING IN THE DARK
The prey may be able to see the lure, but how does the anglerfish see its prey? Many deep-sea anglerfish have poor eyesight, and probably use smell and touch to detect their prey. The lateral line system along their sides can sense slight vibrations in the water that might be made by a passing fish.

Some anglerfish have luminous barbels (fleshy tentacles) on their chins. These barbels may be branched like tufts of seaweed with luminous tips. The light in these barbels is produced not by bacteria, but by the fish's own

chemical reactions. The purpose of these barbels is not clear. They may be used for touch and taste, or they may act as extra lures.

A TENDER TRAP
A deep-sea anglerfish that goes by the rather long Latin name of *Thaumatichthys* has an almost foolproof way of luring fish right into its mouth. Its two-pronged lure actually hangs from the roof of its mouth. It swims along or lies in wait with its mouth wide open to display the lure. The prey swims up to the lure until it is right inside the anglerfish's mouth. Then the angler gently and tightly closes its jaws around it.

WALKING BATFISH
Batfish live in warm shallow seas. Their large pectoral fins spread out like bat wings, and their pelvic fins are used like legs for walking over the sandy seabed. When they find a good spot to wait for prey, they dig into the sand backwards, until only their front end protrudes, propped up on the pelvic fins. Then they wiggle their lures hopefully. Some batfish have long pointed snouts and look almost triangular when viewed from above. Others have a rounded outline.

LONG RIBBONS OF EGGS
Several anglerfish of coastal waters move to deeper water in spring to spawn. They produce large numbers of eggs in a long ribbon-like mass of jelly as much as 9m long. The newly hatched young move to the surface, where they feed on plankton for a time before settling on the seabed.

DOMINATING FEMALES
A female deep-sea anglerfish may be 20 times larger than the male. Spawning takes place in deep water, but the eggs float to the surface. Huge numbers of eggs are produced – up to 5 million at a time – by some species.

Distinct male and female larvae hatch from the eggs. Each female has a small knob on her snout which will grow into a lure. The male has no such structure. As they grow bigger, the larvae move to deeper water. After about 2 months, a very rapid change of form takes place, and they turn into young adults.

The females will take many years to reach maturity, but males already have well-developed sex organs and are capable of mating. But their jaws are weak and shaped rather like pincers, and they grow only slowly. They will use their pincer-like jaws to grip the skin of the female during mating.

MATES FOR LIFE
In some deep-sea anglerfish species, the males do not feed as adults. In order to survive, they must find a mate quickly. Once a male finds a female, he clings to her and gradually his flesh becomes fused with hers. Then he feeds directly from her blood. Most of his body organs are absorbed, but the sex organs continue to grow. When he is mature, he will release his sperm directly into the female's blood.

◀Two species of batfish *Halieutichthys aculeatus* (1); *Ogcocephalus parvus* (2). Batfish shuffle over the seabed on their pelvic fins.

BARRACUDAS, WRASSES

In a quiet corner of the coral reef, a group of large blue and yellow striped fish, Painted sweetlips, wait patiently, watching the antics of a small blue and black striped fish. The cleanerfish appears to be dancing in front of them. A sweetlips moves forward, presenting itself broadside on to the cleanerfish and raising its gill covers. The little fish darts forward, noses its way under a gill cover and starts to feed, picking off several tiny parasites.

BARRACUDAS, WRASSES Order Perciformes
(*about 8,000 species*).

 Habitat: seas and coral reefs.

Diet: fish and invertebrates.

Distribution: warm and temperate regions.

Breeding: produce several thousand eggs. Barracuda eggs float. Wrasse eggs may float, or are laid in nests and guarded by one or both parents.

Size: length 6cm-3m.

Colour: barracudas blue-grey; wrasses in many colours, most often green, marked with red, yellow, blue.

Species mentioned in text:
Bluehead (*Thalassoma bifasciatum*)
Cleanerfish (e.g. *Labroides dimidiatus*)
Yellowtail wrasse (*Coris gaimardi*)

 Barracudas   Wrasses

Wrasses are colourful bottom-feeding fish of shallow coastal water and coral reefs. They feed on a wide variety of invertebrates, including hard-shelled crustaceans and molluscs. They have large pouting mouths with thick lips that can stretch forward to seize a tasty morsel. Their front teeth protrude like forceps to pick up small animals or nip out chunks of fins or flesh from other fish. Their jaws contain strong teeth for crushing and chewing shells. Many species burrow in the sand and sleep at night, but can readily be seen by day, busily hunting for food.

AN INFINITE VARIETY
Wrasses show an enormous range of colours. Many species change colour as they grow older, and adopt yet another colour during their breeding season. The Yellowtail wrasse has a bright red body with large white blotches edged in black and a yellow tail. Males of the bluehead are green with a blue head and black collar, while the females are yellow all over with black blotches.

WHERE FISH STAND IN LINE
Many small wrasses feed on the skin parasites of larger fish and also remove their damaged scales. Each cleanerfish sets up shop in a special territory, and larger fish visit it to be cleaned. Fish that would normally prey on others the size of the cleaner wrasses, or on each other, queue patiently for service, with no sign of aggression. It is as if a special truce exists in the cleaner's territory.

Many wrasses make nests of sand or algae in which to lay their eggs. The nest is usually hidden in a crevice, and the male may invite several females to lay their eggs in it. The eggs and young are guarded by one or both parents.

FEARSOME PREDATORS
Barracudas look like typical predatory fish. They are all long and cylindrical, well streamlined, and with a narrow head. Their long lower jaws stick out beyond the upper jaws to display a fearsome array of needle-sharp teeth. Up to 2m long, they are feared by swimmers, but appear to follow them more from curiosity than from any ill intent. Barracudas seem to be particularly attracted to shiny objects like underwater cameras. When they are small, they travel in groups (schools), but the adults hunt alone.

►This little fish appears to be doomed, but in fact it is quite safe. It is a cleaner wrasse, and it is removing parasites from the mouth of a Monstrous sweetlips (*Plectorhynchus* species). The larger fish has deliberately opened its mouth for the cleaner to enter.

▼A barracuda caught in a shaft of light off the coast of Florida.

SALAMANDERS

It is a dark, rainy evening. From beneath a mossy log a tiny salamander emerges. Tonight the salamander is unlucky. It is seized by a small snake. But the salamander's skin produces so much sticky slime that the snake lets go.

SALAMANDERS Order
Urodela: 6 families (*336 species*)

● ▢ ⚘

 Habitat: water or land; breeding usually in water.

Diet: small animals.

◎ **Breeding:** internal or external fertilization. Most lay eggs; some produce live young.

Size: smallest from about 4cm; largest (giant salamanders): up to 180cm long.

Colour: varies, from dull browns and greys to vivid reds and yellows.

Species mentioned in text:
Alpine salamander (*Salamandra atra*)
Axolotl (*Ambystoma mexicanum*)
Cave salamander (*Eurycea lucifuga*)
Grotto salamander(*Typhlotriton spelaeus*)
Hellbender (*Cryptobranchus allegeniensis*)
Redback salamander (*Plethodon cinereus*)
Spotted salamander (*Ambystoma maculatum*)
Texas blind salamander (*Typhlomolge rathbuni*)
Two-lined salamander (*Eurycea bislineata*).

▲The axolotl usually spends all its life in water, and keeps larval features such as the feathery gills.

Salamanders, newts, and their relatives make up the amphibian order Urodela. They have long bodies, long tails, and two pairs of legs of roughly similar size. Most are found in temperate climates in North America, Europe and Asia, but some live in the tropics of Central and South America.

There are nine different families of the Urodela. Six are dealt with here. Later pages in this book deal with Congo eels and sirens (see pages 92-93) and mudpuppies (see pages 94-95). A few species of salamander are commonly given the name "newt"; these are described on pages 90-91.

WATERY HOMES
Salamanders live in a wide variety of habitats. Some species live entirely on land, some live entirely in water, while others divide their time between land and water. The skin of a salamander allows water to pass through quite easily. Because of this, even the land types need to live in damp places. If they are exposed to hot dry conditions, they soon lose water and die. Land-living species commonly live under rocks and logs or burrow in damp earth. In very hot weather, salamanders retreat into damp refuges, emerging only during the cool of the night. But, like other amphibians, they are a similar temperature to their surroundings. If temperatures are too low, they hide away and become inactive.

BREATHING SKINS
Many salamanders breathe air using lungs. A salamander may also use the damp inner surface of its mouth to get oxygen. Often the soft skin under the salamander's throat can be seen pumping rapidly, helping to change the air in the mouth.

Even when these two methods are used, quite a large part of a salamander's oxygen is obtained through the damp skin. The largest family of salamanders, with over 200 species, do not have lungs at all. They breathe just through the mouth and skin.

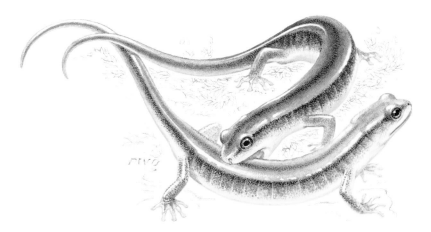

▼The Cave salamander spends all its life on land. It lives in the twilight zone near cave entrances.

▲Many male salamanders bite or grasp the female during courtship, as do Two-lined salamanders.

REPULSIVE SKINS

In a salamander's skin there are many glands. Some of these help to keep it moist and slimy. But some species have other glands that secrete substances which are poisonous or taste nasty. These can deter enemy attacks.

Poisonous salamanders are often very brightly coloured to warn predators to leave them alone. Several species, such as the Spotted salamander, have glands on the back of the neck. When attacked, they crouch to present their bad-tasting neck to the enemy. Others with glands on the neck actually butt an enemy with their heads. Some of the American mole

salamanders do this. It seems effective against small predators such as shrews. Some lungless salamanders have many glands on the tail. When attacked, they wave the tail at an enemy. They may be able to shed their tails, leaving behind a distasteful morsel which thrashes wildly and distracts the predator. The salamanders can then escape and grow a new tail.

SMALL APPETITES

All salamanders are carnivores. They feed on small living animals such as insects, slugs, snails and worms. Some kinds can flick out the tongue to catch prey. Salamanders can be quite ferocious for their size, but because of their slow pace of life and periods of inactivity they do not consume huge amounts of food. The slow pace of their lives may also help them become long-lived. Quite small species may live 25 years, and some individuals are known to have lived 50 years.

HIDDEN MILLIONS

Salamanders are secretive. Most are small (few are more than 15cm long), live in cool shady places, and become active at night, so they usually escape human attention. But in some places they can be very abundant. In the forests of eastern USA, it has been calculated that there is probably a greater weight of salamanders than all the birds and mammals put together.

BIGGEST AMPHIBIANS

Some salamanders are the biggest of all living amphibians. These are the giant salamanders of eastern Asia. As much as 1.6m in length, they never leave the water, which supports their weight. They breathe with lungs and through the skin.

▲Species of salamander *Bolitoglossa schizodactyla* (1) is a lungless species with webbed feet. The Red salamander (*Pseudotriton ruber*) (2) burrows into mud near streams. The Tiger salamander (*Ambystoma tigrinum*) (3) is a close relative of the axolotl. *Batrachuperus pinchonii* (4) and *Onychodactylus japonicus* (5) live in Asia. *Tylotriton taliangensis* (6) has a warty skin.

◄The Spotted salamander of North America lives on land as an adult, but returns to water to lay its eggs.

EGGS AND NESTS

Salamanders have three main types of life cycle. Some breed entirely on land. Some have a "typical" amphibian life cycle, with eggs and larvae in the water and adults on land. (Newts are a good example of this.) Then there are species that spend all the stages of their life cycle in water.

The Redback salamander, found in woodland areas of eastern North America, is a wholly land-living species. After mating, the female lays 20-30

eggs in a rotten log. The eggs are large, and the embryos inside them develop fast. The whole larval development is passed within the egg so the hatching salamander is just a tiny version of the adult. In some salamanders, such as the Alpine salamander of Europe, the egg develops inside the mother, who gives birth to live young.

In salamanders that live entirely in water, the number of eggs laid is often high. The hellbender of America lays up to 450 eggs. The male hellbender digs out a nest and guards it. He allows females to lay their eggs in the nest, then he fertilizes them, and guards them for the 10-12 weeks they take to develop into larvae. The larvae leave the nest and fend for themselves.

STAYING YOUNG

In various species of some families, such as the mole salamanders, gills and other larval features can be kept throughout life. Sometimes populations of the same species develop

differently in different environments. One population may progress to the adult in the normal way. Another population may keep large, frilly gills and a flattened tail. It seems to depend on the living conditions. But these "larval" forms may be able to reproduce. The most famous example is the axolotl of Mexico, which is typically larval looking, but can change to an "adult" if given the chemical iodine. Other species will change into adults if the water they are living in dries up.

▲ The hellbender is the largest of the North American salamanders, reaching 70cm from snout to tail.

BLIND CAVE-DWELLERS

Some of the lungless salamanders live in underground water in caves. The Texas blind salamander is white, with tiny eyes. The Grotto salamander, of the Ozarks in the USA, has a grey or brown larva which lives in streams, but the adult retreats into caves and loses its colour and the use of its eyes.

NEWTS

It is breeding time in spring. A male newt swims in front of the smaller female and blocks her way. He lashes his tail towards her, hitting her with a stream of water. He keeps up this courtship "dance" for some while. Then he deposits a packet of sperm on the pond bottom. It is picked up by the female and mating is complete.

▼ **Newt courtship** The eft or young (1) of the Red-spotted newt is red all over. The adults (2) are duller, with characteristic red spots. The male rubs a cheek gland on the female as he courts her. A breeding male Smooth newt (3) has dark spots, stripes on the head, a crest on the tail and body, and fringed hind toes.

NEWTS Salamandridae
(53 species)

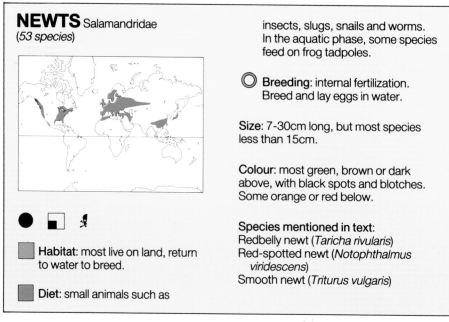

● ◻ ⚶

◻ **Habitat:** most live on land, return to water to breed.

◻ **Diet:** small animals such as insects, slugs, snails and worms. In the aquatic phase, some species feed on frog tadpoles.

◯ **Breeding:** internal fertilization. Breed and lay eggs in water.

Size: 7-30cm long, but most species less than 15cm.

Colour: most green, brown or dark above, with black spots and blotches. Some orange or red below.

Species mentioned in text:
Redbelly newt (*Taricha rivularis*)
Red-spotted newt (*Notophthalmus viridescens*)
Smooth newt (*Triturus vulgaris*)

Newts all belong to the salamander family Salamandridae. There is no special scientific distinction between newts and salamanders, but "newt" is a common name given to several members of this family which live on land and return to the water for a few weeks in spring to breed.

HOMING CLUES

During their land-living stage, newts may be found several kilometres from a pond suitable for breeding. They can find their way back to their "home" waters, often the ones in which they grew up, using clues of various kinds. They all use their senses of smell and sight for direction-finding, but some newts have unusual senses. A number of species navigate by the Sun; others, such as the American Red-spotted newt, can use the Earth's magnetism to check their direction.

WATERY CHANGES

In their land-living phase, newts are generally inconspicuous, and spend much of their time in hiding places. They are often easier to find in water during the breeding season. They may undergo quite a change in appearance between the seasons. On land, the long body and tail are rounded. In the water, the skin becomes thinner and easier to breathe through. The tail becomes deep and flattened to help with swimming. Colours, especially of males, may become more vivid. Males of some species also develop a large body crest. Apart from showing its owner is male, this crest may help to increase the surface area which can absorb oxygen during the active courtship. In the skin, lateral line organs like those of fish develop. These are able to detect movements of prey in the water. Even the eyes change slightly to focus underwater.

COURTSHIP DANCES

In newts, fertilization is internal, but the male has no penis to insert in the female during mating. Instead he produces a little packet of sperm sitting on a base, rather like a golf ball on a tee. He has to persuade the female to walk over this and take the packet from the "tee" into her cloaca. An elaborate courtship dance may be used to manoeuvre her into the right position. Sometimes the male may grab the female, as in the Redbelly newt. Secretions from scent glands are important parts of the ritual.

EGGS AND YOUNG

The females of all European species usually lay their eggs singly on water plants. The eggs hatch into larvae, which have feathery gills. Legs form later. Further on in summer, the gills disappear and the tiny newts (efts) emerge on to land. In some species, they may spend several years on land before returning to water to breed.

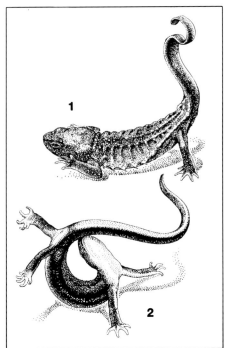

◄Defensive postures The Spiny newt (*Echinotriton andersoni*) (1) in defensive posture. It has long spiny ribs. If grasped by a predator, these push out through poison glands in the skin. A Redbelly newt (2) holds tail and chin high to show the warning colour below.

▼Other courtship behaviour The male Redbelly (1) clasps the female and rubs a gland under his chin on her nostrils. The male Smooth newt (2) fans his tail to send odours to the female.

CONGO EELS AND SIRENS

The mud at the bottom of a ditch stirs. A head appears, fringed with frilly gills, followed by a long, dark body. The siren wriggles lazily across the mud, with no apparent aim. But it is approaching a crayfish from behind, and before this animal can escape, the siren's jaws snap shut to capture it.

There are three species of Congo eel, or amphiuma, and three species of siren. All are long-bodied and completely aquatic. They live in North America. Congo eels have lungs, and four legs, although the legs are too tiny to be of any use in the adults. The sirens have gills on the outside of the body, and no back legs. The weak front legs are just behind the head.

MUDDY HOMES
Congo eels are swamp-dwellers. After rain, they may sometimes wriggle out at the water's edge. Usually, though, they are out of sight, living in a burrow from which they emerge at night to feed on frogs, snails and fish. Sirens live in ditches, shallow streams and lakes, but they too spend much of their time buried in the sand or mud at the bottom of the water.

SURVIVING DROUGHT
Many of the ponds and ditches where sirens live dry up in the summer. As the sand or mud dries out, the slime coat on the siren's skin hardens to form a stiff cocoon, which covers its whole body except the mouth. It can survive like this for many weeks until the water returns.

GUARDING THE EGGS
Congo eels lay a long string of eggs. The mother coils round them and guards them until they hatch, which can be 20 weeks or more. Egg-laying often happens when water levels are high. As it falls, the female and her eggs may be left in a damp hollow beneath a log. When they hatch, the young find their way back to water.

BIG AND SMALL
The Three-toed amphiuma, and the Greater siren, can reach lengths of up to 90cm, making them some of the largest amphibians. Big Congo eels can give a painful bite. At the other extreme is the Dwarf siren, only about 10cm long, which thrives among water hyacinths.

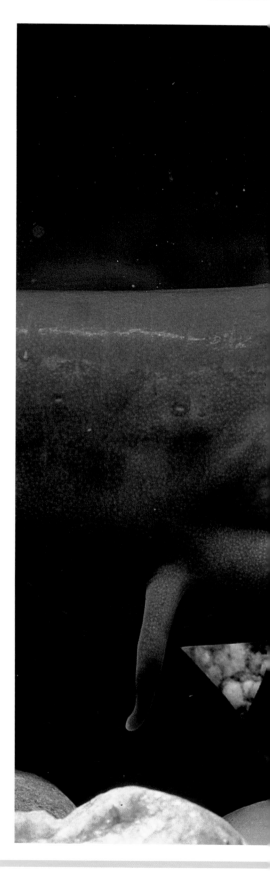

▶A Congo eel in its watery home. These animals have long thin bodies, but are amphibians, not fish. All live in south-eastern USA, not in Africa.

CONGO EELS AND SIRENS Amphiumidae and Sirenidae (*6 species*)

● ■

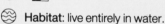 Habitat: live entirely in water.

■ Diet: frogs, fish, worms, snails.

○ Breeding: internal fertilization in Congo eels, which lay up to 200 eggs. Siren breeding little known; eggs laid singly.

Size: 10-110cm long.

Colour: dull colours, browns, blacks, greys and greens.

Species mentioned in text:
Dwarf siren (*Pseudobranchus striatus*)
Greater siren (*Siren lacertina*)
Three-toed amphiuma or Congo eel
  (*Amphiuma tridactylum*)

MUDPUPPIES

Deep in an underground cavern, a cold stream runs beneath the earth. It is totally dark. But the water is not empty of life. In a backwater floats a salamander as long as a man's hand. It is too dark to see, but this animal feels its way through the water and detects its prey without using eyes. But it feels no movement of other animals now. It sinks to the bottom and rests on the cavern floor. Much of its time is spent resting.

The animals in the mudpuppy family live their lives completely in water. Even as breeding adults they keep the feathery gills of larvae, and have small, weak legs. In eastern North America live the mudpuppy and the waterdogs. These names were given in the false belief that these animals bark. In Europe, in Yugoslavia and one small area of Italy, lives the olm.

POT-HOLING SALAMANDER

Olms live entirely in caves, often far underground. Up to 30cm long, including tail, they live in pitch darkness in caves with temperatures between 5 and 10°C. Occasionally, when there are floods, olms may be swept from their caves into open waters. Otherwise they are rarely seen by people. Olms seem to be becoming rarer, perhaps because of pollution.

A DARK WORLD

Skin colour is of no importance in the darkness. The olm has no pigment, so looks a pasty white, except for the gills, which are bright red where the blood shows through. Eyes are also of little use in the darkness, and those of the olm are very tiny.

BREEDING MYSTERY

Olms, as studied in aquaria, seem to have two ways of producing young. Whether both are used in the wild, or whether one is the normal method, is not really known. Sometimes the female lays eggs, in a clutch of up to 70, beneath a stone. Both male and female seem to guard them as they develop.

Alternatively, the female may keep her eggs inside her body. Most eggs break down, providing nourishment for just two, which develop into large larvae and are born alive. Young olms may show some signs of colouring, but this usually disappears before they are adult. If exposed to light, they may become coloured. The olm is rather variable both in size and shape. This is

MUDPUPPIES Proteidae
(6 species)

● ◱ 🐟

〰 Habitat: live entirely in water.

▨ Diet: frogs, fish, worms, snails.

◎ Breeding: internal fertilization. Up to 190 eggs laid. Olm may produce live young.

Size: 11-33cm long.

Colour: dull colours, grey or brown. Olm white.

Species mentioned in text:
Mudpuppy (*Necturus maculosus*)
Olm (*Proteus anguinus*)
Waterdog (*Necturus lewisi*)

▲The olm (1) lives in underground streams and lakes in caves in Yugoslavia. It is usually white, but young ones may show some colour. The mudpuppy (2) lives in North America in ponds, lakes and streams.

▶A mudpuppy shows its blood-filled external gills. The gills vary in size depending on the oxygen content of the water. In stagnant water they are large, but in running water, where there is much oxygen, they may be quite small.

▼A waterdog scrambles over a dead log. Although they breathe mainly by gills, these animals sometimes come to the surface for air, or even emerge briefly on land if the soil is damp.

perhaps not surprising, as the populations in different caves and regions are unable to mix, and are likely to pass on their own peculiarities to their offspring.

DOGGED DEVOTION

In the mudpuppies and waterdogs, mating takes place in the autumn. The eggs are fertilized internally, but remain inside the mother until the next spring. The female lays up to 190 eggs, sticking each to a rock or a log. The eggs are guarded for between 5 and 9 weeks. The male performs this task, which makes a long devotion to duty for an animal that mated months before. Mudpuppies take several years to reach maturity. They feed on fish, insects and crayfish.

FROGS AND TOADS

It is a rainy night in early spring. From a pond comes a sound like small motor-bike engines – male frogs calling to advertise their presence. Other frogs hop to the pond from all directions. The large females, full of eggs, are seized by males as they enter the water. Next morning, the pond is full of round masses of frogspawn.

Frogs and toads are the most numerous amphibians. They are found on most islands and on all continents except Antarctica. The great majority occur in warm areas of the world, but many are found in cool climates. Two species, the European common frog and the Wood frog of North America, can even live within the Arctic Circle. Most frogs and toads live both in water and on land, at least for part

FROGS AND TOADS
Order Anura: 17 families
(2,609 species)

● ▣ ♨

▨ **Habitat:** adults live mostly on land. Some burrow or climb. Some live entirely in water.

▨ **Diet:** insects, worms, snails, some small vertebrates.

○ **Breeding:** typically external

fertilization, laying eggs in water where tadpoles develop. Many variations and exceptions.

Size: smallest (*Sminthillus limbatus*): 1.2cm snout to vent; largest (Goliath frog): 30cm.

Colour: from dull browns and greens to vivid reds, yellows, blues.

Species mentioned in text:
Darwin's frog (*Rhinoderma darwinii*)
European common frog (*Rana temporaria*)
Golden toad (*Bufo periglenes*)
Goliath frog (*Rana goliath*)
Malaysian horned toad (*Ceratophrys dorsata*)
Midwife toad (*Alytes obstetricans*)
Red-and-blue poison arrow frog (*Dendrobates pumilio*)
Surinam toad (*Pipa pipa*)
Western spadefoot toad (*Scaphiopus hammondii*)
Wood frog (*Rana sylvatica*)

of their lives, but some live entirely in water and others entirely on land. Some succeed in living in places that seem at first sight unsuitable, such as savannahs and deserts.

FROG OR TOAD?

How can frogs be told from toads? "Frogs" are smooth-skinned, long-limbed and live in or close to water. "Toads" are stout-bodied with short limbs, and have warty skins. They live in damp places away from water. The word frog or toad really describes the look of the creature. There is no special scientific difference. Some scientific families contain both "frogs" and "toads". In this encyclopedia the tree frogs are dealt with on pages 102 to 105. All other frogs and toads are

▼ Many species of frog gather in large numbers at spawning sites. These are spawning European common frogs.

dealt with in this section. Unless a particular type is specified, the term "frog" includes toads as well.

LONG JUMP EXPERTS

Frogs have a much shorter body than other amphibians. They have nine bones or less in the backbone, which makes it short and rigid. Frogs do not have a narrow neck so the head joins straight on to the body. They do not have a tail either.

These adaptations are connected with the way frogs jump. The long back legs fold into three sections, thigh, shin and foot, of almost equal length. When the leg is suddenly straightened, the frog shoots forward. The short front limbs cushion the landing. The direction of jump is not

▼ Mating Golden toads. During mating, the male clasps the female and fertilizes the eggs as she lays them.

always very well controlled, but it makes an effective means of escaping an enemy. The record for a single leap by a large frog is over 5m; most jumps are much shorter. The long back limbs are also good for swimming. They are pushed backwards in an action similar to the human breaststroke, and the webbed feet push on the water.

Some species of frog are good burrowers. They dig themselves down backwards using a sideways shuffle of the hind feet. The heel in these species has a special hard projection that acts as a scraper and shovel.

BIG EYES AND EARS

A frog's eyes are usually large. They are at the side of the head, so the frog can watch all round for danger. Some kinds of frog have eyes that are specially adapted to detect small moving objects which might be prey. The eyes have lids to protect them, and

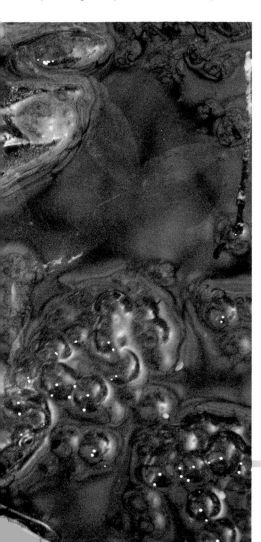

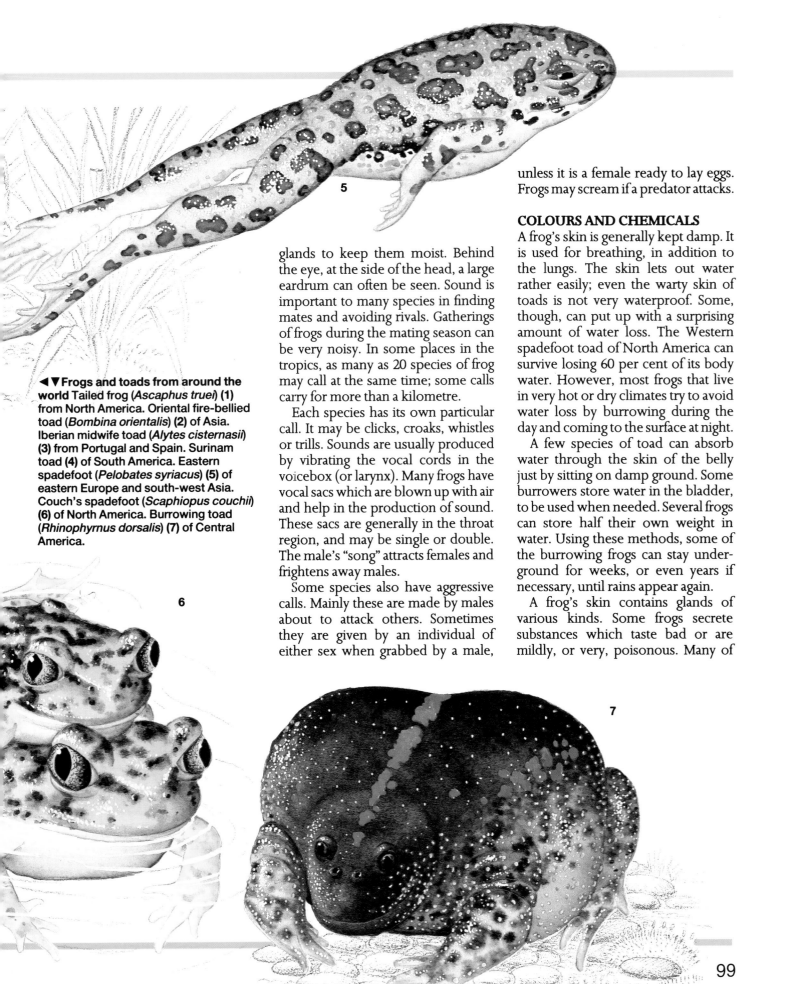

◄▼Frogs and toads from around the world Tailed frog (*Ascaphus truei*) (1) from North America. Oriental fire-bellied toad (*Bombina orientalis*) (2) of Asia. Iberian midwife toad (*Alytes cisternasii*) (3) from Portugal and Spain. Surinam toad (4) of South America. Eastern spadefoot (*Pelobates syriacus*) (5) of eastern Europe and south-west Asia. Couch's spadefoot (*Scaphiopus couchii*) (6) of North America. Burrowing toad (*Rhinophyrnus dorsalis*) (7) of Central America.

glands to keep them moist. Behind the eye, at the side of the head, a large eardrum can often be seen. Sound is important to many species in finding mates and avoiding rivals. Gatherings of frogs during the mating season can be very noisy. In some places in the tropics, as many as 20 species of frog may call at the same time; some calls carry for more than a kilometre.

Each species has its own particular call. It may be clicks, croaks, whistles or trills. Sounds are usually produced by vibrating the vocal cords in the voicebox (or larynx). Many frogs have vocal sacs which are blown up with air and help in the production of sound. These sacs are generally in the throat region, and may be single or double. The male's "song" attracts females and frightens away males.

Some species also have aggressive calls. Mainly these are made by males about to attack others. Sometimes they are given by an individual of either sex when grabbed by a male,

unless it is a female ready to lay eggs. Frogs may scream if a predator attacks.

COLOURS AND CHEMICALS
A frog's skin is generally kept damp. It is used for breathing, in addition to the lungs. The skin lets out water rather easily; even the warty skin of toads is not very waterproof. Some, though, can put up with a surprising amount of water loss. The Western spadefoot toad of North America can survive losing 60 per cent of its body water. However, most frogs that live in very hot or dry climates try to avoid water loss by burrowing during the day and coming to the surface at night.

A few species of toad can absorb water through the skin of the belly just by sitting on damp ground. Some burrowers store water in the bladder, to be used when needed. Several frogs can store half their own weight in water. Using these methods, some of the burrowing frogs can stay underground for weeks, or even years if necessary, until rains appear again.

A frog's skin contains glands of various kinds. Some frogs secrete substances which taste bad or are mildly, or very, poisonous. Many of

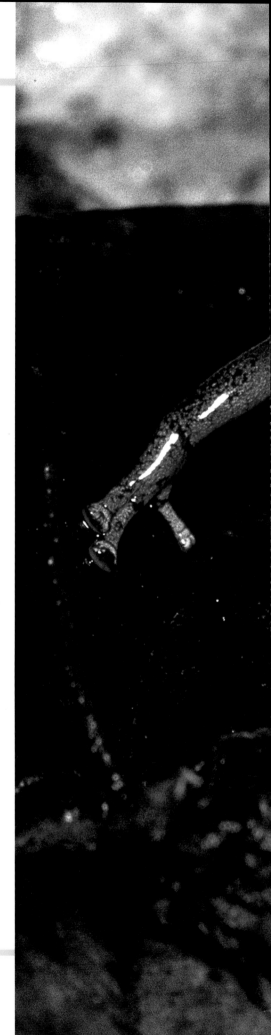

the most poisonous frogs, such as the poison arrow frogs of Central and South America, are decked out in brilliant colours that may serve to warn off enemies. Other frogs may have "flash" colours that suddenly show when they jump, and may confuse a predator. Most frogs, though, have subdued colours which work well to camouflage them. Some, such as the Malaysian horned toad, go one stage better by having bodies which imitate the shape and colour of dead leaves on the forest floor where they live.

MASS BREEDING

Most frogs are scattered over a wide area for much of the year, and must migrate to a suitable breeding site when conditions are right. Hundreds, or even thousands of individuals, may congregate in one spot. Frogs will often return to the same pond or lake again and again, often the one in which they grew up. They may even pass other apparently suitable water on the way there.

Many kinds of clues and landmarks seem to be involved in this navigation. Unfortunately, frogs may continue to return to places ruined as breeding sites by man. They may also cross roads and railways and be killed in large numbers. In some places in Britain "toad tunnels" have been built under roads so they can cross the road in safety.

FROM EGG TO FROG

The typical frog lays large numbers of eggs coated with jelly in the water. The tadpoles that hatch from the eggs have a rounded body containing feeding organs, with a long, coiled gut for digesting plant food. They have gills to breathe, and a long tail which they wriggle to help them swim. After some weeks growing, they "metamorphose". Legs grow. The tail is lost. Gills disappear. Lungs form. The long gut becomes much shorter, and now copes with a diet of insects and other small animals. They are now frogs, and live mainly on land. This is the typical frog life cycle.

Many species of frog have more unusual ways of growing up. Some frogs lay their eggs on vegetation in a nest of frothy foam that hardens like meringue. At hatching time, the foam softens, and the tadpoles drop into the water below.

Some species produce fewer eggs, but look after them so that they stand a better chance of survival. In the Midwife toad, the male winds the string of eggs round his hind legs and carries them about. He takes the eggs to water for hatching. Some species of poison arrow frog put a single tadpole into a tiny pond formed at the leaf base of a plant. The mother lays a clutch of unfertilized eggs to act as food for the tadpole.

The female Surinam toad keeps the eggs embedded in the skin of the back until they develop into tiny toads. Perhaps the oddest of all is Darwin's frog, in which the male swallows hatching tadpoles into his large vocal sac. When they have completed their development there, he spits them out as froglets.

◄Oriental fire-bellied toads are camouflaged above, but display the bright belly colours when attacked.

►Warning colours are found in many frogs, such as these Red-and-blue poison arrow frogs.

TREE FROGS

The reeds at the edge of the pond seem empty. But as a swarm of gnats dances over the water, the reeds erupt in movement. Little green shapes launch themselves into the air after the flying meals. The pond edge is full of hungry young tree frogs, clambering on the plants and watching for easy prey.

There are tree frogs living over most of the warmer parts of the world. The true tree frogs are a large family with over 600 species. They are widespread in many countries with a warm climate but absent from most of Africa and southern Asia. There they are replaced by the Old World tree frogs, which include the "flying" frogs. A third small family of tree frogs lives in tropical America. These are the glass frogs, generally bright green, but with such a transparent skin that many of their bones and organs can be seen from outside.

TACKY TOES

Tree frogs often have rather flattened bodies. This helps them keep balance and they can press close to leaves or tree trunks when they are resting. The flat skin of the belly is loose and can be pressed tightly against a surface to help them stick. Many tree frogs have large areas of sticky webbing between their fingers and toes which also help them hold on. The toes end in round discs which act as suckers, allowing the frog to climb up smooth leaves. Many tree frogs also have extra bones in their toes which help them to curl the toes round very thin twigs to get a grip. All this, together with their small size and lightness, makes them very agile climbers.

The eyes of many tree frogs are very large. They often face forward more than the eyes of other frogs. Both these features help them to judge distances as they jump and climb, and

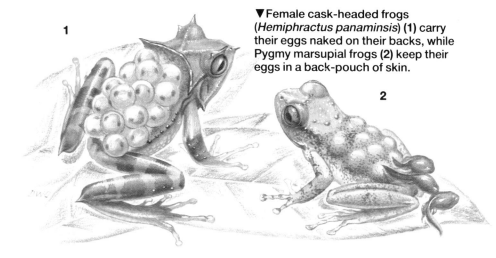

▼Female cask-headed frogs (*Hemiphractus panaminsis*) **(1)** carry their eggs naked on their backs, while Pygmy marsupial frogs **(2)** keep their eggs in a back-pouch of skin.

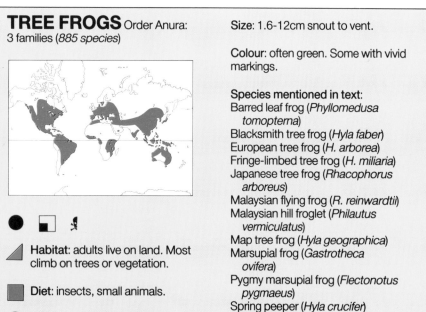

TREE FROGS Order Anura:
3 families (*885 species*)

● ◪ ⚘

▲ **Habitat:** adults live on land. Most climb on trees or vegetation.

◪ **Diet:** insects, small animals.

◎ **Breeding:** typically external fertilization; eggs laid in water, on leaves or in foam nests.

Size: 1.6-12cm snout to vent.

Colour: often green. Some with vivid markings.

Species mentioned in text:
Barred leaf frog (*Phyllomedusa tomopterna*)
Blacksmith tree frog (*Hyla faber*)
European tree frog (*H. arborea*)
Fringe-limbed tree frog (*H. miliaria*)
Japanese tree frog (*Rhacophorus arboreus*)
Malaysian flying frog (*R. reinwardtii*)
Malaysian hill froglet (*Philautus vermiculatus*)
Map tree frog (*Hyla geographica*)
Marsupial frog (*Gastrotheca ovifera*)
Pygmy marsupial frog (*Flectonotus pygmaeus*)
Spring peeper (*Hyla crucifer*)
Water-holding frog (*Cyclorana platycephala*)
White's tree frog (*Litoria caerulea*)

also when attacking prey. Most are active at night, and large eyes may operate well at low light levels. Many insects are active at night, giving the frogs their main food supply.

FLYING FROGS

In the jungles of South-east Asia live several species of "flying" frogs. Flying frogs have even bigger feet than most tree frogs, and long toes with well-developed webs between the toes. They can jump from a tree, spread the webbing, and parachute safely to a lower level. A Malaysian flying frog may travel 15m or so in a single glide from one tree to another. The Fringe-limbed tree frog of Central America has similar habits.

Some species have the ability to change colour greatly. The Malaysian flying frog may change colour through the day from blue to green to black.

▲Tropical leaf frogs, for example *Phyllomedusa bicolor*, lay their eggs wrapped in leaves overhanging water.

▶A shoal of tadpoles of the Map tree frog in Trinidad may gain safety from predators by clumping.

▼A European tree frog springs from its perch. They sometimes leap to catch food, but the usual reason is to escape from their enemies.

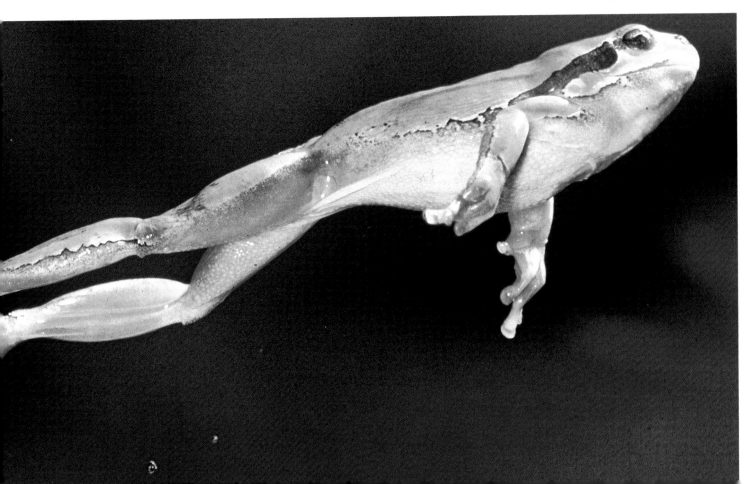

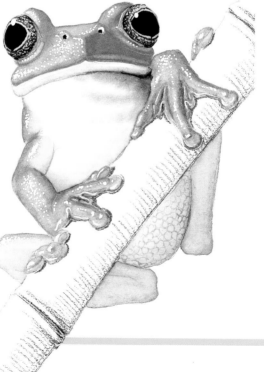

▲ The Barred leaf frog lives in the Amazon rain forest. The huge eyes are a major sense, especially for hunting.

◄ The green colouring of the Japanese tree frog is good camouflage among the leaves.

UNDERGROUND TREE FROGS

Not all of the tree frog family spend their time climbing. Some of the group have become ground-living, including the cricket frogs of North America, in which the toe discs are quite small. A few even go underground. The Water-holding frog of Australia is one. It lives in very dry regions. When it can get water it drinks until it is bloated. It secretes a special outer skin layer, which helps prevent water loss. This allows it to survive the lengthy dry periods by burrowing into the soil with its own water store. When rains come, these frogs may emerge in their thousands to breed. Trains on the Australian transcontinental railway have on occasions had to stop because so many frogs were squashed on the lines, the wheels could not get a grip.

Australia has a variety of tree frogs, some beautifully coloured. They can be pink, blue, violet, yellow or even shiny. Probably the best known is White's tree frog, which often finds its way into houses, water tanks and drainpipes. Like many tree frogs, this species is green, although its scientific name means sky-blue. It was named from a pickled specimen which had lost the yellow colour from its skin.

NOISY SINGERS

Several species of tree frog are noisy breeders, producing loud calls to attract mates to the breeding pond. American species such as the Spring peeper are very well known for their choruses. The Spring peeper blows the floor of its mouth out as a huge resonating chamber. Calling males of the European tree frog are sometimes mistaken for quacking ducks.

Many tree frogs lay clumps of spawn in the water and tadpoles develop into adults in typical frog fashion. In some kinds, such as the European tree frog, the tadpoles are rather solitary. In others, large numbers of tadpoles may clump together. Sometimes these shoals swim in a spiral. The action may stir up food from the bottom of the pond.

PRIVATE POND

The Blacksmith tree frog of South America comes to the ground in the breeding season. The male finds shallow water and makes a nest of mud. This is shaped like a crater, with walls about 10cm high, and collects its own little pool of water. The male sits there until he has attracted a female to lay her eggs. The tadpoles are thus provided with their own private pond, giving them a safer start to life.

LEAF NESTS

The leaf frogs are mostly large and brightly coloured. They live in wet forest in Central and South America. During mating, they hold leaves together, and lay their eggs between the leaves. The sticky, stiff jelly around the eggs keeps the leaves together until the first tadpoles hatch, when the jelly softens and the tadpoles drop in the water. The female may keep the developing eggs moist by repeatedly emptying her bladder over them.

Many of the Old World tree frogs are foam nesters. Several males may compete to fertilize the eggs as the female lays them, and the males'

▲ *Hyla leucophyllata* of South America shows the toe pads which tree frogs use to cling to leaves and vertical surfaces.

▼ Tiny froglets of the Marsupial frog emerge from their mother's pouch, their development completed without water.

thrashing legs beat the foam into a nest. Such a nest may contain up to as many as 150 eggs.

Glass frogs usually lay their eggs on leaves above water. In some species they are known to be guarded by the male. The Malaysian hill froglet lives high in the cloud forests where there are few pools of water. It lays its eggs in huge sheets of damp moss hanging from trees. The eggs develop directly into miniature froglets.

TADPOLE BACKPACKS

In about 60 species of tropical tree frogs, the female lays a fairly small number of eggs which she then carries on her back. They may just be stuck to the skin. In others there is an open pouch in the skin to carry the eggs.

The female Pygmy marsupial frog of South America has an open pouch on her back in which the eggs develop. She releases the tadpoles into little pools formed at the base of the leaves of some plants.

The female Marsupial frog has a pouch on her back which can be closed. She lays eggs with her back up and head downwards. The male fertilizes the eggs and they slip down a groove into the pouch. The tadpoles continue their development riding in the pouch. Their movements can be seen as they wriggle about. The tadpoles emerge as froglets, having been protected for the most vulnerable part of their life. When it is time for them to emerge, the mother opens the pouch entrance with her longest toe.

SEA TURTLES

It is a moonlit night on a tropical island. On a sandy beach a huge black shape pulls itself out of the water. It heaves forward a few metres, then gives a huge sigh, and stops to rest. Slowly it moves above the tide mark and begins to dig. A female Green turtle has come ashore to lay her eggs. By dawn she will have gone back to sea.

All the warm oceans of the world contain sea turtles, and five of the seven species, including the Green turtle, are found right round the world. Yet all species except one are in danger because of human activity.

SEA TURTLES Cheloniidae, Dermochelyidae (*7 species*)

○ ■◻ ☠

~ **Habitat:** tropical and other warm seas.

▨ **Diet:** jellyfish, crabs, sponges, shellfish, some sea grasses.

○ **Breeding:** up to 200 eggs laid in single clutch in special nest. No other parental care. Several clutches may follow single mating.

Size: smallest (Atlantic ridley): 0.75m long; largest (Leatherback): up to 2.13m long, weight up to 680kg.

Colour: mostly dull – grey, olive, brown, black; some with contrasting markings.

Species mentioned in text:
Atlantic ridley (*Lepidochelys kempi*)
Flatback turtle (*Chelonia depressa*)
Green turtle (*C. mydas*)
Leatherback turtle (*Dermochelys coriacea*)

SEA CHANGES

Compared with land tortoises, the sea turtles have a more lightweight shell. The bony part is reduced, but horny plates are still present on the outside, except in the Leatherback turtle. The shell is a streamlined shape. The legs have become flattened to form flippers. The front flippers are particularly long and the turtle flaps them up and down like wings to push itself through the water. In the sea, turtles can travel at speeds of over 30kph, although they usually move at a more leisurely pace of about 6kph.

Like all other reptiles, sea turtles breathe air with lungs. The length of time they can stay underwater depends on the species, the amount of oxygen in the water and how active the turtles are. If they are resting, it can be several weeks.

TURTLE TEARS

Sea turtles swallow seawater as they feed, and much of their food is also salty. To get rid of this extra salt, a sea turtle produces salty tears from a special gland close to each eye. The tears are produced all the time. In the sea the tears wash away, but on land a sea turtle always looks as if it is crying. The sea turtles' eyes are suited to see well in water, but in the air turtles are short-sighted.

BEACH NESTS

Sea turtles spend almost their entire lives in the water. But the pregnant females have to come on to the land to lay their eggs.

A female turtle lays her eggs in a hole on a sandy beach. She uses her back feet to scoop out a nest chamber, which must not get wet with salty water if the eggs are to develop. Turtle eggs are round, with shells like paper, and clutches of 60 to 150 are usual. A female Green turtle can lay 100 or more eggs at a time and may lay 11 clutches in one season, which lasts about 4 months. After laying a clutch,

◀A Green turtle swims through the sea above a coral reef. Clumsy on land, it moves gracefully when supported by water.

◄Hatchling Flatback turtles dash for the water. Birds catch many hatchlings before they reach the sea.

▼**Species of turtle** The Leatherback turtle (1) has a leathery skin over its shell, not horny plates. It feeds on jellyfish, some fish and crustaceans. The Green turtle (2) is so called because of the colour of its fat. Adults feed near the shore on sea grasses.

the mother covers the eggs with sand and then drags herself back to the water. All this activity takes place in a single night, and is a great effort for an animal not built for moving on land.

HATCHING AS A GROUP
Turtle eggs need at least a month to develop, but hatch fastest when they are warm. The whole batch hatches together, and the baby turtles scurry instinctively to the bright light shining off the sea. A hatchling sea turtle weighs little more than 22g, but it may grow into an adult weighing 180kg.

LONG-DISTANCE TRAVELLERS
In some turtle species, although they range widely in the sea, the number of important breeding sites is limited.

1

2

Green turtles in the southern Atlantic feed off the coast of South America, but travel 2,200km across the ocean to Ascension Island to breed. The Atlantic ridley's breeding ground is on the Mexican coast. Here, 40,000 turtles may come ashore in just one night.

Although sea turtles produce many young, few survive to become adults. Some people hunt turtles for meat and for their shells. They also dig up and eat the eggs. In various locations, there are now projects to protect turtles and their breeding beaches. Eggs are dug up and incubated in safe places. When the hatchlings can fend for themselves, they are released.

TURTLES AND TERRAPINS

On a mudbank in a slow tropical river dozens of turtles bask in the Sun. Some turtles walk over the others as if they were part of the ground. The shadow of a large bird passes over them. Many turtles plunge into the water. With frantically paddling limbs they dive to the river bottom. Later, when all is quiet, their heads reappear one by one.

Of the 244 species of tortoise-like animals (chelonians) nearly 200 live in and around fresh water. At first sight an animal with a shell seems an unlikely design for the water, but it works well for a whole range of freshwater turtles. In most species the shell has become flatter and lighter compared with that of a land tortoise. It is also a more streamlined shape for swimming. Some turtles have no outer horny plates and the bony part of the shell has large spaces inside it.

These so-called soft-shell turtles have very flat shells which allow them to hide in the mud at the bottom of the water.

In many freshwater turtles the limbs are flattened and paddle-like. This is usually most obvious in types that rarely leave the water, but some pond tortoises that spend most of their time in water still have rounded limbs just like their land cousins.

BREATHING IN A BOX

The turtle's ribs make up part of the bony box of the shell. A turtle cannot move its ribs in and out to pump air in and out of its lungs as we can. Instead, muscles above the tops of the legs and in the abdomen provide the pumping action. Many aquatic turtles have extra ways of getting the oxygen they need. They may take in oxygen through their skin. The thin lining of the throat, or even special thin-walled sacs in the cloaca (the single posterior opening of the body), can also act as a kind of gill (an underwater breathing

structure). In well-oxygenated water some turtles can remain underwater almost forever. Some species hibernate underwater for weeks without needing to surface to breathe.

FINDING A MATE

In many turtle species the sexes look similar, but some species have markings which distinguish males from females. In the Carolina box turtle, males have red eyes, while those of females are yellow. In some turtles the males are smaller than the females. There may be other clues, such as a longer, thicker tail, or an incurved underside to the shell, which show that a turtle is a male. But in most species it seems to be behaviour, rather than appearance, that allows the sexes to recognize one another.

To attract females, males use a variety of means, from biting and butting with the head, to special ways of swimming and stroking the female with their claws. In some turtles, such as the slider, where the male is much

---

TURTLES AND TERRAPINS Order Chelonia
(families except those of sea turtles and land tortoises) (*196 species*)

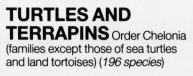

○ ■ ⚘

■ **Habitat:** rivers, lakes, swamps, estuaries; a few always on land.

▨ **Diet:** mainly meat, including insects, crustaceans, fish, molluscs, other animals; some species partly or wholly plant-eating.

○ **Breeding:** lay eggs. Depending on species: round or long, soft or brittle-shelled, clutch from 1-100.

Size: smallest (Bog turtle): 11.4cm long; longest (softshell turtles): up to 1.15m long; heaviest (Alligator snapping turtle): weight 91kg or more.

Colour: mostly drab – brown, olive, grey; some have brightly coloured markings.

Species mentioned in text:
Alligator snapping turtle (*Macroclemys temmincki*)
Australian snake-necked turtle (*Emydura macquarii*)
Bog turtle (*Clemmys muhlenbergii*)
Carolina box turtle (*Terrapene carolina*)
Florida redbelly turtle (*Pseudemys nelsonii*)
Giant snake-necked turtle (*Chelodina expansa*)
Matamata (*Chelus fimbriatus*)
Slider or Red-eared turtle (*Pseudemys scripta*)

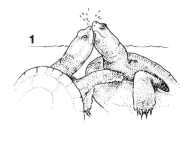

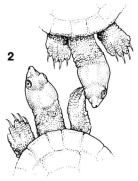

▲A male Australian snake-necked turtle courts a female by nudging her head above water (1), and by stroking her with his foot (2).

▲▼**Species of turtle** This Spiny soft-shell turtle (*Trionyx spiniferus*) **(1)** of North America is "snorkelling". The male Red-eared turtle or slider **(2)** courts a female by fluttering his claws in front of her face. The New Guinea plateless turtle (*Carrettochelys insculpta*) **(3)** is a strong swimmer. The Musk turtle (*Staurotypus salvinii*) **(4)** comes from Central America. Skin flaps and flattened shape camouflage the matamata **(5)** of South America.

smaller than the female, the male has long claws on his front feet to help in his courtship dance. The male swims backwards in front of the female and fans her with his long claws.

EGG-LAYING

All freshwater turtles lay eggs on land, even if they spend the rest of their lives in the water. Species that live in places where conditions are the same throughout the year may breed at any time. But most turtles breed only at certain times of the year, such as in the early summer in cooler climates, or in time with either the wet or the dry season in the tropics.

Eggs are buried in the ground, or, in species such as the stinkpots, under decaying vegetation. As one might expect, the bigger species of turtle lay bigger eggs. The biggest freshwater turtles, with shell lengths of 80cm, lay eggs 8cm long – about the size of a medium-sized hen's egg.

Apart from choosing a suitable nest, turtles do not look after their eggs or young. The eggs are incubated by warmth from the Sun or rotting vegetation. The warmer the eggs are, the sooner they are likely to hatch. The eggs of some kinds of turtle do not develop straight away so there may be a year between laying and hatching. The shortest time for development is about 2 months. In some species,

▲▼More species of turtle A Yellow-spotted Amazon turtle (*Podocnemis unifilis*) (1) takes a breath at the surface. The Yellow mud turtle (*Kinosternon flavescens*) (2) digs a special burrow to lay its eggs. The adult Central American river turtle (*Dermatemys mawei*) (3). The Big-headed turtle (*Platysternon megacephalum*) (4) is a good climber.

the temperature during incubation is known to have an effect on the sex of the hatchlings. When temperatures are high more females are produced, and when temperatures are low more males are produced.

HATCHING AT THE RIGHT TIME
The baby turtle has a peg, or "egg-tooth", on the front of its snout, which helps it to escape from the egg. The egg-tooth drops off soon after hatching. The baby turtle hatches with a supply of yolk still in its body, and may not need to feed for some time.

Once they hatch, the babies do not always leave the nest straight away. In the northern USA, some snapping turtles overwinter in their nests as babies. Some Central American sliders have to wait for rain to soften the ground before they can escape from their nests. The longest waiting time on record was for some baby Giant snake-necked turtles in Australia that had to stay in their nest for 664 days until a drought ended.

GETTING WARM
An important part of the day for many turtles is the time they spend basking in the Sun. They come out of the water on to logs or sandbanks, spread their legs, and sunbathe. This helps raise their bodies to a good working temperature, and may also help digestion.

Mid-morning and late afternoon are the main basking times.

Good basking sites may be used by many turtles at the same time. Rich sources of food can also attract a crowd of turtles. But although these animals may sometimes congregate in large numbers, they do not form family or other social groups with any structure. Most turtles seem little interested in one another except as possible mates or rivals. One exception is the cleaning behaviour seen in young sliders. They take it in turns to pull algae from one another's shells.

FEEDING METHODS
Most turtles feed on slow-moving prey, such as shellfish, worms and insect larvae. Many turtles eat some plants too. Diet may change with age. Baby sliders eat insects and other small animals, but adults have much more vegetable matter in their diet. Many turtles eat whatever plant or animal food they can find.

Some turtles have special ways of catching food. Snapping turtles have long bumpy necks and mud-coloured skins. The shell is often covered in

▲The strong high shell of the Florida redbelly turtle is unlike that of most aquatic species. It is a good defence against the crushing jaws of alligators.

algae. This helps the animals to lie hidden. They suddenly strike out with their powerful jaws at fish or smaller turtles. The matamata has very weak jaws. It catches its prey by opening its mouth wide. Water rushes into its mouth, taking the victim with it.

TOO SLOW AND DEFENCELESS
Populations of many river turtles and terrapins are declining today. Most seriously affected are the large river turtles and species with attractive shells. The main causes are destruction of their habitats, local killing for meat, and the demand from developed countries for luxury items such as turtle shell jewellery, leather goods and pets.

Unfortunately, the turtles' lumbering habits, their predictable nesting behaviour and their passive actions when threatened make them highly susceptible to hunting by people at all times.

LIZARDS

It is a warm day. There is a movement in the heather. A tiny head appears, followed by a long body and an even longer tail. A European common lizard is hunting. It turns its head on one side, listening and watching the vegetation intently. Suddenly it pounces, and snaps up a small spider.

Lizards are found on all continents except Antarctica. Most lizards are found in the tropics, but some live in cooler climates. The European common lizard lives as far north as the Arctic Circle in Scandinavia. There are 16 families of lizards. This article deals with the broad category of lizards. On pages 116-21 you can read about five of the most distinctive families, from chameleons to monitor lizards.

LIZARDS Sub-order Sauria
(3,751 species)

Habitat: all types of habitat from wet forest to desert; on all continents and many islands where temperature not too low.

Diet: usually small animals, but some are plant-eaters.

Breeding: typically lay eggs after internal fertilization. Some give birth to live young.

Size: smallest (Virgin Islands gecko, see page 54): total length 3.6cm; largest (Komodo dragon): length 3m, weight up to 160kg.

Colour: highly variable including green, brown, black and some bright colours.

Species mentioned in text:
Armadillo girdle-tailed lizard (Cordylus cataphractus)
Australian frilled lizard (Chlamydosaurus kingii)
European common lizard (Lacerta vivipara)
Flying dragon (Draco volans)
Komodo dragon (Varanus komodoensis).
Sharp-snouted snake lizard (Lialis burtonis)
Slow-worm (Anguis fragilis)
Sri Lanka prehensile-tail lizard (Cophotis celanica)
Sungazer (Cordylus giganteus)

▶▲Species of lizard Granite night lizard (*Xantusia henshawi*) **(1)** of California. Sharp-snouted snake lizard **(2)** of Australia. Common tegu (*Tupinambis teguixin*) **(3)** of South America. Colorado checkered whiptail (*Cnemidophorus tesselatus*) **(4)**. Flat lizard (*Platysaurus intermedius*) **(5)** of South Africa. Ocellated lizard (*Lacerta lepida*) **(6)** of western Mediterranean area.

A TYPICAL LIZARD

As may be expected in a group with nearly 4,000 species, lizards come in many different shapes and sizes. But a typical lizard is a fairly small animal, perhaps 10 to 20cm long; about half this length is the tail. A lizard has four legs, and its body is covered in small scales. It has good eyesight, and can see colours. The eyelids are usually movable. At the back of the head are small ear openings.

A lizard uses its tongue to help it "taste" the surroundings. It is a hunter, ambushing or hunting down small animals, often insects. To reproduce a typical lizard lays eggs.

OVER AND UNDERGROUND

Some lizards have become especially good at climbing, and a few, such as the Sri Lanka prehensile-tail lizard, even use their tail to hold on to branches. The Flying dragons of Asia are small lizards that have taken to the air. They climb trees and then jump from one tree to another, gliding on "wings" of skin. The skin is stretched over very long ribs, which stick out from the sides of the body.

At the other extreme are lizards that live underground. Many of these lizards have either very small legs or no legs at all. Their eyes may be tiny or even beneath the skin. When the eyes still work, each may be covered by a transparent "spectacle" instead of eyelids. The "spectacle" helps to protect the eye from damage or injury.

Some lizards, such as the water dragons of the Far East, are good swimmers. Others, such as the Australian frilled lizard, are able to run fast on their hind legs for a short distance if they need to escape an enemy.

RITUAL FIGHTS

Most lizards live on their own, but some species do react to other lizards. A few lizards are territorial, and the

113

males threaten any rivals which enter their territory. This may be done by rituals such as head-bobbing, rather than actual fighting. Lizards with this type of behaviour are often brightly coloured to increase the impact of the display. Colours may also be used to attract a mate.

DEFENCE AND ESCAPE
Lizards have many ways of protecting themselves from other animals that may eat them. They often keep very still, and their colours may allow them to blend into the surroundings. Some have specially tough scales. The plated lizards of Africa have bone underneath their scales. Other lizards have long spiny scales, which makes them difficult for an enemy to swallow. The sungazer will lash its spiny tail at an attacker. The Armadillo girdle-tailed lizard often simply wedges itself in a crevice for protection.

▼More species of lizard The Southern alligator lizard (*Elgaria multicarinata*) (1) of America has strong limbs, but is related to the slow-worm. The Chinese xenosaur (*Shinisaurus crocodilurus*) (2) lives along streams. The sungazer (3) uses its spiny tail for defence. The Bornean earless lizard (*Lanthanotus borneensis*) (4) is a good swimmer. The Gila monster (*Heloderma suspectum*) (5) is venomous, with fangs in its bottom jaw. The Asian blind lizard (*Dibamus novaeguineae*) (6) lives underground. It has eyes under the skin.

◄The slow-worm is a European legless lizard that grows to about 45cm long. It can live for more than 50 years.

Quite a different way of using the tail for defence is shown by wall lizards and slow-worms. By contracting some tail muscles, these lizards can make the tail break off at special weak areas in the tail bones. If it is attacked, the lizard drops its tail and leaves it behind, wriggling, as a decoy. The tail may continue to wriggle for several minutes. The lizard escapes; later it grows a replacement tail. Some lizards have specially coloured tails that attract additional attention.

The greatest threats to such lizards, however, are not natural predators, but humans. Especially in sub-tropical regions, the lizards' habitats are being altered or destroyed such that their populations are unlikely to recover.

EGGS OR LIVE YOUNG?

Most lizards lay eggs. A clutch of about 20 is very common. But some lizards produce live young. In most of these live-bearers, the mother lizard keeps the eggs inside her body until they are ready to hatch. The yolk inside the egg nourishes the young in the usual way. In a few lizards, such as the night lizards, a placenta forms so the babies can obtain some nourishment from the mother.

Live-bearing may be useful in difficult conditions, such as in places where summers are cool. The European common lizard produces live young in the north of its range, but lays eggs in the south, where summers are warmer. Strangest of all are a few lizard species in which no males are known. Females are able to produce a new generation of "identikit" lizards on their own.

6

◄The Sharp-snouted snake lizard has no front limbs, and small flaps for hind limbs. It eats other lizards.

CHAMELEONS

A chameleon moves slowly along a twig. As it moves, its body rocks backwards and forwards like a leaf in the wind. It is watching a grasshopper on the next branch. It edges to within 15cm of the unsuspecting insect. Suddenly, faster than the eye can follow, the chameleon's tongue shoots out and back, pulling the grasshopper into its mouth.

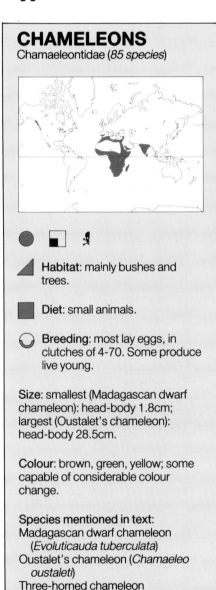

CHAMELEONS
Chamaeleontidae (*85 species*)

● ◼ 🦎

▲ Habitat: mainly bushes and trees.

◼ Diet: small animals.

◯ Breeding: most lay eggs, in clutches of 4-70. Some produce live young.

Size: smallest (Madagascan dwarf chameleon): head-body 1.8cm; largest (Oustalet's chameleon): head-body 28.5cm.

Colour: brown, green, yellow; some capable of considerable colour change.

Species mentioned in text:
Madagascan dwarf chameleon (*Evoluticauda tuberculata*)
Oustalet's chameleon (*Chamaeleo oustaleti*)
Three-horned chameleon (*C. jacksoni*)

Nearly all species of chameleon live in forests in Africa and Madagascar, feeding mainly on insects. One species lives in southern Europe; another is found in southern Asia.

TREE-CLIMBING
Chameleons have many odd features not found in any other lizards. For example, a chameleon has long legs, but they bend at the knee and elbow so that the feet go under the body. To grip a branch, a chameleon puts two toes round one side and the other three toes round the other side. The sharp claws on its feet also help it to grip. Chameleons generally move slowly, and can hold on tightly with at least two feet at once. In addition, most chameleons have a useful prehensile tail, which can be coiled round twigs to act as an anchor.

ALL-SEEING EYES
The eyes of a chameleon are mounted on movable turrets. These can be turned in all directions. Like most lizards, chameleons can move one eye independently of the other. One eye may be looking forward and down, while the other eye looks backwards and up.

A chameleon can scan all round for danger or possible meals. Sometimes, though, it is useful to have both eyes working together. A chameleon can swivel its eyes so that both look forward to focus on the same object. This helps it to judge distances when it is climbing or hunting.

TERRIFIC TONGUE
A chameleon's diet consists mainly of insects and spiders. Some of the larger species eat small birds and mammals. These are rarely caught with the jaws in the usual lizard fashion. Instead, the chameleon relies on its special tongue. The tongue normally rests folded inside the mouth, but it can be squeezed by special muscles and catapulted out to catch prey.

The tongue is often longer than the chameleon's head and body, and it can be used to hit an insect some way away. It can be shot out and pulled back in as little as 0.04 seconds. Its swollen tip can grasp prey and is also sticky so the prey does not escape as it is pulled into the mouth.

COLOUR CHANGE
Chameleons are famous for their ability to change colour. Most kinds are basically brown, green or yellowish, which helps to camouflage them in trees and bushes. But many species are able to change colour and pattern by moving pigments in the skin. They can change from almost white to almost black, with many shades and variations on their "natural" colour.

Colours may change completely in just a few minutes. The chameleon does not seem to be changing colour to match the background colour. The amount of light, the temperature, and the mood of the animal – whether it is angry or frightened for example – may have more effect. But the chameleon's

colours are often sufficiently like the surroundings to make the animal very difficult to see.

LONE LIZARDS

Chameleons prefer to be alone most of the time. They are territorial and males fight to keep other males out of their territory. Fights are rather slow-motion affairs, but they can be long and vicious. Horned species use their horns in combat.

During courtship, male chameleons also display aggressively. After mating, the female may not lay eggs immediately, as she can store sperm for long periods. A few species of pygmy chameleon give birth to live young. The newborn often stay surrounded by the transparent egg membrane for several hours.

◄When threatened, chameleons may inflate their bodies, hiss, and expose the bright skin which lines the mouth.

▼A Three-horned chameleon shooting out its tongue with deadly accuracy to take hold of a fly.

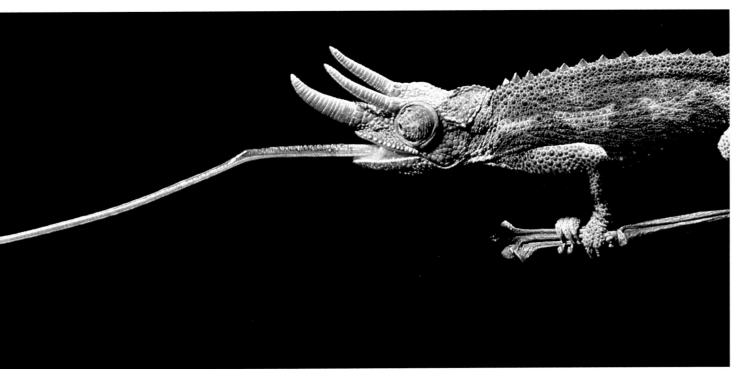

GECKOS

As night falls in a town in the tropics, the people turn on the lights. From its hiding place behind a picture on a wall, a small lizard emerges. It runs up the wall and across the ceiling, close to a lamp that is attracting insects. It snaps up several insects, ignoring the people preparing a meal below. They are pleased to see the gecko at work above them, removing pests from the house.

Geckos are probably best known for their ability to climb on almost any surface, from bark to walls, ceilings and even sheet glass. They live over most of the warmer parts of the world and are common in the tropics. Some species are found on islands right out in the oceans.

EGG TRAVELLERS

Geckos have spread where other lizards could not, probably because of the way they lay their eggs. There are usually two eggs which are stuck underneath tree bark. The eggs have tough shells, and may take several months to develop. During this time storms may wash a log out to sea and the ocean currents may carry it to another island. If the eggs survive the journey and hatch on the new land, the baby geckos may start a colony.

NIGHT NOISES

Geckos are unusual among reptiles in that they have a voice, not just a hiss. Most are nocturnal, and have good hearing, so noises are a good way of communicating. They make chirping, clicking or barking noises and have different combinations of sounds for courting or defending a territory.

▶The Tokay gecko of south-east Asia is one of the noisiest geckos. It can make a barking sound as loud as a dog.

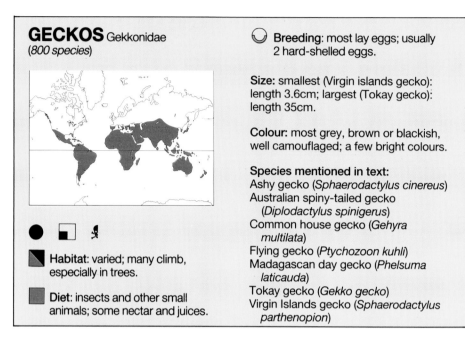

GECKOS Gekkonidae
(800 species)

● ■ 🦗

■ **Habitat**: varied; many climb, especially in trees.

■ **Diet**: insects and other small animals; some nectar and juices.

◐ **Breeding**: most lay eggs; usually 2 hard-shelled eggs.

Size: smallest (Virgin islands gecko): length 3.6cm; largest (Tokay gecko): length 35cm.

Colour: most grey, brown or blackish, well camouflaged; a few bright colours.

Species mentioned in text:
Ashy gecko (*Sphaerodactylus cinereus*)
Australian spiny-tailed gecko (*Diplodactylus spinigerus*)
Common house gecko (*Gehyra multilata*)
Flying gecko (*Ptychozoon kuhli*)
Madagascan day gecko (*Phelsuma laticauda*)
Tokay gecko (*Gekko gecko*)
Virgin Islands gecko (*Sphaerodactylus parthenopion*)

WEARING SPECTACLES

Instead of having the usual lizard eyelids, nearly all geckos have a large transparent "spectacle" over each eye. They are unable to clean this protective covering by blinking, but many put their tongue right out and use it to wipe their eyes.

The pupil of the eye can open very wide, which helps the gecko to see in the dark. In sunlight, the pupil is closed to a slit with a few little chinks in it. These let in enough light for the gecko's sensitive eyes to work well in the daytime.

DEFENCE TACTICS

The tails of geckos vary. Some species have ordinary tapering tails, others have tails that are flattened or shaped like leaves or turnips. All geckos can readily drop their tail if they are attacked. Some geckos, such as the Common house gecko, will also shed large portions of skin if they are picked up. Another method of escape is used by the Flying gecko. This gecko

has flaps of skin along its body and tail, which allow it to glide from one tree to another to avoid danger.

One of the strangest means of defence is used by the Australian spiny-tailed geckos. Instead of losing their tails, these geckos can shoot out sticky, strong-smelling threads from special pits in the tail. These threads can travel up to 30cm and trap a predator in a "cobweb".

CLINGING CLIMBERS

Most geckos have sharp claws and clinging toes, but the interesting part of a gecko's foot is underneath the toes. Here there are many ridges of scales. On these scales are millions of tiny "hairs", which can only be seen under a microscope. The hairs help the geckos to grip the tiny bumps and dips in a surface, even when it appears to be completely smooth. Some tree geckos have prehensile tails, and these too may have microscopic "hairs" underneath them. The animals use their tails to grasp twigs.

◄This male Madagascan day gecko is more colourful than the female which has a drab brownish skin.

►The camouflage pattern of the Australian spiny-tailed gecko usually hides it against tree bark. It is spreading its toes well to get a grip.

▼An Ashy gecko sheds its skin as part of the growth process. This lizard is found in Florida and the Caribbean.

MONITORS

A monitor lizard appears on the river bank. It is searching for food. Half way down the sandy bank, it pauses and tests the ground with its tongue. Then it starts to scratch away the sand with its claws. It puts its head into the hole, lifts out an egg and swallows. It has found a crocodile's nest. It feeds greedily and quickly, before the owner returns.

Monitor lizards comprise a small family of rather large lizards. They live in Africa, southern Asia and the East Indies, and particularly in the Australian region, where 24 of the 31 species are found. As well as feeding on eggs, monitors eat carrion and a wide variety of adult animals.

Monitor lizards have long necks and a relatively short body. The head is rather long and narrow, with a pointed snout. The slit-like nostrils are often near the eyes. The teeth are sharp and fang-like. In all species, the legs are strong, with five strong toes each armed with sharp claws. The tail is not fragile, as in some lizards, but is long and muscular. It is sometimes used as a weapon.

ACTIVE KILLERS

Monitors are active in the day, when most species search for food. All monitors are meat-eaters. The smaller kinds live mainly on grasshoppers, beetles and other insects, but many monitors catch other reptiles, or birds and mammals, as well. The Komodo dragon, the biggest living lizard, has been known to bring down a 590kg adult Water buffalo.

Monitors tend to swallow their prey whole, or in huge chunks. They also have large appetites. A 46kg Komodo dragon once ate in one meal a whole wild pig that weighed 41kg. This species of monitor has been recorded as attacking and killing people.

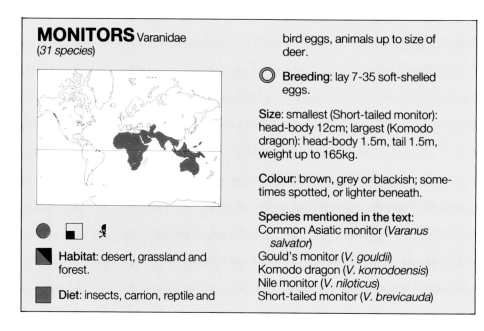

MONITORS Varanidae
(31 species)

🔴 ⬛🔲 🦎

⬛ **Habitat:** desert, grassland and forest.

🟥 **Diet:** insects, carrion, reptile and bird eggs, animals up to size of deer.

⭕ **Breeding:** lay 7-35 soft-shelled eggs.

Size: smallest (Short-tailed monitor): head-body 12cm; largest (Komodo dragon): head-body 1.5m, tail 1.5m, weight up to 165kg.

Colour: brown, grey or blackish; sometimes spotted, or lighter beneath.

Species mentioned in the text:
Common Asiatic monitor (*Varanus salvator*)
Gould's monitor (*V. gouldii*)
Komodo dragon (*V. komodoensis*)
Nile monitor (*V. niloticus*)
Short-tailed monitor (*V. brevicauda*)

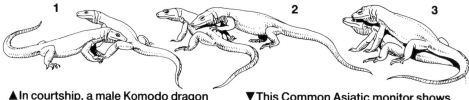

▲In courtship, a male Komodo dragon presses his snout against the female (1), tests her with his tongue, scratches her back (2), and then mates (3).

▼This Common Asiatic monitor shows the typical strong claws of monitors, and the long, forked tongue, which constantly tests the surroundings.

◄Komodo dragons prey on animals as large as deer or wild pigs. They are agile, and swim and climb well.

▼Gould's monitor lives in the deserts of Australia. When threatened by an enemy, it rears up on its back legs.

ALERT AND LIVELY

Many monitors hold their heads erect on their long necks, which makes them look especially alert. Most live on the ground, and some are good climbers and swimmers.

Water monitors are able to catch fish. The Common Asiatic monitor can stay underwater for an hour; it often takes to the water to avoid enemies. It has even been seen swimming far out at sea. It moves through the water by flapping its tail from side to side; the legs are kept motionless close to the body. Several species are able to run fast. Gould's monitor can run faster than a person over a short distance.

SELF-DEFENCE

If threatened, monitor lizards can put on a frightening performance. They hiss loudly, puff their throats out, turn sideways and may rear up to make themselves look as large as possible. They also lash out with the tail, which can give a very hard blow. Finally, if necessary, they will scratch and bite fiercely.

EATEN BY AN ALLY

In the breeding season, fights take place between the males. Monitors lay eggs in holes in river banks or in trees along the edge of rivers or streams. The Nile monitor often lays its eggs in termite nests. As in most reptiles, monitors do not protect their young. Eggs may even be dug up and eaten by other monitors.

SNAKES

In the reeds at the water's edge a Water snake waits. It is partly coiled and lies still. Only the occasional flick of the tongue shows that this snake is alert. A frog hops from the water. Stealthily the snake glides forward, so smoothly that the frog doesn't notice. Then the snake strikes. It seizes the frog in its jaws, and begins to swallow it whole.

Snakes are a large and successful group. They occur on all continents except Antarctica and are found in all regions except the very coldest ones. Water snakes, for example, range from Scandinavia to northern Australia. Snakes have even reached many isolated islands, although they do not live on some islands such as Ireland.

SNAKES OF MANY TYPES

About two-thirds of all snake species belong to the large family Colubridae, which includes familiar species such as the European grass snake and the North American garter snakes. Most members of this family are harmless to humans; a few species have poison fangs at the back of the mouth.

SNAKES Sub-order Serpentes
(*2,389 species*)

● ■ 𓆚

◧ **Habitat:** most ground-living, but many burrow, climb trees, or live in fresh or sea water.

▪ **Diet:** other animals, from slugs and insects to mammals, fish, other reptiles, birds and eggs.

○ **Breeding:** internal fertilization, usually followed by egg-laying. Many species bear live young.

Size: most 25cm-1.5m. Shortest (West Indian thread snake): 12cm; longest (Reticulated python, see p.64): 10m.

Colour: mostly brown, grey or black. Some bright colours or vivid markings.

Species mentioned in text:
African egg-eating snake (*Dasypeltis scaber*)
Boomslang (*Dispholidus typus*)
Costa Rican parrot snake (*Leptophis depressirostris*)
European grass snake (*Natrix natrix*)
Flowerpot snake (*Rhamphotyphlops braminus*)
Milk snake (*Lampropeltis triangulum*)
Redbelly snake (*Storeria occipitomaculata*)
Toad-eater snake (*Xenodon rabdocephalus*)
West Indian thread snake (*Leptotyphlops bilineata*)

▼**Snake species of several families**
Texas blind snake (*Leptotyphlops dulcis*) **(1)**. Shieldtail snake (*Uropeltis ocellatus*) **(2)**. Montpellier snake (*Malpolon monspessulanus*) **(3)**. Cuban Island ground boa (*Tropidophis melanurus*) **(4)**. Malaysian pipe snake (*Cylindrophis rufus*) **(5)**. Schlegel's blind snake (*Typhlops schlegeli*) **(6)**.

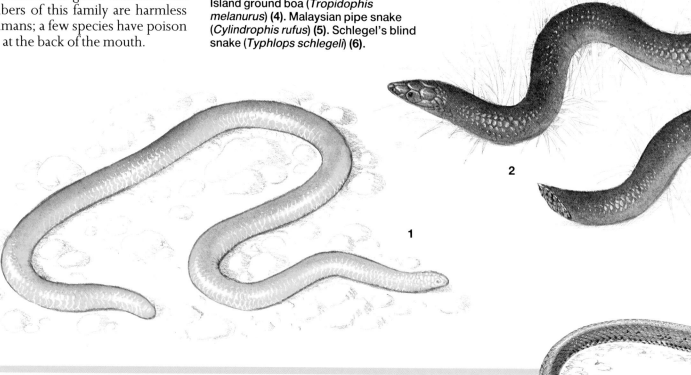

Other types of snake include the primitive pythons and boas (see pages 126-27), the cobras and sea-snakes (pages 130-35) and the vipers and rattlesnakes (pages 136-39).

PIPES AND THREADS

There are also six families of rather odd, mainly small, burrowing snakes, which contain 338 known species.

The 11 species of pipesnake live in the tropical areas of South America and Asia. They are all less than 1m long and burrow in damp soil. They feed on other snakes and eels. To fool enemies, many pipesnakes hide their head and wave the tail, which is red underneath.

The thread snakes number 78 species and include some of the smallest snakes; several are less than 20cm in length and no thicker than a matchstick. They live in tropical rain forests and feed on ants and termites.

FEMALE TRAVELLER

The blind snakes live in the tropics. Their eyes are tiny and hidden under the scales of the head. They are burrowers and most of the 163 species also feed on ants and termites.

One species of blind snake, the Flowerpot snake, has spread from Asia to Europe by being carried in the earth in flowerpots. It is able to colonize a new area easily because the females can produce young on their own; there are no males.

6

5

3

4

A NARROW SQUEEZE

Like other reptiles, snakes have a head, body and tail, but the body, and sometimes the tail, are extremely long and narrow. The long body is supported by a very long backbone; some snakes have more than 400 vertebrae in the backbone. In such a body, it is difficult to fit in all the organs the snake needs. Often a pair of organs are one behind the other; the kidneys are positioned like this. Sometimes, only one of a pair of organs remains. Most snakes have just one lung.

◀The Costa Rican parrot snake is harmless, but can use its brightly coloured mouth to frighten enemies.

SENSES

A snake is always staring and cannot shut its eyes because it has no eyelids. Instead the eyes are covered with a transparent scale. Burrowing snakes can usually just tell the difference between light and dark. In several daytime species, the eyesight is very sharp, although they find it much easier to see moving prey.

Night-time snakes frequently have vertical slit pupils which can open very wide in dim light to let in as much light as possible.

▼Snakes detect prey with their long forked tongues. This Toad-eater snake hunts on the forest floor in Costa Rica.

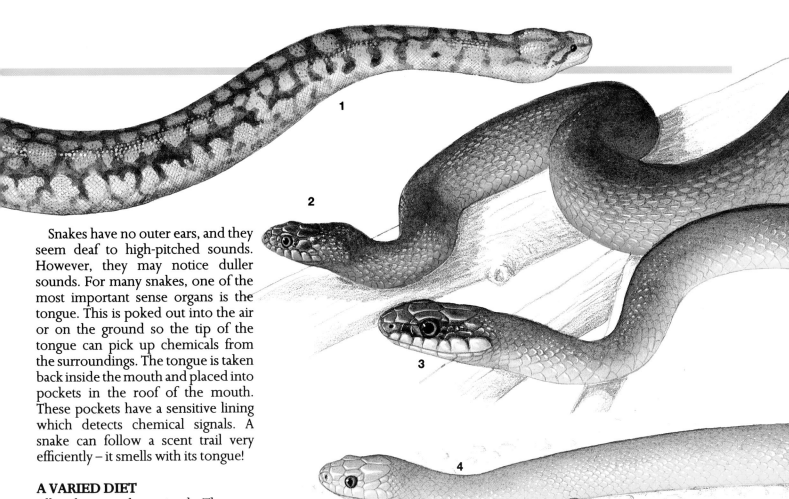

Snakes have no outer ears, and they seem deaf to high-pitched sounds. However, they may notice duller sounds. For many snakes, one of the most important sense organs is the tongue. This is poked out into the air or on the ground so the tip of the tongue can pick up chemicals from the surroundings. The tongue is taken back inside the mouth and placed into pockets in the roof of the mouth. These pockets have a sensitive lining which detects chemical signals. A snake can follow a scent trail very efficiently – it smells with its tongue!

A VARIED DIET

All snakes eat other animals. The prey depends to a certain extent on the size of the snake. Many eat mammals, birds or other reptiles, but some have a very special diet.

The tropical cat-eyed snakes and the Asian snail-eaters eat nothing but snails. They can pull a snail out of its shell. The African egg-eating snake eats eggs and can swallow an egg twice the size of its head. Part of its backbone sticks into its throat. To crack an egg, the snake squeezes it against this bone. The snake then swallows the contents of the egg and spits out the shell. The Redbelly snake of North America feeds exclusively on slugs. American green snakes eat caterpillars and grasshoppers. Perhaps a more typical diet, however, is that of the American garter snakes, which eat anything from worms and insects, to fish and mammals.

SWALLOWING DINNER

When snakes do feed, the meal is nearly always large compared with the size of the mouth. Food is always swallowed whole. A snake's teeth are sharp and point backwards. The teeth are good at holding food, but cannot bite off chunks of flesh. Instead, a snake has an amazingly flexible skull and jaws. It can open its mouth very wide. The bottom jaw can be swung down from the skull, and the two halves of the bottom jaw will swing apart, held together only by elastic tissue. The jaws can be "walked" around the prey, gradually edging it more and more into the throat, until contractions of the gullet can carry the food down to the stomach.

Those snakes of the family Colubridae that have fangs at the back of the mouth often "chew" on the prey. This probably helps them work in their poison, or venom. The most poisonous of these species includes the boomslang, an African tree snake. A

▲ **Harmless snakes** Arafura wart snake (*Acrochordus arafurae*) (1) from rivers in New Guinea and Australia. Red-bellied water snake (*Nerodia erythrogaster*) (2) and the racer (*Coluber constrictor*) (3) from North America. The African house snake (*Lamprophis fuscus*) (4).

bite from this snake has proved fatal to a person in 24 hours.

A LONG SLOW LIFE

For much of the time, a snake's body works at a slow rate. Perhaps this is why they live for a long time. Even a small snake, such as a Milk snake, has been known to live for 18 years. Species of snake from cool areas may hibernate during the winter months. During this time they may be scarcely breathing and do not need to feed at all. Even during their active periods snakes are often still and can survive for long periods without a meal.

PYTHONS

In an African forest a hunter finds signs of a struggle. Worried, he peers into the surrounding trees. Suddenly there is a loud hiss and he draws back in alarm. When he looks again he sees a huge python. But this animal will do him no harm. It has just swallowed an antelope, and for the time being it can hardly move.

Some of the larger pythons have indeed been known to kill and eat people. Pythons are found in Africa, southern Asia and in the Australian region, which is especially rich in species. The exception is the Mexican burrowing python, which is only distantly related to other pythons.

LITTLE AND LARGE

Some of the pythons are giants among snakes, but there are small species too. The dwarf python of Australia is less than 1m long, and the Royal python of West Africa is only 1.5m at most. The Royal python is also called the Ball python because it curls into a ball when it is alarmed. The Calabar python of West Africa is a burrowing species that grows to only about 1m.

At the other extreme is the Reticulated python of South-east Asia, which is up to 10m long. This is the longest snake in the world (but see Boas,

▼The Mexican burrowing python (1), the only python in the Americas, is rarely seen. When frightened, the Calabar python (2) curls up with its head on the inside and "strikes" with its tail.

PYTHONS Pythonidae
(27 species)

● ■ ✦

■ **Habitat:** rain forest, thorn scrub and grassland.

Diet: birds and mammals.

◎ **Breeding:** lay eggs in clutches of up to 60.

Size: most 3-6m. Smallest (West Australian dwarf python): 50cm long; largest (Reticulated python): 10m.

Colour: ranges from uniform brown or bright green to bold patterns of blotches or diamonds.

Species mentioned in text:
African rock python (*Python sebae*)
Calabar python (*Calabaria reinhardtii*)
Green tree python (*Chondropython viridis*)
Indian python (*Python molurus*)
Mexican burrowing python (*Loxocemus bicolor*)
Reticulated python (*Python reticulatus*)
Royal python (*P. regius*)
West Australian dwarf python (*Liasis perthensis*)
Woma (*Aspidites ramsayi*)

▲Some pythons coil round their eggs to guard them. Female Indian pythons may "shiver" to help keep their eggs warm.

◄The colours of the Green tree python match the leaves in the rain forest.

BABY COLOURS

The Green tree python lives in the tropical forests of New Guinea and northern Australia. Its bright colour is effective camouflage as it climbs and hunts in the trees. This helps it to move close to the animals it hunts without being seen. When the babies hatch from the egg, however, they are quite a different colour. Some are yellowish; others are brick red. They have to wait for nearly 2 years before they become emerald green like the adults.

In other pythons, babies look much the same as the adults. A newly hatched Reticulated python is 60-75cm long and weighs 140g. It grows 60cm a year for the first few years.

▼This African rock python has killed a gazelle and is beginning to swallow it. It may be weeks before it feeds again.

pages 128-29). Another giant is the Indian python, which has a thicker body than the Reticulated and grows up to 6.5m long. The African rock python can reach lengths of 9m or more. Few snakes are allowed to live long enough to reach their full size. With the current demand for snake skins for shoes, bags and wallets, the widespread use of rifles and the destruction of rain forests, large specimens are now rare.

SMALL AND LARGE MEALS

The Reticulated python feeds mainly on relatively small animals such as rats. In some places it is welcome because it destroys pests. The African rock python eats wild pigs and small antelopes. The Indian python tackles large animals, including leopards.

At the other extreme the West Australian dwarf python lives in termite nests and feeds on lizards which prey on the termites. The Australian woma eats many different animals, and can tackle poisonous snakes.

SPECIAL SENSES

As well as the usual snake senses, nearly all pythons have a series of special "pits" along the jaws. These pits are sensitive to heat. Pythons may use these pits to help them detect small animals, such as rats or birds, which are warmer than their surroundings. The snakes can determine temperature differences of 0.001°C and so locate prey in total darkness.

BOAS

In a Brazilian river, all is quiet. A caiman lazes at the surface. Suddenly there is a flurry in the water. From a branch above, an anaconda seizes the caiman. There is a struggle as the caiman tries to break free and the anaconda tries to wind its coils around the caiman's body. Eventually the anaconda succeeds, and squeezes the caiman until it is dead.

BOAS Boidae
(*39 species*)

● ◱ ☠

◩ Habitat: forest, swamp, and desert.

◼ Diet: birds, mammals, reptiles.

○ Breeding: give birth to live young, up to 80 per brood.

Size: most 2-4m. Smallest (Pacific ground boa): 0.5m long; largest (Green anaconda): up to 8.45m long, weight up to 500kg.

Colour: brown, grey, green. Some bold patterns with blotches.

Species mentioned in text:
Boa constrictor (*Boa constrictor*)
Emerald tree boa (*Corallus caninus*)
Green anaconda (*Eunectes murinus*)
Pacific ground boa (*Candoia aspera*)
Rosy boa (*Lichanura trivirgata*)
Rubber boa (*Charina bottae*)

Like the pythons (see pages 126-27), boas catch their prey by constriction. They strike and seize animals with their sharp backward-pointing teeth, then wrap their bodies round the victim. Powerful muscles squeeze the prey and stop it from breathing. When the prey is dead, it is swallowed whole, usually head first so that it slides down more easily.

A VARIED DIET

Boas have a scattered distribution. Their main home is in Central and South America, where there are some 20 species, but the small Rosy and Rubber boas live in western North America. Boas also occur on New Guinea, and some Pacific islands. Sand boas live in western Asia and north Africa, and there are three species on Madagascar.

Most boas feed on rat-sized prey. Some specialize in catching roosting birds and bats. Many boas have well-developed heat-sensing pits on their lips. With these they can detect small differences in temperature between an object and its surroundings and so can locate prey by their body heat. The anaconda eats mainly mammals, but also feeds on caimans and turtles.

HEAVIEST SNAKE

Most boas are not enormous. They tend to have slender bodies and longer tails than pythons. The Common boa, or Boa constrictor, of South and Central America, is one of the larger species. It is rarely more than 3m long, but a few reach over 5m. It lives in forests, and climbs well, but can also be found in some dry areas.

The giant of the family is the Green or Common anaconda, which lives in and around water. One large individual was well over 8m long. There are sometimes reports of anacondas which measure 11m or more, but these stories are rarely well documented and so far none of them has been proven true by scientists. An

anaconda this size would be longer than the longest python. However, an anaconda is a heavy, wide-bodied snake, and even one 8m long is much heavier than any python.

CLIMBERS AND BURROWERS

Many of the boas are small lightweight tree-climbers. Most remarkable in its feeding habits is the Emerald tree boa, which looks very like the Green tree python. It feeds largely on birds, and has long front teeth which help it seize birds from tree branches.

A totally different life is led by the sand boas, which burrow in sand and soil in dry areas of Africa and Asia. They have rounded bodies, a nose like a shovel and blunt tails. They reach a maximum length of 1m, but are often only half this length. They stay in burrows during the day, and capture mice on the surface at night. The Rubber boa burrows in damp forests in the western USA. It is up to 60cm long and feeds on mice and lizards.

GIVING BIRTH

Boas are similar to pythons in many ways, but one big difference is that boas do not lay eggs. Instead, they all give birth to live young. After the babies are born, the mother does not look after them. Baby Boa constrictors are 30cm long at birth. Newborn anacondas may be twice this length.

SNAKES WITH LEGS

Boas and pythons differ from most other snakes in that they still have two lungs, although one is much larger than the other. They also have traces of hind legs. Inside the body are tiny leg bones, and on the outside are two claws. These seem almost useless, but they are larger in males and are used to stroke females during courtship.

▶ The Emerald tree boa from South America grips a tree tightly with its prehensile tail as it prepares to swallow a bird whole. The snake had struck, then squeezed the bird until it died.

129

COBRAS

The snake charmer takes the lid off a basket and sits back. He begins to play a pipe. From the basket the head of a cobra rises, with its hood spread out. As the charmer plays, he sways backwards and forwards, and the snake "dances". It is worried, dazzled by the sudden brightness, and is trying to keep in view the strange moving object, the pipe end.

When disturbed, cobras rise up and spread special thin neck ribs to tighten loose skin into a "hood". Cobras and their relations are poisonous snakes found throughout Africa and southern Asia. Their American relatives are the coral snakes (see pages 134-35). In these regions the cobra family is only a small part of the total number of snake species. But in Australia, cobras and their relatives make up 80 per cent of the snakes. There, poisonous snakes outnumber the harmless ones.

VENOM
In members of the cobra family, some of the salivary glands have become modified to produce venom, which is used to paralyse and kill prey. The venom contains a mixture of poisons, but substances that act on the nervous system are the most common. These poisons give rise to breathing or heart problems or paralysis. Most of these snakes have a bite which is dangerous to people; the venom is often effective within only an hour of being injected.

▼Species of cobra The Indian cobra (1) is one of the deadliest of snakes. The ringhals (2) is one of several "spitting" snakes. The Black mamba (*Dendroaspis polylepis*) (3) is one of the fastest-moving snakes, reaching 11kph on the ground. The Eastern coral snake (*Micrurus fulvius*) (4) of the southern USA.

COBRAS Elapidae (land species only *190*)

○ ◻ ⚡

◼ **Habitat:** mainly in forest areas, some in grassland or desert.

◼ **Diet:** rodents, frogs, snakes.

◎ **Breeding:** nearly all lay eggs, some guard them.

Size: most in range 0.75-1.5m. Largest (King cobra) up to 5.6m.

Colour: most grey, brown or black, with collars or bands.

Species mentioned in text:
Australian copperhead (*Denisonia superba*)
Black-necked spitting cobra (*Naja nigricollis*)
Green mamba (*Dendroaspis angusticeps*)
Indian cobra (*Naja naja*)
Inland taipan (*Oxyuranus microlepidotus*)
King cobra (*Ophiophagus hannah*)
Ringhals (*Hemachatus haemachatus*)
Taipan (*Oxyuranus scutellatus*)
Tiger snake (*Notechis scutatus*)

Cobras have short fangs which are a pair of special, needle-like, upper teeth. When the snakes strike, they usually hold on to make sure the venom is injected into their victim. The fangs are hollow, with a channel down the middle to carry the venom. Like most other snakes, cobras are not usually aggressive, and try to avoid trouble from their enemies – mostly people, birds of prey and mongooses. Their venom is usually saved for its proper job – helping to catch animals to eat. But cobras are common in parts of the world where people often go

▲ A baby Green mamba uses its snout to break the parchment-like eggshell.

▼ A female cobra incubates her eggs by coiling round them.

barefoot, and each year they kill many people. Cobras, though, can often deter enemies without biting them by spraying venom, raising their hood or using their skin coloration as a warning signal.

SPRAY OF POISON

Three species of cobra can "spit" their venom in defence. The channel in each fang which carries the venom opens at the front of the tooth instead of at the tip. Muscles squeeze a stream of venom droplets up to 3m away from the open mouth. The cobra usually aims the venom at the eyes, causing irritation or blindness to the attacker. This gives the snake time to escape. The most effective sprayer of venom is probably the ringhals, a small cobra only about 1m long. If this snake is alarmed, it will sometimes "play dead" and loll with its mouth open. If this does not work, it will spray venom at an enemy.

COBRA HOODS

Most true cobras live in Africa, but one species, the Indian cobra, lives in southern Asia. The hood of true cobras is made from skin supported by long ribs. For much of the time a cobra looks as thin-necked as any other snake. However, when it is alarmed, it spreads the neck ribs so that the hood is extended. In some cobras there are marks that resemble "eyes" on the hood to make it appear more frightening. A displaying cobra may frighten off attacking animals without having to strike them with venom. Mambas, which are African members of the cobra family, have no hood, but can inflate the throat when they are irritated.

KING OF THE SNAKES

The King cobra or Hamadryad is not only the largest cobra, but also the largest venomous snake. When it rears up, its head can be level with a person's head. It lives over much of

India and South-east Asia, but is not very common. The Hamadryad has a powerful venom and a reputation for sometimes being aggressive. It feeds mostly on other snakes.

STRIPEY SNAKES

Coral snakes have bands of bright red, yellow, white and black along the body. True coral snakes are found in the Americas, but other similarly coloured snakes are found in Africa, Asia and Australia. They are all rather secretive, living under logs or leaf litter, or even underground.

The function of the bright colours of coral snakes seems to be to startle any enemy that finds them. Although these species are mostly small, they have a powerful venom. The fangs are small, so often they have to inflict several bites to be effective. Many kinds eat other snakes.

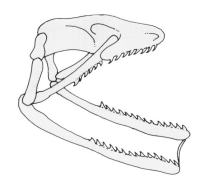

▲ Snakes can open their mouth wide because the lower jaw is connected to the skull by hinge-like bones. Also, ligaments stretched between bones are extremely elastic.

CONTINENT OF KILLERS

Australian snakes include some of the most venomous land snakes. The taipan, which grows to over 3m, is the largest. It has a reputation for being particularly aggressive. Luckily it is not very common. The Inland taipan has perhaps the most potent venom of any land snake. One specimen was found to contain enough venom to kill 125,000 mice. The Tiger snake is much more common and has an extremely dangerous venom.

EGGS AND BABIES

Most cobras lay eggs, but the ringhals of Africa and several Australian species produce live young. The Tiger snake may produce as many as 50 babies in a litter. The Australian copperhead even has a type of placenta through which the babies are nourished inside their mother. Typically, all the young

▼ A Black-necked spitting cobra of South Africa ejects its poisonous spray. The poison is usually aimed at its victim's eyes and can cause permanent blindness.

are born or hatch between 3 and 4 months after mating takes place.

Some species of cobra have more of a family life than is usual among snakes. A few curl around the eggs and guard them. Male and female Indian cobras may help to dig out a nest hole and defend the eggs. The King cobra has the most elaborate care of all. The female scrapes together a large pile of leaves, grass and soil to make a nest. She makes a hole in the top of the pile, lays 20 to 40 eggs in the hollow and covers them with more leaves. Then she stays on guard on the nest until the eggs hatch. The male may also stay close by and help to drive off enemies.

Baby cobras are small versions of their parents, and are able to spread the hood, rear their heads and deliver a venomous bite from the moment of hatching.

▶ A mamba wrapping itself round the branches of a thorn bush. Many cobras are excellent tree-climbers and some can even scale the thin upright trunks of bamboo.

SEA-SNAKES

A snake swims through the clear blue water near a coral reef. It moves slowly and easily, looking around. As it pauses to peer into a crevice, it spots an eel lurking inside. The snake shoots out its head and with its teeth fastens on to the fish. The fish stiffens, then flops lifeless. The sea-snake has caught another meal.

SEA-SNAKES Elapidae
(marine species only *about 50*)

 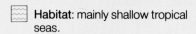

Habitat: mainly shallow tropical seas.

Diet: fishes; some species eat only eels or fish eggs.

Breeding: most give birth in water to live young; a few lay eggs on land.

Size: most about 1.4m long; largest up to 2.5m.

Colour: varied. Some rather dull; others banded light and dark, some black and yellow or black and red.

Species mentioned in text:
Banded sea-snake (*Laticauda colubrina*)
Black-and-yellow sea-snake (*Pelamis platurus*)
Red-and-black sea-snake (*Astrotia stokesi*)

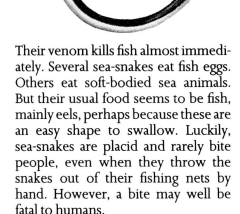

►The Black-and-yellow sea-snake is flattened from side to side. It has been seen hundreds of kilometres from land.

◄Totally at home in the water, a Banded sea-snake hunts across the sea bed near the New Hebrides in the Pacific.

Most sea-snakes live all their lives in salt water. Sea-snakes are commonest in the south-west Pacific from Malaysia to Australia, but a few kinds live in the seas north to Japan, east to the Solomon Islands and west to Saudi Arabia. Most sea-snakes are found in shallow seas relatively close to the coast. The exception is the Black-and-yellow sea-snake, which is found right out in the ocean, from East Africa to the eastern Pacific.

ALL AT SEA

Sea-snakes are closely related to the cobras, and have short fixed front fangs too. But, in several ways, they are specially adapted for the sea. Most do not have the large belly scales usually found in land snakes, as they do not need them to help grip the ground. They have valves on their nostrils which they can shut to keep out the water. The lungs are large, sometimes running almost the complete length of the body, and can act as floats as well as for breathing. Tails are flattened from side to side to help push the snake through the water.

Some sea-snakes have a very small head, a long thin neck and a fat body. These species put their head into rock crevices to catch small eels.

POWERFUL POISONS

Some species of sea-snakes have the most powerful venom of any snake. They need to overcome prey quickly before it escapes into the vast ocean.

Their venom kills fish almost immediately. Several sea-snakes eat fish eggs. Others eat soft-bodied sea animals. But their usual food seems to be fish, mainly eels, perhaps because these are an easy shape to swallow. Luckily, sea-snakes are placid and rarely bite people, even when they throw the snakes out of their fishing nets by hand. However, a bite may well be fatal to humans.

MYSTERIOUS LIVES

Most sea-snakes are unable to move on land, and so cannot come ashore to lay eggs. Instead, they give birth to live young. One small group, which includes the Banded sea-snake, can crawl on land, and does lay eggs, often in caves above the tide level. Sea-snakes may occasionally and briefly rest on islets, but otherwise they live in water all the time.

Sea-snakes sometimes gather in vast numbers. It is thought this may be for breeding, but little is known about much of sea-snakes' lives. In 1932, a huge gathering was recorded by a ship which steamed for 100km past a "solid mass" of sea-snakes about 3m wide. They were all of the Red-and-black species, and there must have been many millions of individuals.

135

VIPERS AND RATTLESNAKES

It is a pitch-dark night out on the prairie. A mouse scurries about, intent on finding seeds. In a hollow lies a rattlesnake. It cannot see the mouse, but it senses the presence of its warm body. It turns its head towards the mouse, waits until it is close, then strikes. It stabs and injects venom, then settles back to wait for its victim's death.

Vipers and rattlesnakes have the best-developed fangs of all the snakes. Members of this family live in all parts of the world that are warm enough for snakes, except for Madagascar and the Australian region. There are two main groups. The 45 species of true viper live in Africa, Europe and Asia. The 142 species of pit viper (including rattlesnakes) live in the Americas and southern Asia.

Instead of the big head shields seen in most other snakes, snakes of this family usually have triangular heads covered with many small scales. The body is thick, and often rather short. The eyes have slit-like pupils.

BIG FANGS

Vipers have a pair of very long fangs. In a Gaboon viper 1.7m long, the fangs can be 5cm long. When a viper is at rest, the fangs are folded back against the roof of the mouth. When it strikes, the mouth is opened wide and the fangs are swung down into a stabbing position.

Many vipers and rattlesnakes stab their prey, give a quick injection of powerful venom, then let go. There is no need to hang on. The prey soon dies, and even if it has moved a little way away, the snake can track it down and find it. Because of their shape and

▶On the Wyoming prairie, a Western rattlesnake hides in low brush, ready to strike a passing lizard or hare.

VIPERS AND RATTLESNAKES
Viperidae (*187 species*)

○ ◼ 𝄢

◼ **Habitat:** all types, from tropical rain forest, to grassland, desert, mountain and moors.

◼ **Diet:** other animals.

○ **Breeding:** most give birth to small number of live young. Some have up to 50 per litter. Some lay eggs.

Size: most 0.6-1.2m. Smallest (Peringuey's viper): 0.30m long; longest (bushmaster): up to 3.7m long.

Colour: generally dull colours, brown or blackish, often with dark blotches on lighter background. Some with bright colours or markings.

Species mentioned in text:
Bushmaster (*Lachesis muta*)
European adder (*Vipera berus*)
Gaboon viper (*Bitis gabonica*)
Hog-nosed viper (*Bothrops nasutus*)
Peringuey's viper (*Bitis peringueyi*)
Side-winder rattlesnake (*Crotalus cerastes*)
Western diamondback rattlesnake (*C. atrox*)
Western rattlesnake (*C. viridis*)

the way their fangs work, vipers are best suited to ambushing their prey rather than chasing it.

DEADLY POISONS

The venom of vipers is not so strong as that of some snakes in the cobra family (see pages 130-33), but it is made in such quantities, and is so efficiently injected, that it does its work well.

Many vipers are capable of killing a person, but they are less aggressive than cobras and are often slow to anger. Some small species, such as the European adder, have a bite that is painful to people, but is rarely fatal. Viper venoms act mainly on the blood and muscle systems, causing pain, swelling, severe bruising, discolouration and other acute symptoms. Recovery may be slow.

HEAT DETECTORS

The major difference between pit vipers and true vipers can be seen in the face. Pit vipers have a pair of large pits below the eyes. Each pit has a membrane inside which can detect heat; it can detect a heat difference of just 0.2°C.

Warm-blooded prey can be sensed with these pits. The snake can line up its head on prey, even in complete darkness, by turning the head so that the same amount of warmth is detected by each pit. A rattlesnake can detect and strike a mouse nearly a metre away with deadly accuracy, even in total darkness.

RATTLE AND BUZZ

Rattlesnakes are found in the Americas. The rattle on the tip of the tail is

▲After injecting venom for the kill, the two fangs of the Hog-nosed viper help to pull a frog into the snake's mouth.

▲Below the eye and nostril of this rattlesnake can be seen the large pit which acts as a heat detector.

made of a series of hollow, horny tail-tips. Like other snakes, a rattlesnake sheds its skin at intervals, but the horny tip of the tail remains permanently in place.

Each time the snake sheds its skin, a new segment is added to the rattle. Many snakes shake the tail if they are alarmed or annoyed; this may make a sound by hitting against and rustling leaves or dry plants. But, if rattlesnakes are disturbed, the tail itself makes a loud, angry buzzing noise. The snake cannot hear the noise, but it can scare off enemies and is a useful method of defence. A rattlesnake's main enemies are foxes and birds of prey.

◄Peringuey's viper of southern Africa leaves characteristic parallel tracks as it moves swiftly across the sand by "sidewinding".

SPRINGING SIDEWAYS
Several vipers and rattlesnakes are adapted to living in deserts. These snakes are often a sandy colour, and may bury themselves in the sand so that only their eyes show above the surface. Many of these desert-living snakes have "horns" over their eyes, which may help to keep the sand out of their pupils.

Some of these desert vipers, and the Side-winder rattlesnake, have a special way of travelling over the sand. It is hard for the snakes to grip the sand to pull themselves along, and, in the middle of the day, the sand may be burningly hot. So the snakes move by

▼Rattlesnakes, such as this Western diamondback, strike prey or an attacker with the mouth wide open and the long fangs erect.

"side-winding", which allows them to touch the sand as little as possible.

A side-winding snake makes an arc with the front part of its body and "throws" its head sideways for some distance before it touches the sand. The rest of the body is then thrown forward in another arc, clear of the ground, so it lands in front of the head. The tail curves over and lands last, but by this time the head has already been thrown to a new position and the body follows. The effect is rather like a spring rolling sideways.

Side-winding is weird to watch, but is an effective, and quite speedy, way of travelling across sand. It is mostly used by vipers of African and North American deserts. A very characteristic series of marks, each shaped rather like a "J", is left behind by the snake as it "side-winds" over the sand.

ALLIGATORS

A big female alligator slips into the water. She has a mouth full of small animals. When she is in the water, she opens her mouth wide and the small animals swim off to hide in the reeds. They are baby alligators. Their mother goes back to the nest for another batch of hatchlings. She continues until all her babies are safely in the water.

Alligators, and their close relatives the crocodiles (see pages 144-47), are unusual for reptiles in that the parents care for their young. Alligators are found in south-eastern North America. Their close family relatives, the caimans, are found in Central and South America. On the other side of the world, in China, lives the Chinese alligator. This species is found, in small numbers, in the Chang Jiang River. It is so far away from other members of the alligator family that western scientists did not believe the first reports of its existence.

▼ Most alligators come out of the water to bask from time to time. These American alligators are warming up on a mud bank in Georgia, USA.

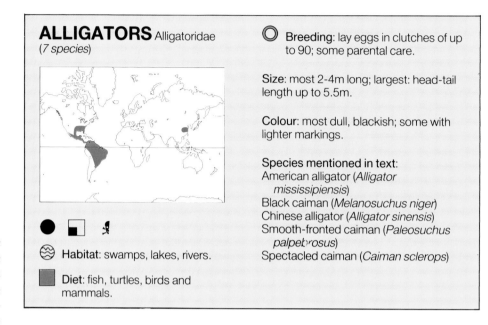

ALLIGATORS Alligatoridae
(*7 species*)

○ **Breeding:** lay eggs in clutches of up to 90; some parental care.

Size: most 2-4m long; largest: head-tail length up to 5.5m.

Colour: most dull, blackish; some with lighter markings.

Species mentioned in text:
American alligator (*Alligator mississipiensis*)
Black caiman (*Melanosuchus niger*)
Chinese alligator (*Alligator sinensis*)
Smooth-fronted caiman (*Paleosuchus palpebrosus*)
Spectacled caiman (*Caiman sclerops*)

≋ **Habitat:** swamps, lakes, rivers.

▪ **Diet:** fish, turtles, birds and mammals.

CROCODILE OR GATOR?
Crocodiles and alligators – together known as crocodilians – are similar, and have many features in common, but a few things set them apart. The animals in the alligator family often have a broad snout; crocodiles usually bear a long snout. Many alligators have bony plates in the skin of the belly; crocodiles do not. When alligators close their mouths, the fourth tooth in each side of the lower jaw fits into a socket in the upper jaw so it cannot be seen. In crocodiles, this pair of teeth sticks up outside the top jaw when the mouth is closed.

A WATERY LIFE
Alligators live in and around water. Their eyes and nostrils are set high on the head so that they can see and breathe when they are almost totally submerged. A third eyelid can be drawn across the eye to give more protection during diving. This eyelid is transparent and does not interfere

with the animal's sharp vision. When alligators and crocodiles dive underwater, they can close their nostrils and their ears. Out of the water their hearing seems good.

One important adaptation to diving is the flap of skin which shuts off the mouth from the breathing tubes. This allows the animal to open its mouth underwater to catch and eat prey, without water getting into its lungs.

GETTING ABOUT

All crocodilians have a large, strong tail with flat sides, which is used to push the animal through the water. The legs may steer or balance a little, but they are often folded back when the animal swims. The back legs are longer than the front legs.

Some crocodilians move only a short distance from water. Others may travel some distance overland when

▼The Chinese alligator was not known to western scientists until 1879. It is a rare animal. It grows to a maximum length of 1.8m and has a short snout.

▲The Spectacled caiman of South America gets its name from the ridge between the eye sockets. This one is swallowing a fish that it has caught.

▼The American alligator occurs in wet habitats in the southern States. During cold winter periods it may dig a mud hole in which to hibernate.

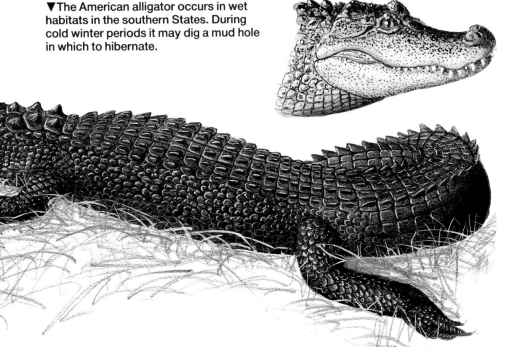

they need to. Sometimes they crawl or slither, but many species can also do a "high walk" with the body raised off the ground and their weight supported by the legs. Some can move fast, or even gallop. The American alligator is generally slow-moving. Compared with many crocodilians, and even its relatives the caimans, it is rather clumsy. It is rarely aggressive.

AMERICAN ALLIGATORS

American alligators eat mostly slow-moving fish, but their prey also includes any birds, mammals, reptiles and amphibians that they can surprise in the water. Large alligators can kill people, though they are not usually interested in attacking humans. American alligators have been known to eat pets when houses have been built near the swamps where they live.

Male alligators are larger than the females, but most individuals do not grow more than 3m long. The record length is for a specimen from Louisiana that was measured at 5.84m. Few present-day individuals approach the size of such giants.

CAIMANS

The largest of the caimans is the Black caiman, which can grow to 3.5m or more. In the 19th century, individuals of over 5m long could be found. It is black above, yellowish beneath. The Black caiman lives in the Amazon and Orinoco regions of South America. At the other extreme is the Smooth-fronted caiman, which grows to a maximum length of only 1.5m. It is found mostly in rocky, fast-running streams.

Caimans have sharper, longer teeth than alligators and strong bony plates on the belly and back. These belly plates have made the animals less attractive to people to hunt for making leather goods than some of the other crocodilians. Like all their relatives, caimans have about 40 pointed teeth in use at any one time.

NESTS AND BABIES

The bellow of a male alligator sounds like thunder and may help him to attract a mate. Mating takes place in the water. When the female is ready to lay her eggs, she makes a nest out of mud and vegetation. The nest may be 1m high and 2m across. After she has laid her eggs, the mother remains on top of the nest to guard the eggs from enemies. The rotting vegetation produces some heat, which helps to keep the eggs warm. After about 9 weeks, the babies are ready to hatch and call out. The mother alligator hears their calls and tears open the nest. She picks up the babies in her mouth and takes them to the water. Sometimes this will be a "nursery pool" which she has dug herself. As the young grow, the mother continues to guard them, for up to a year.

GROWING UP

Many animals will eat alligator eggs or babies if given the chance. Luckily the baby alligators grow fast. At hatching they may be only 20cm long, but will grow some 30cm a year for the first few years. After about 9 years, their rate of growth slows down. An alligator may be 8 years old before it can breed. The maximum possible lifespan may be 100 years.

SAFE FROM EXTINCTION

At one time, the American alligator was seriously endangered. This was partly because it was hunted for its skin and flesh and partly through the loss of its habitat as swamps were drained for farming or for building. This species has, however, been so well protected for the last few years that numbers have now increased to several million. There are so many individuals that controlled hunting is now allowed in some states.

▶ In the water, a large American alligator can move with very little effort, gliding through its swampy home.

CROCODILES

At the water's edge a group of antelope are drinking. A few metres out in the water, a pair of eyes and a nose are the only signs that a crocodile is hunting. Gently it glides towards the bank. With a sudden lunge, it grabs an antelope by the leg, and pulls it into the water. The crocodile holds the antelope underwater until it drowns, then tears off chunks of flesh to eat.

Crocodiles are fearsome predators. Some 14 species live in Africa, tropical parts of Asia and Australia, and in America from southern Florida to northern South America.

One species, the gharial, is found only in the great river systems of northern India. It is also the odd one out among these reptiles on account of its extremely long, narrow snout and weak legs. It is grouped in a separate family of its own, Gavialidae.

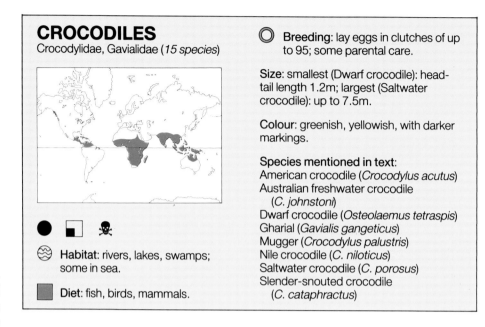

CROCODILES
Crocodylidae, Gavialidae (*15 species*)

⊖ **Breeding:** lay eggs in clutches of up to 95; some parental care.

Size: smallest (Dwarf crocodile): head-tail length 1.2m; largest (Saltwater crocodile): up to 7.5m.

Colour: greenish, yellowish, with darker markings.

Species mentioned in text:
American crocodile (*Crocodylus acutus*)
Australian freshwater crocodile (*C. johnstoni*)
Dwarf crocodile (*Osteolaemus tetraspis*)
Gharial (*Gavialis gangeticus*)
Mugger (*Crocodylus palustris*)
Nile crocodile (*C. niloticus*)
Saltwater crocodile (*C. porosus*)
Slender-snouted crocodile (*C. cataphractus*)

● ◰ ☠

≋ **Habitat:** rivers, lakes, swamps; some in sea.

▧ **Diet:** fish, birds, mammals.

MEATY MENUS

Crocodiles with long snouts, such as the Slender-snouted crocodile, feed mainly on fish.

Species with broader snouts, such as the mugger, tackle bigger prey, including deer and cattle. The Nile crocodile may feed on all sorts of animals from fishes to zebras. In fact, the diet of a crocodile often varies through its lifetime. Newly hatched crocodiles feed on small items such as grasshoppers, but as they grow they start to eat frogs and small fish. Eventually they move on to larger fish, and mammals such as antelopes.

1

The long, thin jaws of the gharial, which are full of pointed teeth, are ideal for snapping at fish in the water. The gharial specializes in eating fish.

HIDDEN KILLERS

Crocodiles usually take their prey by surprise. Most crocodiles are well camouflaged, and will stay completely still, or move slowly towards their prey without being detected.

Crocodile teeth are good for seizing and holding, but not so good at cutting up or chewing prey. To pull apart large prey, which cannot be swallowed whole, crocodiles make twisting movements of the whole body to tear off chunks of meat. Crocodiles may often lose teeth while dealing with prey, but this does not matter, as they are constantly growing new ones. A Nile crocodile 4m long is probably using its 45th "set" of teeth.

Crocodiles swim using their powerful tails, which have flattened sides. On land they often slither along on their bellies, but can also walk with the body lifted clear of the ground.

▼ **Species of crocodile** Dwarf crocodile **(1)** of forest areas of West Africa and the Congo. The False gharial (*Tomistoma schlegeli*) **(2)**, a fish-eater of swamps and rivers in Malaya, Borneo and Sumatra. The gharial **(3)** from northern India. The Slender-snouted crocodile **(4)** of African tropical forests. The mugger **(5)** of India lives in rivers, pools and marshes. American crocodile **(6)**.

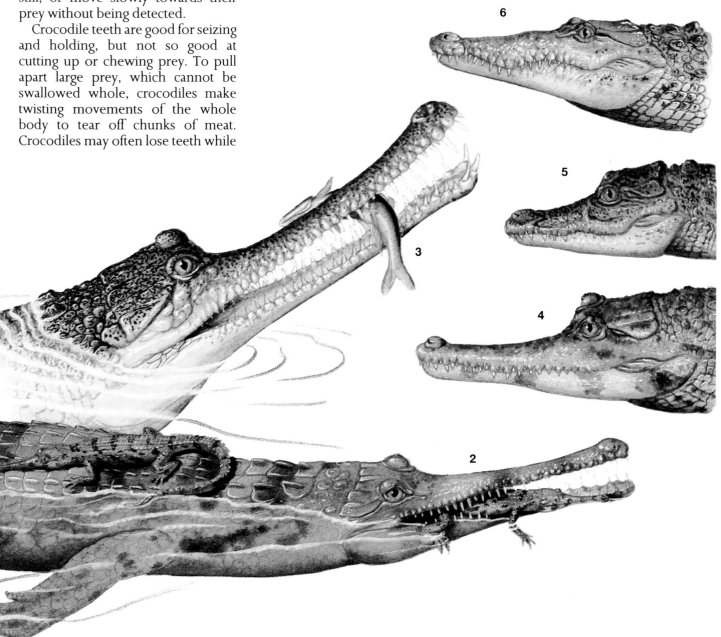

145

Some crocodiles can even gallop, reaching speeds of 13kph. They are all most active at night. Much of the day may be spent basking. When crocodiles are hot they open their jaws and lose water from the skin inside the mouth to cool themselves. The Nile crocodile, when it is basking open-mouthed, will allow birds to pick over its teeth for scraps of food.

SEA-GOING CROCODILES

Crocodiles of several species may venture into estuaries or the sea. The American crocodile often lives in brackish swamps, and may swim out to sea. The Nile crocodile is found in estuaries in parts of Africa. But the most sea-loving of all crocodiles is the Saltwater crocodile, which is found in estuaries and mangrove swamps. Around Indonesia, some individuals may live in the sea all the time. The Saltwater crocodile is a strong swimmer. Stray animals have reached the Cocos-Keeling Islands, 900km from their usual haunts. This species is found from the Ganges delta in India throughout South-east Asia and to as far as northern Australia.

The Saltwater crocodile is also the largest living species, some specimens reaching 6m in length. One skull, owned by an Indian rajah, probably came from a crocodile 7.46m long.

▲A baby Australian freshwater crocodile breaks out of its eggshell.

▼A female Saltwater crocodile sits on guard on top of the huge nest mound in which she has laid her eggs.

Other large crocodiles include the American crocodile at 7m, the Nile crocodile at 6.7m, and the gharial at 6.5m. Nowadays it is difficult to find a crocodile of anything like this size.

LAST OF THE LINE
Crocodiles are an ancient group. They lived alongside the dinosaurs and have changed little in the last 65 million years. But for some species, the chances of surviving for even another 10 or 20 years are poor. Even as recently as 1950, there were large numbers of crocodiles in some parts of the world. But in the 1950s and 60s a demand for crocodile skins for leather bags and shoes led to the deaths of untold numbers of crocodiles.

All species are now on the danger list. Large crocodiles were killed first. Mothers guarding nests made easy targets. Then hunters moved on to smaller specimens. Young animals were not allowed to grow old enough to breed and, with the breeding animals gone, populations crashed.

Although crocodiles produce large clutches of eggs, many eggs and young are taken by predators, floods and other hazards. Even in good conditions, only a tiny percentage of young survives. Most crocodiles take several years to grow into adults. The Saltwater crocodile, for example, may be 10 years old before it breeds for the first time. All species need help if they are to survive.

USEFUL CROCS
It may seem unimportant that a big, sometimes dangerous, animal such as a crocodile does survive. But crocodiles form a vital part of the balance of nature. In some lakes in Africa where crocodiles have disappeared, human fishermen have suffered. The crocodiles ate large fish which fed on the small fish that the fishermen were catching. With the crocodiles gone, more large fish survived and ate more of the small fish.

CROCODILE CONSERVATION
The gharial was nearly hunted to extinction. In 1974, fewer than 60 adults survived in India. But now, large sanctuaries have been created. Eggs are collected and then incubated artificially so more baby gharials will hatch out. Babies are reared until they are about 1.2m long. Then they can be released into the wild. Several thousand gharials now live in sanctuaries, but until they are breeding well we cannot say they are safe. In some places, the mugger and other crocodiles have similar protection.

▼ Crocodiles often wait at water holes to ambush their prey. This Nile crocodile has caught an impala.

EAGLES

High above the Appalachian Mountains of eastern North America, a Golden eagle hangs almost motionless in a clear summer sky. Far below it sees an ideal hunting spot – a long ridge covered with open grassy vegetation. The eagle glides down, and flies fast and low along one side of the ridge. Suddenly it swoops up and over the crest. Fifty metres away, on the other side of the ridge, a hare is feeding, completely unaware of the danger. It has no chance. Even as the hare turns to run, the aerial hunter strikes, killing it outright with its talons.

The Golden eagle is one of the largest members of a group of 30 species of birds of prey called the booted eagles. These birds get their name from the fact that their legs are covered with feathers right down to the foot, instead of being bare and scaly like those of all the other eagles. They are also known as "true" eagles.

EAGLES Accipitridae (part of family) (*53 species*)

Size: length 40-120cm; weight 0.5-6.5kg.

Plumage: plain grey, brown, or striking combinations of dark brown and white. Forest species often with black and white bars on wings.

Species mentioned in text:
African fish eagle (*Haliaeetus vocifer*)
Bald eagle (*Haliaeetus leucocephalus*)
Bateleur (*Terathopius ecaudatus*)
Booted eagle (*Hieraaetus pennatus*)
Golden eagle (*Aquila chrysaetos*)
Little eagle (*Hieraaetus morphnoides*)
Martial eagle (*Polemaetus bellicosus*)
Vulturine fish eagle or Palm-nut vulture (*Gypohierax angolensis*)
White-bellied fish eagle (*Haliaeetus leucogaster*)

Habitat: all land habitats, also sea coasts, lakes.

Diet: mammals, birds, fish and reptiles; also carrion.

Breeding: most species 1 or 2 eggs, incubated for 32-60 days.

The booted eagles are a varied group indeed. The smallest is probably the Little eagle of Australasia, which weighs around 500g. Unlike many of its open-country relatives, this tiny hunter inhabits forests and well-wooded regions. It hunts by dropping on to its prey either from flight about 10m above the ground, or from a perch in a leafy tree. Because of its small size it concentrates mainly on young rabbits, ground-dwelling birds and occasionally lizards.

MAMMAL-KILLER

At the other end of the scale is the magnificent Martial eagle of Africa, which can have a wingspan of well over 2m and weigh up to 6.5kg. It lives in the savannah and thornbush country south of the Sahara Desert, and is even found in semi-desert regions. This eagle spends a great deal of its time on the wing, soaring for hours at a time on the currents of hot air that rise over the Sun-baked hills and plains. Often the bird will fly so high that it appears as little more than a speck from the ground.

Because food is widely scattered over the huge African grasslands, a

◀A European Booted eagle with young. This small eagle, weighing about 600g, inhabits wooded mountains and ravines.

pair of Martial eagles may require a hunting territory of up to 130sq km. The birds usually hunt in one area for a few days and then move on to a new location. In some regions Martial eagles prey mainly on large birds such as guineafowl and bustards. In other regions they take mainly mammals, for example hyraxes. However, these powerful birds will also take prey as big as monkeys and goats.

The Martial eagle may occasionally hunt from a perch, but its main method is to spot a target from high in the sky and then attack in a long fast slanting dive that takes the victim completely by surprise.

WRONGLY ACCUSED?

The most widespread and numerous of the world's large eagles is the Golden eagle. It inhabits mountain country right across Europe, Asia and North Africa, and is the only booted eagle found in North America.

In some parts of Europe and North America the Golden eagle has been persecuted by people, mainly because

▲An adult Golden eagle in Finland. Here, as in 13 other European countries, the bird is protected by law.

▼The female Little eagle incubates her one or two eggs by herself, but her mate usually brings food to her on the nest.

of an undeserved reputation for killing lambs. Lamb carcasses are occasionally found in eagle nests, but although some may be the result of eagle kills, most of the lambs have probably been found already dead. Golden eagles do take some carrion as well as live prey. Their main diet, though, is made up of rabbits and hares, and in North America ground squirrels are often taken. In places where mammals are hard to find, game birds such as grouse and ptarmigan are the main source of food. They are usually caught on the ground, but the Golden eagle can also catch a grouse in flight.

Golden eagle pairs usually have two or three nests on their territory. The nests are called eyries, and are huge affairs made of sticks, placed on rocky ledges high on mountain cliffs. The female usually hatches two chicks, but the first one to hatch often kills the other within the first 2 weeks.

FISH- AND FRUIT-EATERS
Among the most spectacular large eagles are the fishing eagles (11 species) from the Old World and North America. As their name suggests, these birds inhabit coastal regions and the shores of lakes, where they feed on fish, waterbirds and carrion. The only North American species is the Bald eagle – America's national bird. This makes the biggest nest of any eagle. One nest, known to be 36 years old, was 2.6m across and 4m high.

Unlike the osprey, which plunges into the water to catch its prey, the fishing eagles normally snatch their prey close to the surface in a graceful low-level swoop. The one exception in the group is the Vulturine fish eagle or Palm-nut vulture of Africa. The bird does catch fish, but its main food is the fruit of the oil palm tree, and it is never found far from these trees.

SNAKE- AND SERPENT-KILLERS
The snake eagles are a specialized group of 12 species of hunters found in southern Europe, Africa, central and South-east Asia. They have large, owl-like heads, huge yellow eyes, and short toes for grasping their thin-bodied prey. They hunt mainly from perches and drop swiftly on to snakes, frogs and lizards on the ground.

This group also has its odd-bird-out. The magnificent bateleur has black, white and chestnut plumage and such a short tail that it appears in flight like an enormous flying wing. It hunts by gliding across the African plains at speeds of up to 80kph in search of small mammals, birds, carrion and snakes.

▶ Until recently the southern race of the American Bald eagle was an endangered species. Now its future appears safe, due to strict conservation laws.

▲▶Talons outstretched, a White-bellied sea eagle closes in on its target (top). Moments after the strike (centre) its legs are dragged backwards by the weight of the fish, but even a one-footed grip (bottom) is enough to secure the catch.

◀In their spectacular courtship display a pair of African fish eagles grasp each other's talons as they tumble downward through the air like falling leaves.

HAWKS AND BUZZARDS

HAWKS AND BUZZARDS Accipitridae
(part of family) (*150 species*)

⬤ ◧ 🦅

Habitat: all land habitats.

Diet: mammals, birds, snakes, frogs, insects.

Breeding: small species lay 5-7 eggs, large species 1 or 2; incubation period 32 and 120 days respectively.

Size: most species: length 30-70cm, weight 0.5-4kg; largest (Harpy eagle): length 100cm, weight 6kg.

Plumage: very variable, but most species grey or brown, darker above than below.

Species mentioned in text:
Augur buzzard (*Buteo rufofuscus*)
Bat hawk (*Machieramphus alcinus*)
Black kite (*Milvus migrans*)
Common buzzard (*Buteo buteo*)
Cooper's hawk (*Accipiter cooperii*)
Crane hawk (*Geranospiza caerulescens*)
Everglade kite (*Rostrhamus sociabilis*)
Harpy eagle (*Harpia harpyia*)
Hen harrier or Marsh hawk (*Circus cyaneus*)
Northern goshawk (*Accipiter gentilis*)
Philippine monkey-eating eagle (*Pithecophaga jefferyi*)
Red-shouldered hawk (*Buteo lineatus*)
Red-tailed hawk (*B. jamaicensis*)
Sharp-shinned hawk (*Accipiter striatus*)

As darkness falls over a small island in South-east Asia, millions of bats stream out of caves hidden in the depths of the rain forest. Most of them will spend the night feeding, but for some there is danger. Lying in ambush is a Bat hawk, one of Asia's most specialized hawks. Picking its target the hunter dashes in. One strike is enough. The hawk swerves away, transferring its catch from its claws to its bill as it heads back to its nest.

The Bat hawk is found in the rain forests of Malaysia, Sumatra, Borneo and New Guinea, and also in tropical Africa. It is the only known specialist bat-hunter among the birds of prey, and it is also unusual in carrying its catch in its bill. That is something much more typical of owls than of hawks.

UNUSUAL DIETS
The Bat hawk belongs to the group of 31 species of bird called the kites and honey buzzards. Among them are a great many unusual and specialized birds. The Everglade kite, for example, lives in the swamp forests and marshlands of the Florida Everglades, and its main food consists of the large freshwater snails that abound in that habitat. The bird's bill is finely hooked and pointed – the perfect tool for extracting the snails from their shells.

Like all specialists, though, the Everglade kite is at risk. Vast areas of the Florida wetlands have been drained for housing and other types of development. As the swamps are destroyed the snails too disappear, and along with them go the birds that depend on them for food.

The honey buzzards of Europe, Africa and Asia have found another rich source of food – the ground nests and tree nests of various kinds of bee and wasp. The birds tear open the insects' nests with their claws and feed on the honey and larvae inside. However, the adult insects pack a powerful sting and have to be "disarmed" before they can be eaten. The birds do this by snipping off the back end of each insect's body before it is swallowed. Honey buzzards also prey on worms, frogs, small mammals and birds, and some species eat berries.

A TOWN DWELLER

The Black kite of Europe, Africa and Asia is a complete contrast to its specialized relatives. It is a true all-rounder, preying on insects, fish and worms, but often making its living mainly as a scavenger. In the warmer parts of its range, especially across southern Asia, thousands of Black kites inhabit towns and cities. They are often seen on rubbish tips and in the streets. The birds perch on roofs, telegraph poles and dockside cranes then swoop down to pounce on rats and mice or to snatch food from market stalls. There are even cases of them snatching food from astonished shoppers' hands!

THE CUNNING HARRIERS

It is tempting to imagine that all birds of prey catch their food by means of a fast diving attack or a chase. But that is not so. The 10 species of harrier, for example, are birds of open grasslands

▼ **Medium-sized birds of prey** A Grey chanting goshawk (*Melierax poliopterus*) **(1)** calls from the top of a termite mound. A Black-mantled sparrowhawk (*Accipiter melanochlamys*) **(2)** and Red kite (*Milvus milvus*) **(3)** with prey. A Pied harrier (*Circus melanoleucus*) **(4)** hunting.

and marshes which specialize in slow, low-level flight as their main hunting technique.

Harriers are medium-sized hawks with slim bodies and with long wings and tails that provide the lift and control necessary for low-speed flight. They often fly at speeds as low as 30kph, and if a harrier is flying into a light head-wind it may be moving over the ground at only 15kph. (A falcon can fly at over 160kph.) With brief periods of hovering, this gives the bird plenty of time to search the ground below for prey. The harriers have rather owl-like faces, and like the owls they rely on accurate hearing to pin-point their prey. They can locate their quarry even when it is hidden from sight among dense vegetation.

The Hen harrier, known as the Marsh hawk in North America, is a typical member of the group. It inhabits marshlands and heathlands, and sometimes cornfields too. From the air it silently patrols an area with its wings raised to form an instantly recognizable shallow V-shape. Its diet consists of frogs, mice, large insects, snakes and small birds.

Unlike most other birds of prey the harriers nest on the ground, building

▲ In a North American forest, a young Northern goshawk picks at a Grey squirrel carcass with its hooked beak.

large mounds of reeds and rushes, well hidden from view. The female does most of the building, but the male helps by collecting nest material. He delivers the material in a most unusual way. Instead of landing at the nest site, he swoops low overhead and drops the material close by, for the female to retrieve. Later, when the eggs have hatched, the male uses the same method to deliver food to the nest for the female and young.

DOUBLE-JOINTED

The two species of harrier-hawk of Africa and the Crane hawk of Central and South America form a group of medium-sized woodland hawks with a unique adapatation for catching their prey. Their legs can bend either way at the middle (tarsal) joint, and this enables the birds to reach into the most awkward crevices in rocks or tree bark to pull out the lizards, frogs, birds' eggs and nestlings that are their main prey. These hawks get into the most unusual positions when searching for food, and will often hang upside down to reach inside a particularly inaccessible tree-hole. At other times they hunt by flying back and forth, scanning the ground below for food, much as the true harriers do.

A FAMILY OF HUNTERS

The family Accipitridae is by far the biggest of the five bird of prey families, and it includes a huge variety of different birds among its 217 species. The eagles (see pages 148-51) and the kites, harrier-hawks and harriers we have met so far are all fairly small groups. Together they make up just over half of the total number of species. The two biggest groups are the sparrowhawks and goshawks, and the buzzards and harpies, each of which contains 53 species.

WOODLAND PREDATORS

The sparrowhawks and goshawks are small- to medium-sized birds found in

▲A sparrowhawk broods her young in the rain. Like many northern birds of prey, the sparrowhawk is very slowly recovering from the damage to wildlife inflicted by pesticides.

forest, woodland and scrub habitats all over the world. Their wings are short and rounded and their tails are long. These adaptations enable the birds to dash through dense woody vegetation at a breakneck pace, using agility, speed and surprise to run down their prey.

Cooper's hawk is typical of the whole group. It inhabits woodlands of North America from Canada south to Mexico, often roosting perched on one leg in a coniferous tree, but nearly always choosing deciduous woods at nesting time. Its hunting methods are a mixture of skill, speed and trickery. Often the hawk will fly to a partly concealed perch and wait there until a bird or squirrel wanders out into the open, unaware of danger. Then it

dashes out, using its long legs to reach out and snatch the victim on the ground or as it tries to flee.

SWOOPING AND POUNCING

As in most species of sparrowhawk, the female Cooper's hawk is much larger than the male, and while male birds prey on starlings, blackbirds and flickers, the females will take prey as big as grouse.

Both males and females are skilled at using natural cover to get close to their prey. Even a group of birds feeding on the ground in a clearing can be taken by surprise. The hawk swoops in low, using every tree stump, bush and dip in the ground to conceal its approach.

Birds are sometimes deliberately flushed out of cover. The hawk will fly straight towards a bush, then dodge sideways at the last minute, dashing round to the far side to pounce on any birds frightened into coming into the open.

RETURN JOURNEYS

As the abundance of food begins to wane in the autumn, the most northerly Cooper's hawks migrate southwards. Some travel as far as Colombia. As they head south they often join with other hawks – Sharp-shinned, Red-tailed and other unrelated species. The southward mass migration of birds of prey down the "flyway" of the Appalachian Mountains is one of the greatest birdwatching sights in the USA.

The birds return in February and March, usually to the same patch of woodland, although a new nest is made each year. Males and females perform courtship display flights, and the nest-building and mating is accompanied by much displaying and the singing of duets.

BUZZARDS AND HAWKS

The buzzards and their relatives are a very varied group, both in size and in habitat. They range from tiny woodland hawks to the world's biggest, most powerful, and probably rarest birds of prey.

The Common buzzard breeds in woodland, but often hunts over open moorland, plains and mountains. It is found right across Europe and Asia, as far east as Siberia and Japan, but like many birds of prey the buzzard is a migrant. Each year the northern populations move from their summer breeding areas to winter quarters in Africa, India and South-east Asia.

The buzzard is much less striking in colour than its hawk relatives, and spends a lot of time either perched on a fence-post or tree, or slowly soaring back and forth along a rocky hillside as it searches for rodents and small rabbits.

▶Proudly perched on a rocky ledge, a Common buzzard, the most common European bird of prey, surveys its habitat.

In North America, the buzzard's relatives include the handsome Red-shouldered hawk and the Red-tailed hawk. The Red-shouldered hawk inhabits damp lowland forests and marshland in the eastern half of the country. It feeds mainly on mice, frogs and small snakes. The Red-tailed hawk prefers upland regions. Its diet consists primarily of small mammals.

Like several other American species of hawk, these birds have suffered in recent years from the harmful effects of pesticides widely used on agricultural land.

◄The spiky head plume of the Philippine monkey-eating eagle gives the bird an oddly human face.

KINGS OF THE FOREST

Pride of place in the entire bird of prey family must go to the Harpy eagle. This formidable aerial hunter inhabits the lowland tropical forests of South America from southern Mexico to northern Argentina. Despite its great size it is an agile hunter. When hunting it threads its way through the canopy of the Amazon jungle at up to 70kph, pursuing the monkeys that make up a large part of its diet. The Harpy eagle also preys on sloths, opossums and tree porcupines. It will also take snakes and large birds when the opportunity comes along.

Details of the Harpy eagle's breeding behaviour are not well known, but the Harpy's nest is a huge structure of sticks, lined with green leaves. This is

▲Tail fanned like the flaps of an airplane, an Augur buzzard swoops low. This aerial hunter is the most common buzzard of East and southern Africa.

placed in a tree fork 40 to 45m above the ground.

In the rain forests of the Philippines lives another magnificent predator, the Philippine monkey-eating eagle. In every way it is the Asian counterpart of its South American relative – huge, magnificent and, sadly, now listed as an endangered species. Nobody knows how many Harpies survive in Amazonia. In the Philippines there are probably no more than 200 monkey-eating eagles left. In the past, hunting for zoo specimens and trophies was the main threat. Today it is the destruction of the birds' native forests.

FALCONS

A Peregrine falcon shows off its speed and agility in flight as it homes in on a wood-pigeon. Its hunting dive or "stoop" is a breath-taking power dive that reaches speeds of over 200kph.

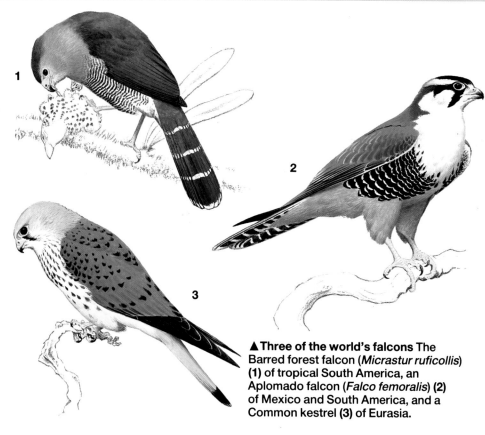

▲ **Three of the world's falcons** The Barred forest falcon (*Micrastur ruficollis*) (1) of tropical South America, an Aplomado falcon (*Falco femoralis*) (2) of Mexico and South America, and a Common kestrel (3) of Eurasia.

FALCONS Falconidae (*60 species*)

● ■

Habitat: very varied, from sea coasts to grassland, woodland, tropical forest and deserts.

Diet: mammals, birds, reptiles, insects; also carrion.

Breeding: caracaras 2 or 3 eggs, laid in a nest. True falcons up to 9 eggs, (usually 4 or 5), laid on bare rock, in a rough scrape, or in an abandoned nest. Incubation period up to 30 days.

Size: smallest (Asian falconets): length 15cm, weight 40g; largest (caracaras): length 35-60cm, weight 280-1,600g.

Plumage: varied; usually brown or grey, and dark above, pale below. Many species with strong colours and bold markings.

Species mentioned in text:
American kestrel (*Falco sparverius*)
Common kestrel (*F. tinnunculus*)
Gyrfalcon (*F. rusticolus*)
Lanner falcon (*F. biarmicus*)
Mauritius kestrel (*F. punctatus*)
Peregrine falcon (*F. peregrinus*)
Red-throated caracara (*Daptrius americanus*)

The Peregrine falcon is the most widespread and successful of all the birds of prey. It is found in every continent except Antarctica, and on many of the world's island groups too. It is one of the biggest members of the falcon family, measuring up to 48cm long. With its grey-blue back, beautifully banded pale buff undersides, yellow eye-rings and black "moustache", it is also one of the most handsome.

SPEED AND PRECISION
The superb hunting skills of the Peregrine falcon have made it the favourite bird of falconers in many countries. The birds are caught in flight using nets and then trained. They can be used to hunt gamebirds the size of bustards. The Peregrine's hunting method is unique. Unlike the hawks, which usually attack in fast level flight and strike with their front toes, the Peregrine plummets down on to its prey in a dive that has been

estimated at speeds ranging from 170kph to a staggering 400kph.

Just before reaching its target the Peregrine slows and levels out, striking the lethal blow with the needle-sharp talons of its rear "toes". The victim is often allowed to tumble to the ground, but the attacker closely follows it. The Peregrine's main prey varies according to where it lives, but its favourite quarry includes pigeons, grouse and small sea-birds. Young Peregrines take smaller prey such as finches.

The Peregrine falcon is found in many different habitats. It seems to prefer rocky crags, and is most common on rocky sea coasts. But it is a versatile bird, and is also found in moorland, open grassland, scrub and desert areas, and even in forests.

A YEAR IN THE LIFE
There are 18 separate races of Peregrine falcon, living in regions as varied as Alaskan river valleys and the

tropical grasslands of Africa. The tropical species are year-round residents, but most northern birds migrate in winter to areas with better food supplies. European birds migrate to southern Africa, and North American birds fly far into South America.

▼A Common kestrel returns to its young with a large rodent. Like most falcons it does not build a proper nest.

At the start of the breeding season the male Peregrine chooses a good breeding ledge on a cliff. When he sees a female he flies out, calling to her, then returns to the ledge. The performance is repeated until a female accepts the male's invitation. After that the two birds swoop and dive and chase each other in a spectacular series of display flights. The birds make no nest and the eggs are simply laid on the bare rock. The male usually shares the task of incubating the eggs, and also brings food to the nest for himself and the female.

THE PESTICIDE THREAT

During the 1960s the Peregrine populations of North America and Europe began to fall alarmingly. Scientists then discovered that the shells of the birds' eggs were so thin and fragile

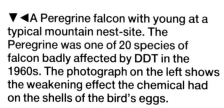

▼ ◄A Peregrine falcon with young at a typical mountain nest-site. The Peregrine was one of 20 species of falcon badly affected by DDT in the 1960s. The photograph on the left shows the weakening effect the chemical had on the shells of the bird's eggs.

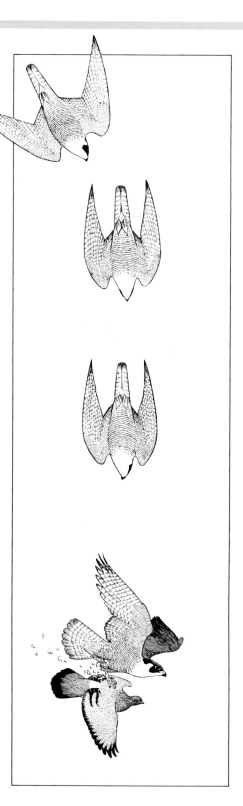

▲Folding back its wings to reduce air resistance, a Peregrine falcon plunges in a near-vertical dive. If it misses its quarry, or is simply "playing", it swoops up again and repeats the attack.

that they were breaking when the incubating birds sat on them. The cause was DDT, a common farm pesticide. The chemical was building up in the bodies of seed- and insect-eating birds, and it passed on to the falcons when they ate these birds.

Many countries have now banned the use of DDT, and in these the Peregrine is making a recovery. (In the developing countries of the tropics and subtropics especially, the use of DDT is on the increase.) It was a sharp lesson in the dangers of using chemicals that remain in the environment long after their job has been done.

THE SMALLER FALCONS

The Peregrine, and the magnificent grey and white gyrfalcon of the Arctic wastelands, are two of the bigger falcons. But there are many smaller species too. One of the most familiar in Europe is the kestrel. This is often seen hovering over the verges of motorways.

The kestrel holds its position in the air with rapid beats of its long pointed wings and with constant adjustments to the angle of its unusually long fan-shaped tail. It is the only falcon to hunt in this way, scanning the ground below for the mice, frogs and small

▲ The Lanner falcon of Africa and the Mediterranean often attacks its prey head-on, instead of approaching from above or behind as most falcons do.

birds like larks, pipits and buntings that make up its diet.

The European kestrel is mainly a bird of grasslands, heaths and open farmland. The American kestrel inhabits much drier country and is even found in the desolate desert around Lima in Peru. There the bird preys on lizards, scorpions and large insects. In the gentler climate of North America it feeds mainly on grasshoppers and other large insects in summer and on

mice and small birds like sparrows during the winter months.

LIZARD- AND MOTH-EATERS

The Mauritius kestrel is now one of the rarest birds in the world. It is a forest-dwelling species, with short rounded wings that are perfectly adapted for twisting and turning among tree trunks and branches. The bird hunts for tree-lizards, beetles and flying insects. Sadly, most of the forest has been cut down for its valuable timber, and for farmland. In 1985 there were only 16 breeding pairs left in the wild. Fortunately this kestrel

breeds well in captivity, and several captive-bred birds have already been reintroduced to the few remaining patches of forest. The species may just survive, but only with total protection for the bird and its habitat – and a good deal of luck.

Smaller still are the pygmy falcons and falconets. One species inhabits the desert areas and grasslands of northern Argentina. There are two pygmy species, one inhabiting woodlands in southern Asia, the other living in the desert and thornbush country of Africa. But smallest of all – barely 15cm from bill to tail tip – are the falconets of tropical Asia. These sparrow-sized hunters are boldly coloured, with black above and white or chestnut-brown below. Their main prey are the large forest dragonflies and moths, usually caught on the wing in a darting attack from a perch.

SOUTH AMERICAN COUSINS

The caracaras are large (buzzard-sized) birds with long legs and broad wings. At first glance it is hard to think of them as falcons. Unlike their dashing relatives they are rather slow, sluggish birds that spend much of their time either perched in the trees or walking about on the ground.

The caracaras are found only in South America, where they inhabit open country, woodland, forest and grassland. They feed mainly on large insects, but they are also carrion-eaters and are often seen in the company of New World vultures, squabbling over the remains of an animal carcass.

The Red-throated caracara is rather vulture-like in appearance. Its plumage is glossy black, shot with green and blue. Its cheeks and throat are bright red and bare of feathers, and it has a habit of perching on a branch screaming and cackling loudly. Its feeding habits are just as strange as it specializes in tearing open wasps' nests to feed on the larvae.

SKIMMERS

It is very nearly dark over the inland Salton Sea in California, yet some birds are still active. They are flying low over the water with their wingtips nearly touching the surface. The body is angled forwards so that the lower part of the open bill dips into the water. They are Black skimmers going fishing. Here and there a bird strikes lucky as the lower bill touches a fish. It snaps the head down and closes the bill over the fish. Then it lifts the head up and swallows its catch.

Skimmers are named after the way they skim over the surface when feeding. They have an extraordinary bill, with the lower mandible much longer than the upper one. Both mandibles are flat, like the blades of a pair of scissors. This gives the birds their popular name of scissorbill.

The muscles and bones in the head of the bird are specially adapted to the method of feeding. They act as a shock absorber when the head snaps down and the bill shuts as prey is caught.

Skimmers usually fish either alone or in pairs, only occasionally in small groups. They mostly feed at dusk and often during the night. Unusually, their eyes have a vertical slit pupil, like a cat's eye. This may help them see better in the dark.

CLOSE RELATIONS
The three species of skimmer are found mainly in tropical and subtropical regions of the world. They are of similar size and appearance.

Apart from the bill, skimmers resemble the sea terns. They have an elegant body, short legs and a black cap and nape. Their wings are very long and sharply tapered, with a span 2½ times their body length. The wings and back are dark, the underparts white or pale grey. The main differences between the species are in the colour of the bill and legs.

The Black skimmer represents the skimmers in the New World. It has bright red legs and an orange bill tipped with black. It breeds in the United States and in Central and South America. The slightly smaller Indian skimmer is similar except for an all-orange bill. It ranges from Pakistan, through India to the Malay peninsula. The African skimmer, of Central and East Africa, has yellowish legs and a yellowish-orange bill.

In the United States, the Black skimmer is a bird of the coasts and the inland Salton Sea. In South America it inhabits the river systems. The Indian and African skimmers are also found mainly along inland waterways.

BELLY WETTING
Skimmers nest in colonies, typically in the open on sand bars in rivers and estuaries. They sometimes nest alongside terns. This probably helps protect

SKIMMERS Rynchopidae
(*3 species*)

● ■

🌊 **Habitat:** coastal and inland waters, marshes.

■ **Diet:** small fish, shrimps, other crustaceans.

○ **Breeding:** 2-5 white to brownish, dark-blotched or spotted eggs; 22-24 days incubation.

Size: length 35-45cm; weight up to 400g.

Plumage: upper parts dark, underparts pale.

Species mentioned in text:
African skimmer (*Rynchops flavirostris*)
Black skimmer (*R. niger*)
Indian skimmer (*R. albicollis*)

▼The Black skimmer of the Americas is the largest member of the family. But all skimmers have this odd-looking bill.

them better against predators, because the terns are more aggressive against intruders.

Before mating and nesting, skimmers become very active and noisy, especially at night. Their courtship displays include vigorous high-speed aerial chases. Skimmers make their nests in shallow hollows in the sand which they excavate with the breast.

▼A Black skimmer foraging for food. The bill snaps shut instantly when the long lower part touches a fish.

Both males and females incubate the eggs. At tropical nest sites in particular, the birds swap duty frequently during the day when the temperature of the sand soars. Before relieving its mate, each bird dips its belly and feet in the water. When back on the nest, this wets the eggs and helps prevent them from becoming overheated.

The parents feed the young with small fish. The young can pick them up because to begin with the two mandibles of the bill are the same size.

They also feed themselves on insects at this time. Only when the young start to fly does the bottom mandible begin to lengthen. Then the birds fly with their parents on fishing trips and learn to skim for themselves.

Although a nesting pair can successfully raise as many as four young, most pairs do not do so. On the open low-lying nest sites, the eggs are often washed away by high tides or flooding. Snakes, lizards and herons may prey on the eggs too and also on newly hatched chicks.

NIGHTJARS

In an experiment, a Common nighthawk was released in a darkened tunnel festooned with ropes. The bird flew through the maze without once colliding with the ropes. Then the test was tried again, but with the bird's ears covered. The nighthawk was unable to find its way through. The ear-muffs had robbed it of its "secret sensor".

The nightjar family is divided into two groups: the nighthawks of North and South America, and the nightjars, which are found in Europe, Asia and Africa as well as in the Americas. Like the Common nighthawk, many species hunt at night using echolocation to find their prey. As with most specialist insect-hunters they are commonest in tropical regions where insects are available all year round. But many species migrate into temperate regions in the summer months.

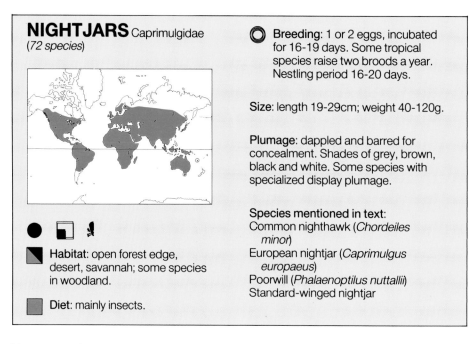

NIGHTJARS Caprimulgidae
(*72 species*)

● ▢ ❦

◪ **Habitat:** open forest edge, desert, savannah; some species in woodland.

▦ **Diet:** mainly insects.

◎ **Breeding:** 1 or 2 eggs, incubated for 16-19 days. Some tropical species raise two broods a year. Nestling period 16-20 days.

Size: length 19-29cm; weight 40-120g.

Plumage: dappled and barred for concealment. Shades of grey, brown, black and white. Some species with specialized display plumage.

Species mentioned in text:
Common nighthawk (*Chordeiles minor*)
European nightjar (*Caprimulgus europaeus*)
Poorwill (*Phalaenoptilus nuttallii*)
Standard-winged nightjar

THE GHOSTLY HUNTERS

The nightjars and nighthawks are true specialists. During the day they rest on the forest floor, or perched on branches, or among the stones and dry scrub of a savannah or desert region. Their patterned plumage of black, brown, grey and white blends into the background so well that the birds are almost impossible to see unless they are disturbed and forced to move.

▶ A European nightjar shows its dappled camouflage plumage as it raises its wings in an angry threat display on its nest on the ground.

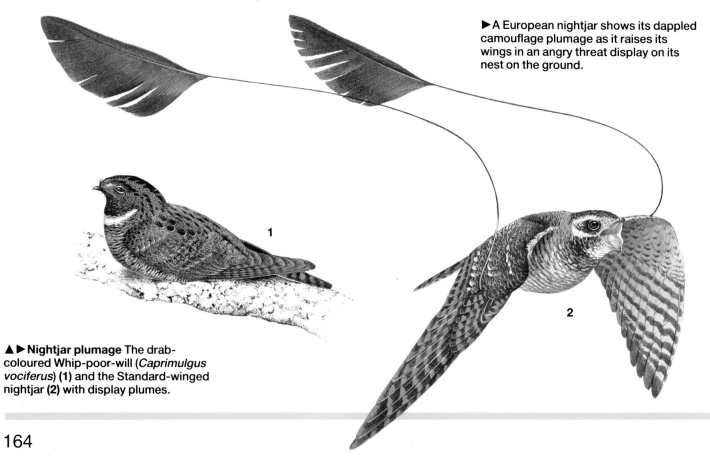

▲ ▶ **Nightjar plumage** The drab-coloured Whip-poor-will (*Caprimulgus vociferus*) (**1**) and the Standard-winged nightjar (**2**) with display plumes.

As night falls, the birds become active. Their soft plumage makes hardly a sound as they start to hunt, bobbing and weaving in a graceful dancing flight that makes them look like large moths. There is nothing so charming about the nightjar's mouth. It is enormous! When a nightjar opens its bill wide it becomes a gaping cavern that can take in a cloud of mosquitoes or a huge tropical moth in one go. Some of the larger species will even snap up a small night-flying bird if the chance comes along.

Most nightjars remain in flight all the time they are hunting, but some woodland species hunt from a perch, dashing out to snap up a passing insect then returning once more to their look-out.

TUMBLERS AND FLAG-WAVERS

The males of some nightjar species perform spectacular courtship displays to attract their mates. Some involve diving and tumbling display flights. Others make use of long specialized display feathers that are grown just for the mating season. The male may have several females, each with her own nest, and throughout the mating season he must be constantly on guard to chase away other males. Elaborate display plumes are a hindrance to a bird caring for young in the nest, so the males tend to leave care of the young to the females.

"THE SLEEPING ONE"

In 1946 an astonishing discovery was made about a small American nightjar called the poorwill. The bird inhabits the deserts of Mexico and California, and during the winter a bird was found hidden in a crack in the wall of a canyon. The scientists at first thought it was dead. Its body temperature was well below normal and it was barely breathing, but it was alive. The bird was hibernating – something no other bird has ever been found to do. The local Hopi Indians had chosen well when they named the bird "Holchko" meaning The Sleeping One.

▲**Nightjars in display** The Common nighthawk male dives towards the female (1), swooping upwards at the last moment with a booming sound made by the air rushing through specialized feathers. The male Standard-wing nightjar flutters round his chosen mate (2), displaying his 45cm-long plumes.

HOOPOE

An eagle flying over a hoopoe's nest fails to see the chicks until one of them opens its colourful wings to preen. The eagle swoops down to attack. As it approaches, the young birds flutter their wings, both to dazzle the eagle and to strike it should it pounce. The eagle turns tail.

▶An adult hoopoe flattens itself against the ground and points its bill skywards to poke at an attacker from above.

▼A hoopoe bringing food to its brood. When the bird lands, it briefly flicks its crest upright then lowers it again.

HOOPOE *Upupa epops*

● ◼

◼ **Habitat:** open woodland, farmland and savannah.

◼ **Diet:** insects and lizards.

○ **Breeding:** 2-5 eggs in tropical regions; 7-9 in temperate regions. Incubated for 15 or 16 days, nestling period 28 days.

Size: length 27-29cm; weight 50-80g.

Plumage: pinkish-brown with black and white bars; South African race redder, with less white on wings. Plumage the same on males, females and juveniles.

The hoopoe's pinkish-brown plumage and dramatic black-and-white wing bars are quite unmistakable, but they are also part of this unusual bird's defences. When it is feeding quietly on the ground in a field or woodland clearing, the hoopoe is surprisingly difficult to see. It will often remain unnoticed until it opens its wings to fly. When danger threatens, the dazzling pattern of bars on its long tail and short broad wings helps to confuse the attacker as the hoopoe dashes for the safety of trees or scrub vegetation.

BIRD OF THREE CONTINENTS

The hoopoe is found right across southern Europe, all over Africa (apart from the dense tropical rain forest) and throughout southern Asia. It is such a popular and familiar sight that it crops up again and again in the folklore and legends of many lands.

It feeds on the grubs and adults of insects such as grasshoppers and beetles, and on snails. It probes in the grass and soil with its long slender bill, or searches among the cracks and crevices of tree bark or stone walls. In the southern parts of its range it also catches small lizards. These are an important source of food in the breeding season when the bird has hungry youngsters to feed.

The hoopoe's nest site is always a hole of some kind – in a tree or wall, or among rocks. African hoopoes often use holes in termite mounds, or abandoned woodpecker holes. There is no attempt to build a proper nest, and the eggs are simply laid on the bare floor of the nest hole. The female hoopoe incubates the eggs alone, but is kept supplied with food by her attentive mate. She does not leave the nest hole until the young are

▲ The striking bars on the hoopoe's back, wings and tail help to confuse a chasing bird. The bars have the same effect as camouflage patterns painted on military aircraft.

big enough to survive without the warmth of her body. By that time the hole is usually fouled with droppings and the characteristic strong smell of the birds themselves.

The young hoopoes have several ways of defending themselves. If danger threatens, they hiss, stab upwards with their bills, strike out with their wings and squirt their droppings at the intruder.

The bird's common name, hoopoe, and its scientific name, *Upupa epops*, both have the sound of its call – a soft "oop...oop...oop", which carries far and wide through its open habitat.

SHRIKES

1

2

3

◯ **Habitat:** tropical forest, dry savannah woodland, cultivated land, coastal scrubland.

◨ **Diet:** mainly insects; larger species take lizards, frogs, birds. Some also eat fruit.

◯ **Breeding:** true shrikes usually lay 4-7 eggs; incubation 12-18 days. Other groups vary; details unknown for some.

Size: length 14-38cm; weight 10-110g. Details unknown for many species.

Plumage: some species mainly black, white and grey, others brightly coloured in crimson, yellow, green; often with streaks, spots and blotches.

Species mentioned in text:
Gonoleks (genus *Laniarius*)
Great grey, or Northern, shrike (*Lanius excubitor*)
Helmet shrikes (*genus Prionops*)
Helmet vanga (*Euryceros prevostii*)
Minivets (genus *Pericrocotus*)
Red-backed shrike (*Lanius collurio*)
Red-tailed vanga (*Calicalicus madagascariensis*)
Sicklebill (*Falculea palliata*)

Perched on a fence-post on a New England farm, a Great grey shrike scans the ground for prey. A movement in the grass catches the bird's eye, and like a miniature hawk it pounces. Returning to its perch with a large beetle in its bill, the bird moves out along the fence wire and with a brisk movement of its head impales the beetle on one of the sharp steel barbs.

Many members of the shrike family hunt from a look-out perch in this way, and several species have the "butcher-bird" habit of storing food. These birds impale insects on sharp thorns or, in farming areas, on the spikes of barbed wire fences.

The main prey of the smaller

◄**Shrikes and their relatives** Large cuckoo-shrike (*Coracina novae-hollandiae*) **(1)** of India, south Asia and Australia. The Great grey or Northern shrike **(2)** of North America, Europe, Africa and Asia. Red-shouldered cuckoo-shrike (*Campephaga phoenicia*) **(3)** of East Africa. The Long-crested helmet-shrike (*Prionops plumata*) **(4)** from Africa. The Helmet bird (*Euryceros prevostii*) **(5)** of Madagascar holding a lizard's tail. A palmchat (*Dulus dominicus*) **(6)** from Hispaniola, and a Burchell's gonolek (*Laniarius atrococcineus*) **(7)** of South Africa.

COATS OF MANY COLOURS

There are seven families of shrikes and their relatives. The true shrikes (family Laniidae) are the most widespread. As well as being found throughout Africa south of the Sahara Desert, they are also found in Europe and Asia and across most of North America.

Another big family, the cuckoo-shrikes (Campephagidae), lives in the forests and scrublands of southern Africa, South-east Asia and Australia. These birds range from drab-coloured forest birds the size of pigeons to dainty and brilliantly coloured birds called minivets, which have slender wings and long tails. They are all highly sociable birds, and often move through the tree-tops in noisy bands of 20 or more as they search among the leaves for insects.

The vanga-shrikes, or vangas (family Vangidae), are found only on the huge island of Madagascar. Their ancestors probably belonged to the helmet-shrike family (Prionopidae) of Africa, but for millions of years they have evolved in complete isolation. Madagascar has very few other groups of native birds, and so the vangas have been able to take over many different life-styles. The Helmet vanga preys on large insects, chameleons and frogs – it is like a small bird of prey. The Red-tailed vanga has a small pointed bill and searches the tree bark for small insects, just as a tit does. Other species behave like flycatchers.

shrikes, like the Red-backed shrike of western Europe, consists of bumble-bees, grasshoppers and other large insects. The much more powerful Great grey shrike often takes mice, lizards and even young birds, which are snatched from the nest while the parents are away gathering food.

Three-quarters of the shrike species are found in Africa. Some inhabit rain forests, others deciduous woodlands or savannah country. Many species are brightly coloured, for example the spectacular gonoleks, but all have the powerful hook-tipped bill that is the main family characteristic.

MARSUPIAL CARNIVORES

The Moon shines down brightly on a group of sand-hills in the Australian outback. From a shallow burrow comes a buff coloured "mouse" about 15cm long, with a 10cm black-tipped tail. It is a mulgara. Peering into crevices, it searches busily. In one hole it finds a beetle, which it flicks out with a front paw and snaps up. Finding a lizard nearly as large itself, it attacks it sav-agely, biting the lizard behind the head. After feeding, for a while its hunger is satisfied. Nearby, still searching for her food, is a female mulgara, dragging six little pink young attached to her teats. Morning comes. Before it is hot, the mulgaras are back home underground.

MARSUPIAL CARNIVORES

Dasyuridae (*51 species*)

● ■□ 𝄐

◤ **Habitat:** forest, stony desert, mountain heath.

▮ **Diet:** insects, worms, spiders, lizards, mice, other small animals, carrion; some also eat flowers and fruit.

◯ **Breeding:** 2-12 young after pregnancy of 12-27 days.

Size: smallest (Pilbara ningaui): head-body 4.5cm, tail 6cm, weight 2g; largest (Tasmanian devil):head-body 65cm, tail 25cm, weight 8kg.

Colour: many smaller species greyish, mouse-coloured; larger species often brown or black with white markings.

Lifespan: 11.5 months (Brown antechinus) to 7 years (Tasmanian devil).

Species mentioned in text:
Brown antechinus (*Antechinus stuartii*)
Common planigale (*Planigale maculata*)
Dibbler (*Parantechinus apicalis*)
Dusky antechinus (*Antechinus swainsonii*)
Eastern quoll (*Dasyurus viverrinus*)
Fat-tailed dunnart (*Sminthopsis crassicaudata*)
Mulgara (*Dasycercus cristicauda*)
Pilbara ningaui (*Ningaui timealeyi*)
Spotted-tailed quoll (*Dasyurus maculatus*)
Tasmanian devil (*Sarcophilus harrisii*)
Tasmanian wolf (*Thylacinus cynocephalus*)

The marsupial carnivores are a large family found in many habitats through Australia and New Guinea. They live in tropical rain forest and light wood-lands, up mountains and even by the coast. Many kinds are able to survive in deserts.

Many of the species look rather similar. Small species are often mouse-like in appearance, although their habits are very different to true mice. Larger species are the equiva-lents to the stoats, civets and cats of other parts of the world. Instead of the mouse-like coloration of the small carnivores they are red-brown or black and may have spots of white.

SAVAGE ATTACK
Over half of the marsupial carnivores are small animals weighing less than 100g. Some are less than a tenth of this weight and are among the smallest mammals. But they have sharp teeth and attack their prey savagely. The Common planigale, little more than

▼Four month old Eastern quolls are too old to stay on their mother's teats. She leaves them in a grass-lined nest. Six tiny young fix to the teats in the pouch at birth and stay there for 10 weeks.

►The Dusky antechinus usually lives on the ground. Like many of the small "mouse-like" marsupials it is a fierce predator.It catches insects and small vertebrates such as lizards.

5cm long, plus a 5cm tail, can overcome grasshoppers as big as itself.

Many of the marsupial carnivores feed mainly on insects. Even those that are cat-sized rely to a large extent on beetle larvae, although they can catch and kill reptiles, birds and mammals. The mulgara kills its prey by biting and shaking. The final bite is always at the head or neck.

Most marsupial carnivores hunt by stealth or surprising prey. Few chase prey far. One exception is the Spotted-tailed quoll of Tasmania, a large cat-like animal with a body up to 0.75m long and a long tail. It is active and agile and can run down prey. It takes wallabies, gliding possums and reptiles. It also kills with an accurate and powerful bite to the back of the head.

Spotted-tailed quolls are sometimes

◄A Tasmanian devil shows its strong jaws and sharp teeth. It can chew and swallow all of a carcass, even bones.

▲The Tasmanian wolf or thylacine was one of the largest marsupial carnivores. Its fossil bones are found in Australia, but in historical times it lived only in Tasmania. It looked like a dog, about 60cm high at the shoulders, but fell away to the hind legs. It had a long stiff tail and a coat that was sandy with darker stripes. It had teeth like a dog and caught animals such as wallabies. It was said to kill sheep, so people hunted it. The last known specimen was caught in 1933 and died in 1936.

known as tiger-cats, because of their size and behaviour. They make sudden hisses when alarmed, and an angry animal produces unnerving screams. Quolls are mainly active at night. They are able to track prey by following scent trails. These animals are relatively long-lived, becoming adult at 2 years old, and living 6 years or more.

FEEDING ON CARRION
The Tasmanian devil, the largest living marsupial carnivore, is black, with a white mark across the chest. It has a rather tubby body and short legs. It is sometimes said to look like a small bear. In habits it is really more like a hyena. Although rarely able to kill active prey, it is very good at eating carrion. It can crunch up dead animals' bodies, bolting large lumps. It has been seen cramming intestines into its mouth with its front paws as though it was eating spaghetti.

DESERT AND TREE SPECIES
Many small carnivores are able to survive well in the Australian deserts. The mulgara, for example, can exist where there is no drinking water. All water must come from the insects and small vertebrates it eats. It holds on to water by producing very concentrated urine. It cuts down on evaporation of water from its body by living underground during the day. This avoids the high daytime temperatures.

In dry areas where food is only plentiful for part of the year carnivores may store food. The Fat-tailed dunnart has a tail which it uses for storing fat. It uses the fat up in time of need. When food is scarce it may also save energy by becoming inactive and allowing its body to slow right down. Even the body temperature drops.

Many marsupial meat-eaters, such as the quolls or "native cats", can climb well when the need arises, although they may spend much time on the ground. The phascogales are smaller species that are good climbers. They are usually in trees, either in forests or in open woodland.

Phascogales have long tails, the end-part of which is a brush of long hairs. The tail is used for balance and also probably as a signal. Phascogales are as agile as squirrels and are mainly active at night.

MATING AND BREEDING
Some of the small carnivores have a very short lifespan. Females of the Brown antechinus and related species may live for over a year, but the males are "annuals". They are born in early spring and are weaned by mid-summer. In late winter comes the mating season. The antechinus males are frantically active, searching for females and mating with them. Then they all die. At the end of the winter only pregnant females are left to carry on the species.

TOO MANY BABIES
Like kangaroos, the marsupial meat-eaters have their babies born in a very undeveloped stage after a short pregnancy. But few have a well developed pouch to hold the babies. In most cases there is just a fold of skin.

The exposed young are carried attached to the mother's teats for the first weeks of life.

There may be more babies born than the mother has teats. Those that do not find a teat to attach to will die. Some species, for example the planigales, have as many as 12 teats and may produce 20 babies.

SHRINKING NUMBERS
Since Europeans settled in Australia many carnivores have decreased in both distribution and numbers, often because habitat has been destroyed or used for farming. The larger species, such as the quolls, have suffered most. The Eastern quoll, for example, is endangered in parts of its range, although this may be due to competition from domestic cats that have become wild. Five species are believed in danger of extinction. These include the dibbler, a little mouse-like species which may already be extinct.

▼**A range of marsupial carnivores**
Kultarr (*Antechinomys laniger*) (**1**).
Pilbara ningaui (**2**).Three-striped
marsupial mouse (*Myoictis melas*) (**3**).
New Guinea marsupial cat (*Satanellus
albopunctatus*) (**4**). Fat-tailed or
Red-eared antechinus (*Pseudantechinus
macdonnellensis*) (**5**). Marsupial mouse
(*Phascolosorex dorsalis*) (**6**). Red-tailed
phascogale (*Phascogale calura*) (**7**).
Little red antechinus (*Dasykatula
rosamondae*) (**8**). Long-tailed marsupial
mouse (*Murexia longicaudata*) (**9**).
Fat-tailed dunnart (**10**). Common
planigale (**11**).

BANDICOOTS

Two male bandicoots patrolling neighbouring territories come face to face. On other nights one has chased the other away. Tonight both stand their ground, and a fight breaks out. Up on their hind legs, they lunge and lock jaws, wrestling each other to the ground. One struggles free, leaps high into the air and rakes the other with its hind claws. Squealing in fright, the other runs away. The victor gives chase for a while, then resumes the nightly patrol.

Bandicoots are stocky, coarse-haired mammals with a pointed snout. They are the size of a rabbit. They have the small, even teeth of a typical insect-eater. Their feet have strong claws,

▶ The white markings on the rump give the Eastern barred bandicoot its name.

▼ Some typical postures of a short-nosed bandicoot. Squatting to sniff the air when hunting (1). Male hopping aggressively (2). Digging for insects with strong foreclaws (3). Female giving birth (4). Mother carrying 7-week-old young in pouch (5).

which they use for digging into the ground for insects and worms.

Bandicoots live in Australia and New Guinea and on neighbouring islands. Like many Australian mammals, they are marsupials, raising their young in pouches. The pouch opens at the rear, not at the front as with other marsupials.

THE LONG AND THE SHORT

The hind limbs of the bandicoot are longer than the forelimbs, especially in the Greater bilby. This increasingly rare animal lives in the Australian deserts. Unlike other bandicoots, it has very long ears and a furry tail.

The common Brindled bandicoot has short ears and a nearly naked tail. It lives in the wetter regions near the coasts of eastern and northern Australia and further inland along rivers. The Brindled bandicoot is one of the short-nosed bandicoots, which gener-

BANDICOOTS Peramelidae, Thylacomyidae (*21 species*)

● ■ 🦡

Habitat: desert to rain forest.

Diet: insects, worms, other small animals, fruit and seeds.

Breeding: up to 7 young after pregnancy of 2 weeks or less.

Size: smallest (Mouse bandicoot): head-body 15cm, tail 11cm, weight 30g; largest (Giant bandicoot): head-body 56cm, tail 34cm, weight 4.7kg.

Colour: grey or brown coat.

Lifespan: up to 5 years.

Species mentioned in text:
Brindled bandicoot (*Isoodon macrourus*)
Eastern barred bandicoot (*Perameles gunnii*)
Giant bandicoot (*Peroryctes broadbenti*)
Greater bilby or Rabbit-eared bandicoot (*Macrotis lagotis*)
Long-nosed bandicoot (*Perameles nasuta*)
Mouse bandicoot (*Microperoryctes murina*)

▲ A female Greater bilby and young. The animal's alternative name, Rabbit-eared bandicoot, describes it well.

5

ally live in long grass and shrub where there is good ground cover. The long-nosed bandicoots prefer more open ground such as short grassland. They have longer ears as well as longer muzzles.

The long-nosed bandicoots of the grasslands, such as the Eastern barred bandicoot, have striped or barred markings on the coat to provide camouflage. Such markings are absent in the forest species.

FAST REPRODUCTION

Male bandicoots patrol their home territory each night to find females ready to mate and to keep out rival males. This is when they may fight.

The female gives birth usually in less than 2 weeks. Unlike those of other marsupials, the young are attached to the mother at birth by a placenta, as most mammals are. The young crawl into the mother's pouch and attach themselves to a nipple and begin to feed. They remain in the pouch for about 7 weeks and begin to eat normal food about 10 days later.

By this time the female may be pregnant again or may already have another litter in the pouch. But despite this high rate of reproduction, the population of Australian bandicoots has fallen rapidly in recent years. The desert species have been especially reduced. Overgrazing by cattle, sheep and rabbits is probably one of the main causes.

TENRECS

The female Common tenrec has been pregnant for almost two months, and her time is due. She settles in her cosy nest and soon feels the first pangs of birth. Then the babies start appearing – one, two, three, four, five... more than 20 babies emerge from her body. Although all but helpless, they manage to find the mother's teats and take their first feed of milk. None goes without, for there are more than enough teats to go round.

The Common tenrec is the largest member of the major animal group of insectivores or insect-eaters. Like most other insectivores it has a long narrow snout covered with sensitive whiskers. Its eyesight is not good, and it relies more on its excellent hearing and sense of smell to detect its prey. Its brown coat is coarse and has spines along the back.

When fighting, it opens its mouth in a wide gape, exposing long canine teeth. It slashes sideways at its opponent, then bucks with its head. This brings into action the stiff spines on its neck. Similar behaviour is found in other tenrecs.

MADAGASCAN HEDGEHOGS
The Common tenrec is found in large numbers on the island of Madagascar in the Indian Ocean. It is one of 31 tenrec species on the island. One of its close relatives is the Streaked tenrec, so called because of the white stripes on its blackish coat.

The Streaked tenrec looks much like the young Common tenrec. Both practise stridulation. This means they rub together stiff spines on their back to make a noise. The young do this when alarmed or just to communicate with one another and with their mother when foraging.

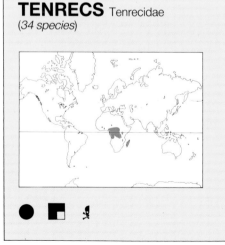

TENRECS Tenrecidae
(34 species)

Habitat: wide range, from semi-arid to rain forest, also mountains, rivers and human settlements.

Diet: worms, insects, birds, crustaceans, some fruit.

Breeding: 2-32 offspring after pregnancy of 7-9 weeks.

Size: smallest (Microgale parvula): head-tail 9cm, weight 5g; largest (Common tenrec): head-tail 40cm, weight 1.5kg.

Colour: brown to grey, sometimes streaked.

Lifespan: up to 6 years.

Species mentioned in text:
Aquatic tenrec (Limnogale mergulus)
Common tenrec (Tenrec ecaudatus)
Greater hedgehog tenrec (Setifer setosus)
Large-eared tenrec (Geogale aurita)
Lesser hedgehog tenrec (Echinops telfairi)
Long-tailed tenrec (Microgale melanorrachis)
Rice tenrec (Oryzoryctes tetradactylus)
Streaked tenrec (Hemicentetes nigriceps)

Two other members of the tenrec family have stiff spines all over their body except the underside, just like a hedgehog. They are called the Greater and Lesser hedgehog tenrecs. The latter spends some of its time in the trees. Both roll themselves into a protective ball when threatened.

Quite different in appearance are the soft-furred Long-tailed and Large-eared tenrecs, which look rather like shrews. Some are able to climb trees, while others sometimes burrow in the ground. The Rice tenrec is a more persistent burrower, while the Aquatic tenrec is a water creature, whose webbed feet make it a powerful swimmer.

RECORD BREEDERS
The female Common tenrec has been known to produce as many as 32 young in one litter. This is a record among mammals. Like most tenrecs, the Common tenrec is usually nocturnal. But nursing mothers with large families have to forage in the daylight hours as well. Their young have a striped coat, which gives them good camouflage in the relatively dangerous daylight hours. The young tenrecs become more nocturnal as they acquire the darker adult coat.

◀**Species of tenrec** Tenrecs vary widely in appearance, from the hedgehog-like Lesser hedgehog tenrec **(1)** to the shrew-like Long-tailed tenrec **(2)**. Largest is the Common tenrec **(3)**, here displaying its powerful jaws. The Streaked tenrec **(4)**, is easy to recognize. The Rice tenrec **(5)** is also shrew-like. The aquatic Giant otter shrew (*Potamogale velox*) **(6)** and Ruwenzori least otter shrew (*Micropotamogale ruwenzorii*) **(7)** live in streams, lakes and swamps in tropical Africa.

▼When cornered, the Lesser hedgehog tenrec curls itself up into a ball. Its prickly spines will keep off most predators.

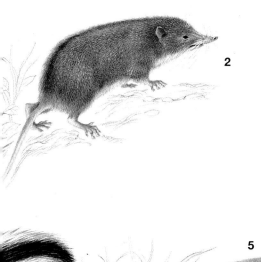

2

5

6

7

SOLENODONS

A rather large rat-like creature is feeding among the leaf litter and stones on the forest floor. It lifts up its head, showing an unusually long snout. The animal is a solenodon. After sniffing the air, it goes back to using its snout to probe under stones and into crevices. Soon its labours are rewarded, as a beetle scurries out from shelter. The solenodon lunges and pins down the beetle with its snout, then scoops up its prey into its mouth. The beetle soon stops struggling, poisoned by the solenodon's saliva.

Solenodons live in the forests of Hispaniola (Haiti and the Dominican Republic) and Cuba. The solenodons on Hispaniola belong to a different species from those on Cuba, but they are closely related. Both species have the same sized body, but the Cuban species has a shorter tail. They also have a different coloured coat. The Cuban solenodon's coat is dark grey, except for a pale head and belly. The Hispaniola solenodon has a much coarser coat, which is grey-brown on the back and yellowish on the flanks; the forehead is black.

SOUND EFFECTS

Solenodons are active at night. Their eyes are small, and their eyesight is poor. They learn about their surroundings mainly with their other senses. They have a good sense of touch through the long sensitive whiskers on the snout. Their senses of smell and hearing are also well developed, helping them locate their prey in the dark.

An interesting sound solenodons make is a high-pitched clicking noise.

▼ When hunting, solenodons use their long sharp claws to upturn stones and tear off bark in search of prey.

SOLENODONS
Solenodontidae (*2 species*)

▲ Habitat: remote forest.

■ Diet: millipedes, beetles and other insects, worms and termites, sometimes birds.

◡ Breeding: 1 or 2 offspring; length of pregnancy unknown.

Size: head-body 28-33cm; tail 22-25cm; weight 700g-1kg.

Colour: Hispaniola species mainly brownish-grey; Cuban species dark grey.

Lifespan: unknown.

Species mentioned in text:
Cuban solenodon (*Solenodon cubanus*)
Hispaniola solenodon (*S. paradoxurus*)

They probably use this as a kind of sonar to find their way around. They give out the clicks and listen for echoes, which will tell them if there is something in their path. Solenodons also twitter, chirp and puff as they move around.

DWINDLING NUMBERS

Before the Europeans arrived in the Caribbean region, solenodons were found on several other islands besides Hispaniola and Cuba. But the animals the Europeans introduced – cats, dogs and mongooses – preyed on the solenodons and killed them off. The same predators have today reduced the remaining solenodon populations to danger levels. On Hispaniola and Cuba they are found now only in the remotest regions.

Another reason why solenodons have become scarce is that they have a much lower rate of reproduction than their predators. Only one or two offspring are produced at a time. The young rely on their mother for several months, much longer than with other insectivores.

During the first few weeks of their life, young solenodons are carried around by their mother in a unique way. They cling to her long teats. Later they follow her on foot around the nest burrow. They get a taste of grown-up food by licking the mother's mouth as she feeds.

◀One of the most unusual features of the solenodon is its long, tapering and whiskered snout. The snout is made of cartilage, not bone, and extends beyond the jaw. In the Hispaniola species it is joined to the skull by a ball-and-socket joint, which makes it very flexible.

HEDGEHOGS

Crawling into the nest it has made under a pile of logs, the European hedgehog settles down and falls asleep. It is late autumn, and the temperature is dropping fast. Next day, the hedgehog is still asleep, and the next, and the next. Its hibernation may last until the spring. During this time it appears dead, but its heart is still beating – albeit slowly.

Hedgehogs are among the most familiar small mammals there are. Their stiff spines give them good protection against most predators, so they are not too worried about being caught out in the open. When they are attacked, they roll themselves into a prickly ball, shielding the soft underparts.

Hedgehogs have the long snouts that most insectivores have. But although insects form a major part of their diet, they will also feed on other small creatures and have even been known to attack quite large birds.

Hedgehogs are adaptable animals, which is why they are found so widely throughout Europe, Asia and Africa. Most is known about the European hedgehog.

HEDGEHOGS Erinaceidae (*about 17 species*)

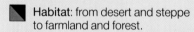

Habitat: from desert and steppe to farmland and forest.

Diet: mainly worms, beetles, slugs and caterpillars, also birds, eggs and young, seeds and fruit.

Breeding: up to 10 offspring after pregnancy of 5-7 weeks (European hedgehog).

Size: smallest (Lesser moonrat): head-body 10cm, tail 1cm, weight 40g; largest (Greater moonrat): head-body 45cm, tail 21cm, weight 1.4kg.

Colour: coat brown, paler on underside; Greater moonrat black and white.

Lifespan: up to 8 years.

Species mentioned in text:
European hedgehog (*Erinaceus europaeus*)
Greater moonrat (*Echinosorex gymnurus*)
Lesser moonrat (*Hylomys suillus*)
Mindanao moonrat (*Podogymnura truei*)

HIBERNATION

The European hedgehog often hibernates, or sleeps, through the cold of winter, because during this time food becomes scarce. Its relatives in other regions with a cold season also hibernate. Hedgehogs that live in Africa's tropical regions, however, have no need to hibernate, because there is a plentiful supply of food for them all year round.

In desert regions hedgehogs may sleep through the driest and hottest periods of the year. This summer sleep is known as aestivation.

To prepare for hibernation, the hedgehog eats well in the summer, almost doubling in weight. It builds up a thick layer of fat beneath the skin, which sustains it during its long sleep. The layer also acts as insulation to keep it warm when the temperature outside drops to freezing and below.

The hedgehog's own temperature may fall until it is only a few degrees higher than its surroundings. In this state it is barely alive. It takes only a few shallow breaths every minute, and its heart beat is so slow and feeble that it can scarcely be felt.

STRANGE HABITS

There are many folk tales about the hedgehog's behaviour. They are supposed, for example, to carry fruit on their spines and to suck the milk from

◄This all-white Greater moonrat is unusual. Most members of the species are mainly black, with white just on the head and shoulders.

cows, but this seems most unlikely. They certainly have one or two strange habits, though, such as self-anointing. They produce lots of foamy spit and then flick it over their spines with the tongue. Nobody knows why they do this. It could be a way of attracting the opposite sex, of cleaning the spines or of ridding the skin of parasites.

The European hedgehog is equally at home in the town garden or in the countryside. Many people treat hedgehogs as pets, leaving out bread, milk and other food for them. People often think that "their" hedgehog lives somewhere near by, but this is not necessarily true. During their search for food, which for many species is at night, hedgehogs may travel as far as 1.5km from their nest site, sometimes

▶ **Species of hedgehogs and moonrats**
The Desert hedgehog (*Paraechinus aethiopicus*) (**1**) often digs and lives in burrows. The Shrew hedgehog (*Neotetracus sinensis*) (**2**) is much smaller and has a softer hairy coat, not spines. It is a kind of moonrat and has a long tail, as do the Mindanao moonrat (**3**) and the Greater moonrat (**4**).

farther. Also, they change their nest site frequently.

Hedgehogs are mostly solitary animals. The male and female come together only to mate. During courtship the female keeps her spines erect if she does not want to mate and may butt the male with them. She flattens her back spines when she is ready to mate. The male gets on her back, but

has to hold on to the spines on the female's shoulders to prevent himself slipping off.

After mating, the male departs, showing no interest in bringing up the young. The female prepares a nest in which to give birth. She uses dry leaves, grasses and moss to create a warm dry bed, usually beneath a bush but sometimes underground.

SPINELESS YOUNG

When the young are born they are naked and blind. Their spines lie beneath the skin to prevent them damaging the mother during birth. They are embedded in a watery fluid, but this soon disappears, and 150 or so white spines soon force their way through the skin. Within two days more dark spines start to grow out.

The young stay with the mother until they are about 7 weeks old (European hedgehog), then they leave or are driven away by her. The European hedgehog may breed twice a year if the food supply is good. The hedgehogs that live in the tropics breed all through the year.

THE HAIRY HEDGEHOGS

Related to the familiar spiny hedgehogs are a group of animals that look more like rats. They have a coat of hair, not spines, and are often called hairy hedgehogs. These are the moonrats or gymnures, animals native to China and South-east Asia.

Like their spiny relatives, moonrats have a well developed sense of smell. They are also very smelly themselves. They have scent glands that give out what is to humans a quite unpleasant scent, sometimes described as being like rotting garlic.

The Greater moonrat is the largest member of the hedgehog family, being about the size of a cottontail rabbit. Not a great deal is known about the habits of moonrats because they are very shy creatures, unlike hedgehogs. Some species are under threat of extinction because of the destruction of their jungle habitat. The Mindanao moonrat of the Philippines seems in the most danger.

▶A family of European hedgehogs goes foraging in the grass. From the age of about 3 weeks the young leave the nest and follow their mother. There may be up to seven young in the litter.

LEOPARDS AND JAGUAR

A loud, raucous rasping noise comes from near the top of a thorn tree in East Africa. It is a male leopard, signalling his dominance over the area he surveys from his prickly perch, high above the ground. At night he will leave this tree and prowl in search of prey.

There are three species of leopard, the largest and most familiar being the ordinary African leopard. This beautiful spotted cat lives in all of Africa south of the Sahara and extends through Asia as far east as China.

It is the most widespread member of the cat family and can live in almost any habitat so long as there is some cover. This solitary hunter is mainly active at night. Using a combination of silence, speed and cunning, it preys on a wide range of small mammals and birds. Leopards may ambush their prey or stalk it before making a final rapid pounce. Because of its wide choice of rather small prey, the leopard avoids competition with lions, tigers, African wild dogs and hyenas, all of which hunt larger animals.

Like other large cats, the leopard is territorial. Each animal has its own home range and it will not allow other leopards of the same sex to come close to it. The home range of a female leopard is 10 to 30sq km and overlaps very little with the territories of neighbouring females. Male territories are larger and include one or more female territories.

Both sexes defend their areas by fighting, and scent-mark widely by

LEOPARDS AND JAGUAR Felidae (*4 species*)

● ◪ ☠

■ **Habitat:** most areas with good cover, from tropical rain forest and dry savannah to cold mountains.

■ **Diet:** very varied, from fish and birds to small- and medium-sized mammals.

○ **Breeding:** litters of 1-6 after pregnancy of 85-110 days.

Size: head-body 60-190cm; weight 15-113kg; males often much larger than females.

Colour: black to black-ringed brown spots of varying size on a fawn to pale brown background.

Lifespan: up to 12 years, 20 years in captivity.

Species mentioned in text:
Clouded leopard (*Neofelis nebulosa*)
Jaguar (*Panthera onca*)
Leopard (*P. pardus*)
Snow leopard (*P. uncia*)

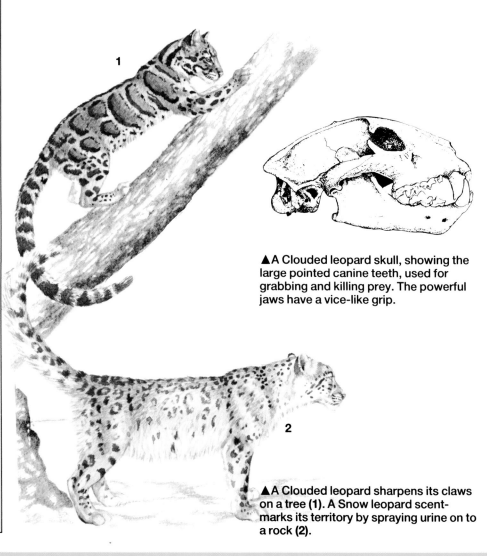

▲A Clouded leopard skull, showing the large pointed canine teeth, used for grabbing and killing prey. The powerful jaws have a vice-like grip.

▲A Clouded leopard sharpens its claws on a tree (1). A Snow leopard scent-marks its territory by spraying urine on to a rock (2).

spraying urine on to tree trunks, branches and logs. They also signal their presence by calling with a saw-like rasping sound.

RAISING YOUNG
The leopard begins to breed when it is about 2½ years old. Females come into heat every 3 to 7 weeks, and mating occurs at all times of the year. The male plays no part in rearing his offspring.

The female produces up to six blind, furry cubs, each weighing between 430 and 570g. She keeps her young hidden in a safe place for the first few weeks, and they soon begin to follow her around. They depend on her for 18 to 20 months, after which she mates again. Female cubs may then take over part of their mother's home range, while male cubs leave when they are 2 or 3 years old and set up separate territories of their own.

HUNTED FOR FUR
Although there are well over 100,000 African leopards still in the wild, the species is endangered. Farmers sometimes kill leopards because of their attacks on livestock and many are

▲ Making a larder. This leopard drags its prey to a tree, storing it out of reach of scavengers.

▼ Relaxed and unconcerned, a leopard dozes in an acacia tree, shaded from the midday sun.

hunted for their fur, which is highly prized for making coats and jackets for rich but unthinking women. In Africa the leopard is still hunted for "sport" by Western visitors. In parts of Asia leopards sometimes become man-eaters, and some individuals have been known to kill over 100 people.

Although the leopard is probably declining in numbers in many parts of its range, attempts to save it can be successful. In the deserts of Israel the number of leopards has actually increased.

RARE AND MYSTERIOUS

The Snow leopard or ounce lives in Asia. It is a rare and shy inhabitant of mountain country, living in steppe and coniferous forest at altitudes of 1,800 to 5,500m. Here it preys on a wide range of animals, from birds and mice to marmots, musk deer, wild sheep and ibex, which it follows as they migrate higher up the mountains during summer. In winter the Snow leopard seeks lower ground, where it preys on hares, wild boar, gazelles and deer. Each Snow leopard has a large territory of up to 100sq km. It stalks its prey and pounces from a distance of 5 to 15m.

During the breeding season, from January to May, the Snow leopard gives up its solitary life, and males and females hunt together in pairs. Before giving birth, in spring or early summer, the female finds a safe den which she lines with her own fur. She produces up to four cubs. They are blind at birth, then open their eyes after several days. By about 2 months they are active and playful, remaining with their mother throughout their first winter.

At the approach of winter, the fur of the Snow leopard becomes thicker and this helps it survive the intense

▶The "black panther" is really just an all-black leopard and is not a separate species.

186

cold. In summer the fur becomes finer again. Sadly, its wonderful coat may well be the Snow leopard's downfall – this cat is now very rare because of the illegal trade in its fur.

Also rare is the Clouded leopard, which lives in dense forests in India and South-east Asia. Although heavily built, it is the smallest of the leopards. Birds, squirrels and monkeys form much of its prey. This beautiful cat spends most of its time in trees, where it is a skilled climber.

The Clouded leopard is rarely seen in the wild, and nothing is known about its social life.

GOOD SWIMMER

The jaguar is the only big cat found in the Americas and is similar to the leopard in its way of life. It lives in forests, swamps, and even deserts, from the south-western United States south to Patagonia.

The jaguar preys on fish, frogs, turtles and their eggs, birds, caymans, rats, mice and larger animals like capybara, deer and monkeys. It is a good swimmer and prefers to live near water.

Except during the mating season, the jaguar is solitary. Each has a territory of between 5 and 500sq km. For some unknown reason, a jaguar may travel up to 800km each year. Jaguars breed from about 3 years of age. A female gives birth to two to four blind cubs, each weighing between 700 and 900g. After about 13 days, the eyes open; the young remain with their mother for about 2 years.

WILD CATS

In a remote forest in the far north of Scotland, a solitary European wild cat steals through the night. Despite the darkness, he knows his area well, guided by landmarks scented with his own urine. Always on the prowl by night, seeking food or a mate, he is alert to danger and whatever opportunities he comes across. The faint rustling of a mouse attracts his attention. Quietly and patiently he stalks it. Then, with a rapid pounce, he has it in his jaws, and the mouse is dead.

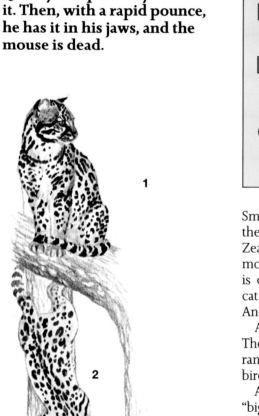

WILD CATS Felidae
(28 species)

● ■▢ ✦

■ **Habitat:** varies; desert, steppe, savannah, tropical and cool temperate forest.

■ **Diet:** range of small animals, ranging from insects, fish and frogs to rodents, peccaries, small deer and monkeys.

◡ **Breeding:** litters of 1-6 born in den after pregnancy of 56-90 days.

Size: smallest (Leopard cat): head-body 40cm, weight 3kg; largest (puma): head-body 196cm, weight 103kg.

Colour: varying patterns of dark spots or stripes on pale grey, fawn or tawny background, coat sometimes unpatterned; black "tear stripe" often running from eye.

Lifespan: up to 12-15 years (European wild cat).

Species mentioned in text:
African wild cat (*Felis sylvestris lybica*)
Bobcat (*F. rufus*)
Domestic cat (*F. catus*)
European or Scottish wild cat (*F. s. sylvestris*)
Fishing cat (*F. viverrina*)
Geoffroy's cat (*F. geoffroyi*)
Leopard cat (*F. bengalensis*)
Lynx (*F. lynx*)
Margay cat (*F. wiedi*)
Ocelot (*F. pardalis*)
Puma (*F. concolor*)
Sand cat (*F. margarita*)
Serval (*F. serval*)

Small wild cats are found in all parts of the world except Australia and New Zealand. There are 28 species, and the most familiar is the Domestic cat. This is descended from the African wild cat, which was domesticated in Ancient Egypt about 4,000 years ago.

Almost all species are nocturnal. They hunt and stalk small animals ranging from insects, lizards and birds, to small rodents and monkeys.

All the "small cats" are similar to the "big cats" in build and behaviour but they are different in other ways. They cannot roar, they eat in a crouching position, and there is a bald strip along the front of the nose. Unlike the big cats, the small wild cats tuck their front paws under the body when resting and they also wrap the tail around the body. Big cats rest with the front paws in front of them and the tail extended behind them.

CATS OF FIVE CONTINENTS
Wild cats live in many different habitats. The European wild cat makes its home in the cool forests of Northern

◄Taken by surprise, a Scottish wild cat bares its teeth in a fierce threat display. Not even a fox can get the better of it.

▼**Stalk, pounce and kill** Twelve species of small wild cat, arranged by their distribution from west (America) to east (Asia). Ocelot **(1)**. Margay cat **(2)**. Tiger cat (*Felis tigrinus*) **(3)**. Jaguarundi (*F. yagouaroundi*) **(4)**, European and African Wild cat **(5)** and **(6)**. Black-footed cat (*F. nigripes*) **(7)**. Sand cat **(8)**. Jungle cat (*F. chaus*) **(9)**. Leopard cat **(10)**. Asiatic golden cat (*F. temmincki*) **(11)**. Fishing cat **(12)**.

Europe, while the African subspecies lives in dry, open forest and savannah. The Sand cat lives in hot, dry desert, where it preys on insects and lizards.

Some species, like the lynx, are very widespread. This lovely cat lives in forest and thick scrub from Western Europe to Siberia and in Canada and the northern United States. Also widespread, and with several subspecies, the puma can be found from southern Canada to Patagonia in South America, living in grassland, forest, steppe, desert and tropical forest. This is the largest of the North American cats and is also known as the panther, cougar or, more rarely, the Mountain lion.

Other wild cats are more special-ized or restricted in their habitats. The serval lives in African savannah coun-try, where it preys on game birds, rodents and small deer. Never going far from water, the serval has long legs which help it run through long grass.

Even more specialized is the Fish-ing cat of India and South-east Asia. With its slightly webbed feet and exposed claws, the Fishing cat is well adapted for catching fish and crabs in the swamps and wet forest where it lives. It also preys on insects, birds and small mammals.

SOCIAL BEHAVIOUR
Little is known about the behaviour and social organization of most of the

wild cats. The individuals of most species are probably territorial. As every cat-owner knows, territories are scent-marked with urine and/or faeces.

Ownership of a territory is important. It allows an individual to keep control of access to prey and mates. The size of the territory depends on the abundance of prey and the number of cats in the local area. Domestic cats living wild (feral cats) may live as solitary individuals if prey is scarce and widely scattered, or they may be in groups of 30 or more where prey is abundant.

The European wild cat also may live as a solitary individual or in a group. The territory of a solitary individual is usually larger than for the wild Domestic cat, adult males having the biggest territory.

DESIGNS FOR LIVING

The lynx and North American bobcat are similar in size and shape but are adapted for life in different kinds of habitat. The lynx lives in the cool northern forests of North America, while the bobcat extends from southern Canada to the south of Mexico.

North American winter temperatures may drop to −57°C. For this reason, the lynx has a shorter tail, which reduces heat loss, and also has a dense covering of fur on the pads of its feet. Longer legs allow it to walk through deep snow, where the bobcat may be at a disadvantage. But the bobcat's shorter legs are ideally suited for scrambling on steep rock screes and dense brush on mountain-sides.

In the dense forest where the lynx preys on mice and small deer, hearing may be more important than sight. The lynx's longer ear tufts are thought to improve its hearing abilities.

As stalk-and-pounce hunters, both lynx and bobcat need to get as close to their prey as possible before making their final leap. Being able to blend in with the background is important.

The plain brownish-grey of the lynx camouflages it against the moss-covered forest trees and swamps, while the black-spotted brown coat of the bobcat blends with a background of dense brush and rock screes, where it preys mainly on cottontail rabbits.

THREAT OF EXTINCTION

Of the 28 species of small wild cat, nine are rare or threatened in some way. In some areas the danger comes from the destruction of habitats to create farmland. When this happens, wild cats may start to attack farm animals and then are killed as pests.

Another serious threat comes from the fur trade. This especially affects those small cats which have beautiful spotted fur. The Margay cat, of Central and South America, and the Leopard cat, of South-east Asia, the Philippines and Taiwan, are the victims of intense hunting pressure. Some species, such as the North American lynx and bobcat, are trapped in large numbers. But both are protected by laws that prevent too many from being killed. Geoffroy's cat from South America is another threatened species. Each year sees the slaughter of 20,000 of these lovely cats.

The ocelot is the most beautiful of the small wild cats and it is being brought near to extinction by the fur trade. Its range extends from Arizona in the southern United States through Central and South America as far as Argentina. The ocelot is a skilled swimmer and climber and preys on reptiles, birds and small mammals. In 1975, 76,838 ocelot skins were imported into Britain alone. It takes many skins to make a single fur coat. Unfortunately, there are still enough rich and selfish people in the world to keep the trade in wild cat skins going.

▶A North American bobcat pads through the snow. Winter is a lean time, when prey is scarce.

WILD DOGS

A herd of wildebeest graze in the cool of an East African dawn. Suddenly, they smell danger in the air and are off, with a pack of African wild dogs hard at their heels. Two of the dogs pick out an old wildebeest which is lagging behind. With a burst of speed, one has the wildebeest by the tail.

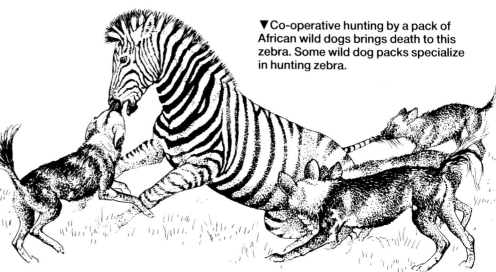

▼Co-operative hunting by a pack of African wild dogs brings death to this zebra. Some wild dog packs specialize in hunting zebra.

WILD DOGS Canidae
(*6 species*)

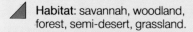

◗ ■ ☠

◢ **Habitat:** savannah, woodland, forest, semi-desert, grassland.

■ **Diet:** berries, insects, reptiles, mammals from rodents up to wildebeest and zebra.

◯ **Breeding:** litters of 2-5 after pregnancy of 60-73 days.

Size: head-body 50-105cm; weight 5-27kg.

Colour: from white and yellow blotching on dark background, through tawny and foxy red to grizzled-grey.

Lifespan: where known, 10-14 years.

Species mentioned in text:
African wild dog (*Lycaon pictus*)
Bush dog (*Speothos venaticus*)
Dhole or Asian wild dog (*Cuon alpinus*)
Dingo (*Canis dingo*)
Maned wolf (*Chrysocyon brachyurus*)
Raccoon dog (*Nyctereutes procyonoides*)

Wild dogs live in packs of 2 to 20 adult animals, but the most common number is 7 or 8. Each pack has a home range, of up to 1,500sq km. They criss-cross their range in search of prey and only have a fixed base when there are young pups.

African wild dogs prey mainly on impala, gazelles and sometimes smaller animals such as rats. The pack travels, rests and hunts together. They kill their prey quickly. If there are any pups, they are allowed to eat first.

UNUSUAL SOCIAL LIFE
The African wild dog lives in savannah woodland and desert. There are probably no more than 10,000 left, and the species is regarded as endangered.

The social life of the African wild dog is the opposite of other predators. Males remain in the pack they were born into and so are related to each

▼Two female African wild dogs in a tug of war over a pup in a battle for breeding dominance. Pups are often killed by this.

192

▲ Sizing each other up, two Maned wolves circle each other, the one on the right arching its back to make itself look larger.

▼ A dingo, Australia's wild dog, attacks a lizard in a shallow lake.

blind pups weighing about 400g. Pups are born in a den, where both mother and young feed on regurgitated food from other members of the pack.

FOREST AND GRASSLAND DOGS

The dhole or Asian wild dog has a similar family life to the African wild dog. It lives in forests, from India to China and South-east Asia, where it eats berries, insects, lizards, rodents and deer.

The wild dog of Australia is the dingo. Like the Domestic dog, this species is descended from the wolf and was probably brought to Australia by Aboriginal peoples about 20,000 years ago.

In Eastern Asia the Raccoon dog is most un-dog-like in appearance. As its name suggests, it looks more like a raccoon. A forest dweller, this small dog has been introduced into parts of Europe.

The Maned wolf of Central South America looks rather like a fox on stilts. Its long legs help it to move through long grass. The little-known Bush dog of South America has short, squat legs, tiny ears and a blunt face.

other. The young females – usually more aggressive than the males – leave the pack as a group of litter-mates to join the males of another pack.

The African wild dog mates once a year, when food is plentiful. Usually only the dominant male and female of the pack mate. Females give birth to

JACKALS

On the Serengeti Plain in Tanzania, African white-backed vultures swoop down to a dead zebra. But their meal is interrupted. A pair of Silver-backed jackals trot into view across the plain. They gather speed as they approach, yelping and snarling around the zebra carcass until all the birds have gone, leaving the pickings to them.

Jackals are small, slender dogs with large ears and bushy tails. Their long legs make them powerful runners. Besides carrion (the flesh of animals already dead), jackals eat almost anything, from fruit, insects and frogs to birds and small mammals.

FOUR SPECIES

There are four species of jackal. The Golden jackal is the most widespread and common. It lives in dry, short grassland in North and East Africa, South-east Europe and Southern Asia. All the other jackal species live only in Africa. The Sidestriped jackal lives in wet forest, the Silverbacked in dry, scrubby woodland.

The rarest species is the endangered Simien jackal, which inhabits the remote mountains of Ethiopia. There are only about 500 left in the wild. Jackals are often killed for their fur, and many are killed in farming areas to prevent them attacking livestock.

FAMILY "HELPERS"

Like wolves jackals mate for life. They live in family groups consisting of the

▼ Silverbacked jackals feed at a zebra carcass, having driven away vultures.

JACKALS Canidae (4 species)

● ■ ☠

● **Habitat:** dry grassland, dry woodland, wet forest, mountains.

■ **Diet:** fruit, small animals, carrion.

○ **Breeding:** litters of up to 9 after pregnancy of 63 days.

Size: head-body 65-106cm; weight 7-15kg.

Colour: yellow-pale gold (Golden jackal); black and white saddle, otherwise russet (Silverbacked); reddish, with white chest and belly (Simien); grey, with white from elbow and white-tipped tail (Sidestriped).

Lifespan: up to 9 years, 16 years in captivity.

Species mentioned in text:
Golden jackal (*Canis aureus*)
Sidestriped jackal (*C. adustus*)
Silverbacked jackal (*C. mesomelas*)
Simien jackal (*C. simensis*)

▲A family group of Silverbacked jackals. A pup begs regurgitated food from the mother, while she suckles two more pups (1). A helper (2) adopts the submissive posture towards its father (3).

▼Playtime for the four species of Jackal. A Golden jackal pup plays with an adult's ear (1). Juvenile Silverbacked jackals in a tail-pulling game (2). Two nearly grown Simien jackals play a chasing game (3).A Sidestriped jackal plays with a dead mouse (4). Play is an important learning time for young hunting animals.

parents, young pups, and juveniles of about 1 year old, which sometimes for several months help their parents rear the next litter.

Each group has a territory of up to 2.5sq km, which it maintains all year round. Together, the parents scent-mark the boundary of their territory with urine. Both parents and juveniles hunt together. This way they can run down larger prey which would be too big for a single jackal.

Golden and Silverbacked jackals mate in October, at the end of the dry season. Pups are born in a den during

December and January, the wet season, when food is plentiful. Females produce up to nine pups, which remain in the den for up to 3 weeks. Their mother spends nearly all her time with them, but the juveniles guard the pups when the mother is away hunting.

Jackal pairs which have a team of juvenile "helpers" can raise more young than those without helpers. The advantage to helpers is that they become familiar with the home range of their parents, part of which they may inherit.

FOXES

It is a warm, moist evening. The Red fox is quietly padding across the grassy meadow, ears pricked for the slightest sound. Then he hears it, the rasping of an earthworm's bristles on the grass. Finding the exact source of the sound, he poises, before plunging his muzzle into the grass to grab the worm. The worm, though, still has its tail in its burrow. So the fox pulls it taut and tugs until the worm comes free.

FOXES Canidae (*21 species*)

● ◼ 🦊

◼ **Habitat:** general, including urban.

◨ **Diet:** small mammals, birds, insects, eggs, fish, fruits, berries, carrion.

◎ **Breeding:** up to 8 offspring after pregnancy of 3 months (Red fox).

Size: smallest (Fennec fox): from head-body 24cm, tail 18cm, weight 1.5kg; largest (Small-eared dog): up to head-body 100cm, tail 35cm, weight 9kg.

Colour: grey to reddish-brown coat, sometimes white, silver, cream or black.

Lifespan: up to 6 years.

Species mentioned in text:
Arctic fox (*Alopex lagopus*)
Argentine grey fox (*Dusicyon griseus*)
Azara's fox (*D. gymnocercus*)
Bat-eared fox (*Otocyon megalotis*)
Colpeo fox (*Dusicyon culpaeus*)
Crab-eating fox (*D. thous*)
Fennec fox (*Vulpes zerda*)
Grey or Tree fox (*V. cinereoargenteus*)
Indian fox (*V. bengalensis*)
Kit or Swift fox (*V. velox*)
Red fox (*V. vulpes*)
Small-eared dog (*Dusicyon microtis*)

◀ A Grey fox keeps watch from its vantage point up in a tree. It has the white throat typical of many species of fox.

▼ **Eight vulpine species** Foxes of the genus *Vulpes* shown dashing after and swiping at a bird. Grey fox (1). Swift fox (*Vulpes velox*) (2). Cape fox (*V. chama*) (3). Fennec fox (4). Rüppell's fox (*V. rüppelli*) (5). Blanford's fox (*V. cana*) (6). Indian fox (7). Corsac fox (*V. corsac*) (8).

Foxes, like dogs, belong to the family of canids. Compared with dogs, they have a flattened skull, a pointed muzzle and a long bushy tail. Their triangular ears are fairly big and stand erect. The tip of the tail is often a different colour from the rest of the coat, usually black or white. Several species, including the Red fox, have a white chin.

THE TYPICAL FOX

The Red fox is often thought of as the "typical" fox because it is found so widely. But, with a head-to-tail length of over 110cm and weight up to 6kg, it

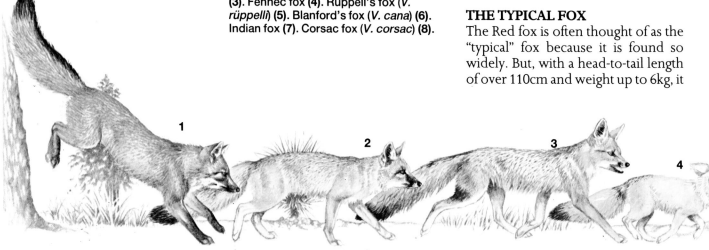

is bigger than its relatives in the genus *Vulpes*. More typical is the slighter-built Indian fox, which inhabits the open forest, scrub and steppe land of India, Pakistan and Nepal. This fox has a sandy-brown coat, with darker legs and tail.

The Grey fox of North and South America can grow nearly as big as the Red fox. It is also known as the Tree fox because it has the habit of climbing trees. It often sleeps in trees.

MOST ADAPTABLE
The Red fox is the most widespread and most successful of all the fox species. It is found from the far north of North America, Europe and Asia, south to the deserts of Central America and North Africa. It can adapt to a variety of climates from the frigid cold of the Arctic to the searing heat of the desert. It can also adapt to life in the city.

The Red fox is also very adaptable when it comes to food. It will eat almost any food that is available, not only small mammals, birds, eggs, worms, rabbits, but also in season fruits such as blackberries and apples and even rose hips. Fruits can form as much as 90 per cent of its diet.

▲Two male North American Red foxes battling in the woods on an autumn day. It is a test of strength to see which one will be dominant.

5

6

7

8

HUGE EARS

One species of fox is immediately recognizable by its huge ears. It is the well-named Bat-eared fox of Africa. This animal is also notable because of its diet, which is mainly of insects. Termites and dung beetles and their larvae are among its favourite foods. Its hearing is so sensitive that it can detect the sound of larvae gnawing their way out of dung balls.

The cream-coloured Fennec fox, smallest of all the foxes, also has very large ears. It lives in the sandy deserts of Africa and Arabia. Its large ears not only enable it to locate its prey. They also act as "radiators" to get rid of excess heat, helping the animal stay cool. Other adaptations to desert life include furry feet, which help the Fennec keep its footing in the sand.

The ears of the Arctic fox, by contrast, are small and rounded. The muzzle is shorter than in the typical fox. These are ways in which this fox has adapted to living in a bitterly cold climate. The very thick underfur of its winter coat insulates the fox. This fur conserves body heat until the temperature falls to below minus 70°C. Only then does the fox start to shiver!

▲The coat colour of the Arctic fox can vary from animal to animal and from season to season. A polar form has an all-white coat in winter (1), which becomes darker in summer (2). Other foxes may have a steel-grey or brown (3) coat in winter. An Arctic fox vixen in her brown summer coat is seen here with younger brothers and sisters, each of which has a different coloured summer coat (4).

▼South American foxes of the genus *Dusicyon*. Small-eared dog (1). Colpeo fox (2). Argentine grey fox (3). Azara's fox (4). Crab-eating fox (5).

IN THE DEN

Foxes breed once a year. The vixen, or female fox, gives birth to her young in a den, which is often a burrow or sometimes a hollow in a tree or a rock crevice. The young pups, or cubs, are helpless at first and remain in the den suckling their mother for several weeks. By the age of 6 months they can hunt by themselves.

Most species of foxes lead solitary lives, coming together only at mating time. But members of some species may share their dens with other foxes. Red and Arctic foxes sometimes do this. A typical group would include one male and several vixens, probably all related. They feed in different parts of the group's territory, but their paths may cross many times each night.

◄The Kit fox lives on the prairies of North America. Now classed as one of the Swift foxes, it is smaller and has larger ears than the other North American foxes.

►Like other members of the dog family, foxes mark their territory with urine, especially the places they visit often.

WIDE-SCALE HUNTING

The skins of foxes have long been prized for making fur coats and wraps. Foxes are still hunted on a large scale to satisfy the demand. In North America alone, more than half a million Red, Grey and Arctic foxes are killed each year for the fur trade. The white and blue furs of the Arctic fox are especially in demand. Several states now limit fur licenses severely and restrict fox hunting to just a few weeks each year.

Large numbers of foxes are also killed where they have become pests, and also to combat the spread of the deadly virus rabies. Other foxes are hunted for sport. But despite destruction of their habitat, few species of fox are in danger of extinction. Perhaps the most at risk are three South American species, the Argentine grey fox, the Colpeo fox and the Small-eared dog of the tropical forests. This is the largest of all the foxes.

▼Two alert Bat-eared foxes, unusual among the foxes in living mainly on insects. They use their large ears to detect insect prey.

AMERICAN BLACK BEAR

A black bear forages among the bushes. Her two cubs clamber up a nearby tree and slither down the trunk. They jump on one another and wrestle, rolling over on the ground. They bump into their mother, and she cuffs them with her paw. But they carry on playing. The mother bear puts up with their games. She is too busy eating to join in. She is thin after having the cubs, and she is making good use of the late summer to feed on berries.

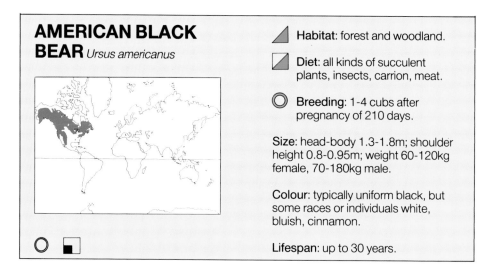

AMERICAN BLACK BEAR *Ursus americanus*

Habitat: forest and woodland.

Diet: all kinds of succulent plants, insects, carrion, meat.

Breeding: 1-4 cubs after pregnancy of 210 days.

Size: head-body 1.3-1.8m; shoulder height 0.8-0.95m; weight 60-120kg female, 70-180kg male.

Colour: typically uniform black, but some races or individuals white, bluish, cinnamon.

Lifespan: up to 30 years.

▼Apart from an occasional dash to catch prey, the pace of life for an American black bear is slow. For many, in the northern parts of their range, food is scarce and slow-growing. Bears are often seen scratching the ground for food, like the one shown here. A female black bear may wander over an area of 100sq km in a year to find enough food.

The American black bear once roamed over most of the woods of North America from central Mexico to Canada. Where people have built towns or cleared the woods, the bears have vanished with their habitat. But where there are forests, American black bears can still be found. They do not often go into open country.

In spite of their name and usual colour, there are several varieties of black bear. Near the west coast in British Columbia there are even pure white "black bears", as well as brown and bluish forms. In the east pure black bears are usual. This is also where the largest bears come from, the biggest on record being a male that reached 272kg and almost 2m from nose to the tip of its stubby tail.

▼Black bears like meat if they can catch it, or will feed on carrion. This one has found a cow killed in a storm.

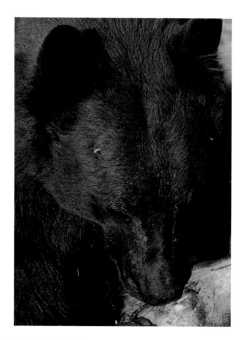

SWEET TOOTH

An American black bear needs up to 8kg of food a day. It feeds on bulbs, tubers, young shoots, and nuts and berries in season. It also kills animals from the size of mice to young deer if it has the chance. It digs up insect grubs and is fond of honey and sweet things. The black bear is a good climber and sometimes goes up trees in search of food.

Black bears mate in the summer. In the winter most den up, sometimes for as long as 7 months, so they spend more than half their lives asleep. While asleep during the winter the heartbeat slows down, and the body's temperature drops a little. This cuts down the bear's use of energy.

It is in the den, in January or February, that the cubs are born. Each cub is naked and weighs only 250g. They stay denned with the mother through the cold weather until the spring and suckle until the late summer. They may stay with the mother as long as 2½ years.

When the cubs first emerge from the den they weigh about 2kg. The mother is very protective. Her alarm grunt may send the youngsters scrambling up a tree out of reach of enemies. Accompanying their mother, the cubs learn how to dig out all kinds of delicacies.

Bears do not begin to breed until they are from 3 to 5 years old. Even in good conditions a female has cubs only once every 2 years.

BEGGING BEARS

Black bear numbers have declined as people have settled across North America, but there are more left than there are Brown (Grizzly) bears. They usually avoid people, but when hungry they may scavenge for scraps. In National Parks, where they are not molested, some bears get into the habit of begging for food beside roads. They can become dangerous if not given what they want.

◄Black bears scavenge at waste dumps or dustbins. This habit brings them into conflict with people.

▼An American black bear kills an unwary beaver and pulls it ashore to eat. Such meals supplement a mainly vegetable diet.

SMALL BEARS

High in the tree a buzz sounds from a crack in the bark where wild bees have a nest. On the ground below a Sun bear pauses and listens. Then it shins up the tree trunk straight to the nest. It scratches at the bark with its big claws until it has ripped open the nest. Pulling out the honeycomb, it eats honey and bee grubs.

Three of the four smaller bears live in the south of Asia. The fourth, the Spectacled bear, is found in the Andes in northern South America. Although they are small as bears go, all can weigh as much as an adult human. Males are bigger than females and (except the Sun bear) may be much heavier than a man.

SMALLEST BEAR

The Sun bear, from the tropics of South-east Asia, is the smallest bear and has the shortest and sleekest coat. Like the other Asian small bears it has a light coloured mark on its chest. The Sun bear is a forest dweller. It is light, and its big curved claws and large naked soles can give a good grip as it climbs.

The Sun bear spends much of its time in the trees. Active at night, it often sunbathes during the day, and this gives the animal its name. It eats all kinds of foods, from fruits and young tips of palm-trees to insects, small mammals and birds.

SMALL BEARS Ursidae
(4 species)

● ◧ ☠

◢ Habitat: forest, some grassland and scrub.

◪ Diet: omnivorous.

◯ Breeding: 1-3 (usually 2) cubs after pregnancy of 7-8 months (3½ months for Sun bear).

Size: smallest (Sun bear): head-body 1.1-1.4m, weight 27-65kg; largest (Sloth bear): head-body 1.5-1.9m, weight 90-135kg.

Colour: black, with lighter markings on muzzle and chest.

Lifespan: up to 30 years.

Species mentioned in text:
Asian black bear (*Selenarctos thibetanus*)
Sloth bear (*Melursus ursinus*)
Spectacled bear (*Tremarctos ornatus*)
Sun bear (*Helarctos malayanus*)

▼ Performing bears, once common, are a rare sight today. Bears like this Sloth bear can look "human" standing on their hind legs.

▲ The four smallest species of bear The Sloth bear (1) makes good use of its long curved claws and flexible snout to forage, on the ground for termites and grubs, or in trees. A Sun bear (2) licks termites from its paw after scooping them out of the mound it has broken open. The Spectacled bear (3) is a good climber. It eats tree fruits, palm frond bases and other succulent plant food. The Asian black bear (4) sometimes kills large animals or feeds on carrion like this deer carcass.

SUCKING UP INSECTS

The Sloth bear has shaggy fur and long claws. It eats many things, but prefers insects. It uses its claws to break open termite mounds, then sucks up the inhabitants. Its flexible lips can be formed into a tube, and there is a gap in the front teeth. The nostrils can be closed to prevent insects and dust getting in.

The Sloth bear blows dust from its prey before sucking them up. It is mainly nocturnal and likes to live in forested areas.

Further north lives the Asian black bear. This bear is omnivorous, feeding largely on plants, but also eating animals. At times it has made itself unpopular with people by killing domestic animals or eating crops. It usually avoids humans, but can be aggressive if cornered. Although it is called "black bear", some individuals are brown or reddish.

MOUNTAIN BEAR

The Spectacled bear lives mainly in damp forests, but also goes into mountain grassland and lowland scrub deserts. It can be found at any height up to 4,200m in the Andes. The eye markings that give this bear its name are very variable. The spectacled bear is solitary and rather shy, so it is difficult to observe and study.

This bear is mainly a plant-eater but can catch young deer and guanacos. Like the other bears in the tropics it seems to be active all year and may produce young at any time. Black bears in colder regions may retire to their den for the winter.

COATIS

The tree is full of coatis. On every branch one or two are resting, scratching or grooming one another. From a nest of sticks on the next tree a female coati emerges. Soon she is down with the troop, bringing three youngsters just ready to leave the nest. The troop members look and sniff at the new arrivals, then carry on with what they were doing before. One female, especially friendly with the mother, stays and grooms the young coatis.

Little is known about two of the species of coati. One of these lives only on Cozumel Island off the eastern coast of Mexico. Another lives in the mountain forests of Ecuador and Colombia in South America. The best known species are the White-nosed coati, which lives in the southern USA, and as far south as Ecuador, and the Ring-tailed coati, which lives in tropical forests east of the Andes mountains. Coatis are good climbers and are mainly active during the day.

COMPANIONS AND LONERS
Female coatis are very sociable animals. They usually live in troops of 5 to 12 animals. Sometimes there can

COATIS Procyonidae
(*4 species*)

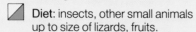

Habitat: tropical lowlands, dry mountain forest, forest edges, some grassland.

Diet: insects, other small animals up to size of lizards, fruits.

Breeding: 2-5 young after pregnancy of 77 days.

Size: head-tail 0.7-1.3m, over half tail, weight 3.5-5.6kg.

Colour: reddish, greyish or olive brown with some contrasting markings.

Lifespan: up to 10 years.

Species mentioned in text:
Ring-tailed coati (*Nasua nasua*)
White-nosed coati (*N. narica*)

▲Coati "friends" will often groom one another (1). Some group members stay on watch (2). Mothers groom their young (3), and the young often play together (4).

▼A White-nosed coati drinks with its tail up. The tail is often held high when searching for food.

be as many as 40. A troop lives in an area about 1km across. Females may form close friendships. They groom one another and look after each other's young. At night the troop members sleep together in the trees.

Adult males, on the other hand, are usually solitary. They join the troop during the mating period, but at other times of the year they live alone, although their home range overlaps with a troop. Because they behave so differently, and are more heavily built, these solitary males were once thought to be a different species called coatimundi.

FOLLOWING THEIR NOSES
A troop of coatis forage for food by pushing their noses into every likely log and piece of leaf litter or under stones. Their sense of smell is good, and the coati's nose is a good digging organ, as are the claws.

◀A Ring-tailed coati shows its strong front claws and the long mobile snout it uses to dig and sniff out prey.

Coatis find a whole range of small animals to eat, including beetles, grubs, ants, termites, spiders, scorpions, centipedes and land crabs. They also catch frogs, lizards and mice and will eat the eggs of birds and reptiles. They also enjoy fruit.

TELLING TAILS
A coati has a long tail which acts as a balancing rod while it is climbing. The ring markings on the tail make it a good flag to show where a coati is, what it is doing and what kind of mood it is in. Coatis also make high-pitched twittering noises that help them keep in touch with one another while they move through the forests.

◀A White-nosed coati finds an insect among the leaves. The curiosity of these animals often helps them find food.

WEASELS AND POLECATS

A weasel crosses the open ground between two hedges. Its movements are so swift and flowing that anyone watching would hardly realize that an animal had passed across. It dives into the hedgerow and works its way along at speed, poking its head into every hole and crevice in case there is something to eat. A movement in the leaves alerts it. A mouse is there. Like lightning, the weasel goes in pursuit. The mouse dives down its burrow, but there is no escape. The weasel goes down after it. At the bottom of the burrow it bites savagely at the back of the mouse's head. The weasel eats the brain and head, then the rest of its victim.

There are some 67 species in the mustelid family, which includes such animals as badgers and otters. There are 21 relatively small members of the family that make up the species of weasels, stoats, polecats and mink. They are found over most of the world in many habitats.

FEROCIOUS HUNTERS
All of this group are ferocious hunters. They differ from most carnivores in that they are able to kill, single-handed, animals bigger than themselves. They are intelligent and energetic. The smallest weasels are, if anything, even more lively and ferocious than the larger ones.

Weasels have long slim bodies and short legs. The head is narrow too, and the animal can get through a tiny space. A European common weasel is said to be able to squeeze through a wedding ring.

The European common weasel feeds on mice, voles and any other small animals it can capture. It is

▲A stoat in its summer coat, chestnut with a light bib. In cold areas stoats change to white (ermine) in winter.

►The long low shape of weasels and polecats allows them to squeeze through small openings after prey. Here a European polecat hunts down a rabbit burrow. This is the species from which the domestic ferret was bred.

WEASELS AND POLECATS Mustelidae; sub-family Mustelinae (*21 species*)

● ▣ ♪

▨ Habitat: all types.

■ Diet: rodents, rabbits, birds and other animals.

○ Breeding: 2-13 young after pregnancy of 5-7 weeks, plus delay in some species.

Size: smallest (Least weasel): head-body 12.5 cm, tail 2.5cm, weight 30g; largest (grison): head-body 47-55cm, tail 16cm, weight up to 3.2kg.

Colour: usually brown above, light below; others with black and white markings or other bold patterns.

Lifespan: up to 10 years, usually much less in wild.

Species mentioned in text:
Black-footed ferret (*Mustela nigripes*)
European common weasel (*M. nivalis nivalis*)
European polecat (*M. putorius putorius*)
Grison (*Galictis vittata*)
Least weasel (*Mustela nivalis rixosa*)
Long-tailed weasel (*M. frenata*)
Stoat or ermine (*M. erminea*)

capable of killing rabbits, although these are more usually prey for the larger stoat. Polecats eat rodents, worms, carrion and also birds, which is why gamekeepers dislike them.

Most of this group hunt on or under the ground, but mink are also at home in the water. They have partly webbed feet and catch fish as well as land animals.

Most of the weasel group feed entirely on other animals, content to eat whatever they can catch. The Black-footed ferret of the American prairies, though, is a specialist, feeding just on prairie dogs. Because these rodents have been exterminated as a pest in many places, the ferret is endangered.

COAT FOR ALL SEASONS

Some of the weasel family change their coat for the winter months. The Least weasel in North America and the European common weasel in Northern Europe turn white in winter. Some other Asian species also get a lighter coat. The stoat can also change, except for the tip of the tail, which always remains black.

In the snows of the northern winter these animals are as well camouflaged from their prey as they are with a brown coat in summer.

ROUGH COURTSHIP

Weasel species are usually solitary. At most times of the year even a male and a female will try not to come close.

Males in most species are larger than females. In small species, such as

▶Species of the southThe North African banded weasel (*Poecilictis libyca*) (1). The African striped weasel (*Poecilogale albinucha*) (2). The Marbled polecat (*Vormela peregusna*) (3) lives on the Asian steppes. The zorilla (*Ictonyx striatus*) (4) of Africa. The Little grison (*Galictis cuja*) (5) of South America and the European polecat (6). The Patagonian weasel (*Lyncodon patagonicus*) (7) and the Black-footed ferret (8) are shown hunting.

the European common weasel, the size difference is very great, and males are twice as heavy as females. An advantage may be that the sexes hunt different prey and do not compete for food.

Courtship is rough, with the male grabbing the female by the scruff of the neck before mating. Afterwards the male takes no further interest in female or young.

UNUSUAL PREGNANCY

After mating, the fertilized egg begins to develop, but in many species of the weasel family the development is interrupted. The embryo remains dormant for a while, before attaching to the inside of the mother's womb and developing through to birth.

Not all weasels have this "delayed implantation", but it occurs in the stoat and Long-tailed weasel, as well as in some of the related badgers, otters and martens. It may have come about to help birth take place at a season when there will be plenty of food.

Most of the weasel group are quite small animals, and one would expect the females to be pregnant for only a few weeks. But because of delayed implantation the time gap between mating and giving birth can be up to as much as one year.

DEVOTED MOTHERS

Female weasels are devoted mothers. They give birth to blind and thinly furred babies in a secure nest. Even after weaning the youngsters stay with their mother and learn to hunt. The European common weasel can have up to three litters a year and may be capable of breeding at only about 4 months of age.

►The European polecat has distinctive face markings. In England it was hunted so much that it became extinct.

MARTENS

From high in a pine tree a Pine marten looks out, searching for prey. It surprises a squirrel sunning itself near by. The marten leaps at it. The squirrel is already running out along a branch and jumps to the next tree. The marten follows, running through the tree-tops. It gains on the squirrel. But then the squirrel runs out along some thin twigs and jumps across a clearing. The marten cannot follow.

Most martens live in Europe and Asia. Two species, the American marten and the fisher, live in North America. Martens spend some time on the ground, but all can climb well. The long bushy tail helps with balance. Their large paws have strong claws and are furred below, giving a good grip on tree trunks and branches.

AGILE HUNTERS
Martens make leaping from branch to branch look easy. They are fast and agile. They look into likely hiding-places for prey. If they see prey they make a quick rush and kill it with a bite to the back of the neck. Sometimes they chase prey through the trees. Squirrels are the main prey for some.

The fisher, being less agile in trees, spends more time on the ground than

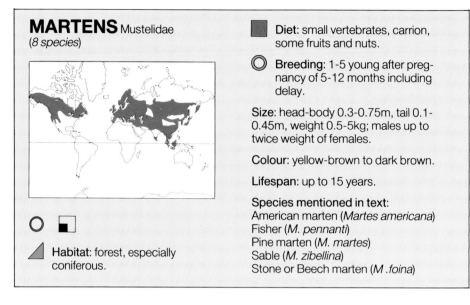

MARTENS Mustelidae
(8 species)

○ ■

▲ Habitat: forest, especially coniferous.

Diet: small vertebrates, carrion, some fruits and nuts.

Breeding: 1-5 young after pregnancy of 5-12 months including delay.

Size: head-body 0.3-0.75m, tail 0.1-0.45m, weight 0.5-5kg; males up to twice weight of females.

Colour: yellow-brown to dark brown.

Lifespan: up to 15 years.

Species mentioned in text:
American marten (*Martes americana*)
Fisher (*M. pennanti*)
Pine marten (*M. martes*)
Sable (*M. zibellina*)
Stone or Beech marten (*M .foina*)

most martens. It is one of the few animals that can catch a porcupine. It attacks and worries it around the head, avoiding the quilled back and tail. When the porcupine tires, the fisher rushes in, bowling it over and attacking and eating the soft belly with its sharp teeth and strong jaws.

BEHAVIOUR AND BREEDING
Martens are usually solitary. They mark their pathways, in trees or on the ground, with scent from the anal glands and urine.

Young are usually born in early spring. Babies are blind and deaf and have little fur, but by 2 months old they are weaned. By 4 months they

can kill prey, and soon after this they leave their mother and live alone.

Martens are active by both day and night. Even in the bitter cold of the northern winter they leave their dens to hunt – they have very warm coats. Martens, in particular sables and fishers, are prized for their fur. Huge numbers used to be trapped. Some protection is now given, and the species are not in danger.

▶ The Stone marten lives across most of Europe. It often lives on rocky ground, and will also enter built-up areas.

▼ The Stone marten (1) is more heavily built than the Pine marten (2) and spends less time hunting in the trees.

BADGERS

A badger out hunting moves along a familiar path. At intervals he squats and leaves scent from the glands under his tail. It is a damp night, and he finds many worms to eat. Returning to his sett he meets other animals of his group. They scent-mark each other.

Six species of badger, among them the ferret badgers, are found only in Asia. The Eurasian badger lives in Europe and Asia, the American badger just in North America. The ratel or Honey badger is widespread in Africa and across Asia as far as India.

Badgers have well developed anal glands. Ratels can produce a foul liquid to deter enemies, and the teledu or Malayan stink bagder can squirt its scent at attackers.

LARGE BURROWS

Badgers have powerfully built wedge-shaped bodies with a small head and a short thick neck. The long snout is used to find food. Their sense of smell is the most important one. Their front feet have long claws and are used in digging out food and making burrows.

The Eurasian badger makes burrows ("setts") with several entrances and chambers. Larger setts may be hundreds of metres long with many entrances. These are usually the work of several generations of badgers.

▼Two young Eurasian badgers peer from the entrance to their sett. They do not venture out until 2 months old.

BADGERS Mustelidae; subfamilies Melinae and Mellivorinae (*9 species*)

● ■

◢ Habitat: wood and forest, some in mountains or grassland.

◩ Diet: small animals, fruit, roots.

◎ Breeding: 1-5 young after pregnancy of 3½-12 months, including delay.

Size: smallest (Oriental ferret badger): head-body 33-43cm, tail 15-23cm, weight 2kg; largest (Eurasian badger): head-body 67-81cm, tail 15-20cm, weight 12kg.

Colour: black, white and grey, some species yellowish or brown.

Lifespan: up to 15 years.

Species mentioned in text:
American badger (*Taxidea taxus*)
Eurasian badger (*Meles meles*)
Oriental ferret badger (*Melogale orientalis*)
Ratel or Honey badger (*Mellivora capensis*)
Teledu (*Mydaus javanensis*)

HUNTING PARTNERS

Most badgers eat all kinds of food items. The ratel is especially fond of bee grubs and honey. A small bird, the honeyguide, alerts and attracts a ratel by its cries, leading it to a bees' nest. The ratel, which has enormous strength and a tough skin, rips open the nest, and both ratel and bird have a feast. American badgers are also said to form hunting partnerships with coyotes, and share a kill with them.

Some types of badger are solitary, but the Eurasian badger lives in groups of up to 12 related animals. These relatives share a main sett and outlying setts within their territory. They use special dungpits to deposit scent, droppings and urine. Pits at the edge of the territory help keep out intruders.

A female Eurasian badger makes a nursery chamber in the sett for the birth of the cubs at the end of winter. At birth the cubs are pale, but are striped before leaving the den.

▲The American badger lives in open country, eating mainly meat. This one has caught a rattlesnake.

▼The teledu (1) lives in Sumatra, Borneo and other nearby islands. It is a ground dweller with a tiny tail. The Oriental ferret badger (2) has a long tail and sometimes climbs trees. It lives in forests in Java and Borneo.

WOLVERINE

On the spring snow a large bloodstain shows where a wolverine has killed a deer. The wolverine has fed well. Now it is breaking up what remains of the carcass with its strong jaws. It drags a deer leg away to some rocks on a hillside and rams it deep into a crevice. Marking the place with scent, the wolverine then returns to the carcass. It takes the next piece to another hiding place. The hidden food will be useful when the wolverine is hungry.

WOLVERINE *Gulo gulo*

○ ◩

◣ Habitat: Arctic and sub-Arctic tundra and taiga.

■ Diet: deer, small mammals, birds, carrion and some plants.

◎ Breeding: 1-4 kits after pregnancy of about 9 months.

Size: head-body up to 0.83m, tail 0.2m; weight 10-25kg; males about 1½ times size of females.

Colour: dark brown to near black; long coat with lighter band along flanks.

Lifespan: up to 12 years.

▶The wolverine covers large distances in the search for prey. Its sharp sense of smell finds carrion from far away.

The wolverine is the heaviest of the land-living members of the weasel family. It lives in the most northerly lands and is active all year, even in the depths of the Arctic winter.

Because of its warm coat, the wolverine is sometimes trapped for its fur. Over-hunting and human disturbance have reduced numbers in some areas, but these animals have always been thinly scattered.

WOLVERINE WANDERERS

In the course of a year a wolverine's movements cover a huge area. A male's territory can span up to 1,000sq km, an area as big as some medium-sized English counties. Female territories are one third the size or less and may overlap with those of males.

Wolverines keep others of the same sex away by scent marking, using urine, droppings or secretions of the scent glands. They may fight if they meet. Wolverines need to be well spaced to find enough food in their barren surroundings.

POWERFUL PREDATOR

The wolverine is enormously strong. It is also intelligent and determined. Sometimes it drives off larger animals from their prey, such as a solitary wolf from a sheep. It can kill reindeer and other large deer. It drags down large prey by jumping on their backs and holding on. It can give a neck bite that kills a smaller mammal and disables a big one.

Large deer mostly fall prey to the wolverine in the winter, when it has the advantage in moving over snow. In summer it catches smaller mammals, eats nesting birds and their eggs and digs out wasps' nests for grubs. Some berries and other plants are also part of the diet, and at all times of the year the wolverine finds carrion.

The wolverine has an alternative name, glutton, which comes from its supposed greedy habits. In fact the wolverine will often bury or hide

▲ The wolverine is heavy and powerful, almost bear-like in appearance. It can climb trees fast and runs with a tireless, loping action.

▼ The broad paws of the wolverine spread its weight and stop it sinking in snow (1). On soft snow the narrower feet of a deer sink in (2). So in winter the wolverine can catch deer. On hard ground in summer, deer can usually outrun the wolverine.

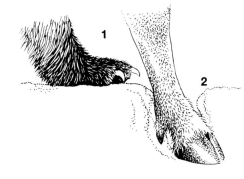

some of its food and come back to it in time of need. This may be as much as 6 months later. In the meantime the food is preserved in a natural deep freeze. A breeding female makes good use of such stores.

KIT CARE

Wolverines mate during the summer. The babies ("kits") are born at the end of the winter. They are blind and helpless. The mother gives birth in an underground den, often dug beneath a snowdrift.

The kits stay in or near the den until early summer, although the mother may move them to a new den if disturbed. The young emerge from the den with lighter coats than adults. They forage with the mother until the autumn, by which time they are nearly full grown and have an adult coat. Once they leave their mother, wolverines live solitary lives. The animals first breed when 2 years old.

TIGER

A lone tiger pads softly through the dappled sunlight of an Indian forest. Silently, he picks his way through the undergrowth, stopping at frequent intervals to sniff the air. Perhaps he is searching for a female on heat or for a suitable animal to prey on. Soon he will take to a stream to cool down in the heat of the day. There, he drinks and may rest, or simply wait for an unwary deer to come for a drink.

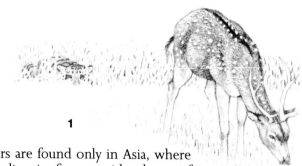

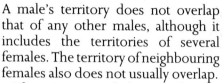

1

2

Tigers are found only in Asia, where they live in forests with plenty of cover. They are the largest living cats and, unlike lions, are solitary hunters. There are eight races or subspecies of the tiger, some of which are now extinct. All surviving races are endangered, despite the setting up of tiger reserves in India.

The tiger is well armed for its life as a stalk-and-ambush hunter. The hind legs are longer than the forelegs, for powerful leaping, and long sharp claws on the front feet enable it to grasp and keep hold of struggling prey. The tiger eats whatever it can catch, but most of its prey are medium to large-sized animals, including wild pigs and deer.

HOME RANGES
Each tiger has its own home range or territory. Those of females (tigresses) are about 20sq km in area, while male territories range from 60 to 100sq km.

A male's territory does not overlap that of any other males, although it includes the territories of several females. The territory of neighbouring females also does not usually overlap.

The tiger regularly patrols the borders of its home range. It marks the borders with urine mixed with a scent from the anal gland, which it sprays on to trees, bushes and rocks. It also deposits droppings throughout its area.

For a female tiger, owning a territory has advantages. She gets to know the area well and discovers the best places to find prey. Having control over the prey in her area is important

▼Camouflage – dark stripes on a pale background break up the body outline of a tigress lying in ambush.

TIGER *Panthera tigris*

○ ◻ ☠

◤ Habitat: tropical rain forest, northern coniferous and broad-leaved forest, mangrove swamp.

◼ Diet: wild pig, deer, sometimes rhinoceros and elephant calves.

◎ Breeding: litters of 3 or 4 after pregnancy of 103 days.

Size: male Javan and Sumatran: head-tail 2.2-2.7m, weight 100-150kg; male Indian head-tail 2.7-3.1m, weight 180-260kg.

Colour: black stripes on a tawny, brownish or yellowish background.

Lifespan: up to 15 years, 20 in captivity.

◀▼This tiger may have walked 20km in search of prey. **(1)** It stalks a deer to within 20m, before **(2)** leaping on it with a few bounds, **(3)**, seizing it with powerful claws and **(4)**, bringing it to the ground. With a long-held bite to the throat, the tiger suffocates the deer, before dragging it off into cover to feed on until only skin and bones remain.

3

4

▼A zoo-bred "white tiger", whose ancestors came from north and central India.

if she has cubs to look after. For a male, with his much bigger territory, access to prey is probably not so important. His advantage lies in being able to monopolize the females living within his borders.

SOLITARY MOTHERS

Tigers begin to breed when they are 3 to 4 years old. They mate at any time of the year in the tropics, but only in winter further north. A female has a litter of three or four cubs, each weighing about 1kg. The cubs live in a den until they are 8 weeks old, after which they follow their mother around.

The female looks after the cubs until they are 18 months, and they may remain in her territory for 2½ years before leaving to find their own home ranges.

LION

It is dawn on the East African plains. A herd of wildebeest and zebras graze in the pale sunlight. Suddenly, the early morning quiet is shattered by the roar of a lion. But the zebras and wildebeest carry on feeding peacefully. They have nothing to fear. The lion is a male and his fearsome roars are not directed at them. Instead, they are a signal to other males: "This is my home area and these are my females. Keep away!" For the grazing animals, danger will come later in the day. Then, a group of lionesses begin their prowl in search of animals to kill and eat.

LION *Panthera leo*

● ◪

● **Habitat:** grasslands of E. Africa, desert areas. Some in India.

◼ **Diet:** antelope, gazelle, warthogs, wildebeest, zebra, smaller animals.

◖ **Breeding:** litters of 1-5 after pregnancy of 100-119 days.

Size: head-body 2.4-3.3m; weight 122-240kg; males larger.

Colour: light tawny, belly and inside legs white, backs of ears black, mane of male tawny to reddish or black.

Lifespan: 15-24 years.

The lion's strength and haughty expression have led people to call it the "King of Beasts". Like all the cats, the lion has a sleek, muscular body with a deep chest. The short powerful jaws are well-armed with a fine set of sharp teeth, designed for chewing and tearing meat and even for cracking open bones. The feet have a set of powerful claws and, together with keen hearing and sight, a lion is superbly equipped for the hunting life.

Male lions are heavier than females (lionesses) – sometimes half as big again. Being larger enables the male to push his way between females at a kill and get at the best meat. Males sometimes steal carcasses killed by other animals, but mostly they feed on animals killed by the females.

Only the male lion has a mane of long hair on the head and shoulders. This makes him look larger and fiercer than he really is, and is useful in arguments with other males – a smaller male will retreat before starting a fight. If there is fighting, the thick mane protects its owner against the teeth and claws of a rival. The main role of male lions is to defend the home area of the family group and to protect females from other groups of male lions.

THE MIGHTY HUNTER

Male lions rarely hunt. Most hunting is carried out by lionesses. The prey consists of large animals such as gazelles, antelopes, warthogs, zebras and wildebeest. Lions also kill and eat lizards, birds and smaller mammals such as rats. An adult male lion needs about 7kg of meat a day, while the smaller female requires 5kg each day.

Lionesses usually hunt together. Several females stalk and spread out to surround a prey animal. They try to get as close as possible, using long grass or bushes as cover. A lioness can run as fast as 58kph, but some of its prey can run much faster than this, so a slow, quiet approach is just as important as speed.

Only one in four charges by lionesses ends with a kill. After being knocked to the ground, the animal is

▼This male lion has killed a horse which strayed from a farm. Now, using all his might, he drags it to cover.

◀Two males from the same pride groom each other. They are probably brothers or half-brothers, and grooming maintains the bond between them.

▼Family life in a resting pride of lions. A lioness **(1)** suckles three cubs, only one of which **(2)** is hers. The others belong to females **(3)** and **(4)**. Two dozing males **(5)** seem not to mind the playing cubs **(6)**.

killed by a bite to its throat, which breaks the windpipe, or by having its jaws clamped shut by the lioness. Either way, it chokes to death.

Although lions are good hunters, up to three-quarters of the animals they eat are killed by hyenas and stolen by the lions. People usually think of hyenas as being scavengers, but in fact lions are more so.

A PRIDE OF LIONS

Lions are the most social of all cats. They live in groups called prides. A pride usually has 4 to 12 adult females and their young, with 1 to 6 adult males. The females are usually related to each other, most often as cousins. The males are also related to each other – mostly as half-brothers – but not to the females.

A pride has its own home area or territory. The size of this area depends on how many prey animals it contains. A pride of lions lets other prides know where its territory ends by patrolling the boundary, roaring, and marking it with urine at regular places. Although both sexes will defend territories against intruding males, it is the males of a pride that do most of this.

Lions first breed when they are between 36 and 46 months old, and females can breed several times a year. Within a pride, there is little fighting between males over females. Instead, the first male to meet a willing female mates with her.

At between 109 and 119 days after mating, a lioness gives birth to a litter of 1 to 10 cubs. The cubs stop suckling milk from their mother at about 6 months old, although they start eating meat earlier than this. As many as three-quarters of all lion cubs die of starvation before they reach 2 years of age.

LIONS AND PEOPLE

For thousands of years, people have respected lions for their strength and bravery. Many royal families in Europe had lions on their flags and coats-of-arms.

Because lions are thought to be so fierce and strong, people could show how brave they were by killing a lion. Many hunters went to Africa from Europe and North America to kill lions and bring .ck their heads or skins as trophies.

Nowadays, the hunting of lions in Africa is strictly controlled and most visitors go to photograph animals instead.

Although there are still many lions in Africa, they are under some threat. When scrub is cleared for farming,

◀A group of resting lionesses on a rocky outcrop. Lions spend much of their time sleeping, especially during the heat of the day and after a heavy meal. But these seven lionesses have woken suddenly after being disturbed and are very alert.

prey becomes scarce and lions may then disappear from the area, or may be shot if they begin to hunt farm animals.

Lions and their prey animals are both threatened when the vegetation in the areas they inhabit changes. Lions used to be found all over northern India, the Middle East and Africa north of the Sahara Desert. As the deserts increased in size and encroached on scrubland, the lions disappeared.

Up to 2,300 years ago, lions lived in Greece, and cave paintings show that in much earlier times the lion was widespread in most of Europe. The last lions in the Middle East were wiped out by hunting about 100 years ago. Today, lions live only in Africa south of the Sahara and in one forest nature reserve in north-west India.

MAN-EATERS

The Romans imported lions from North Africa and used them to kill prisoners as a kind of public entertainment. Many early Christians were killed in this way. Lions, though, are not normally man-eaters. Stories of man-eating lions in Africa usually result from old or sick lions attacking humans because they are easier to catch than normal prey.

Sometimes, though, healthy lions will eat people if their supply of game has been reduced by farming or other human activities. A famous example took place in the late 1800s, when the railway between Kenya and Uganda was being built. So many workmen were killed by a pair of lions that work on the railway had to be stopped until the lions were shot.

If lions are to survive, we must ensure that they and their game animals have plenty of space. This is provided by the great game parks and nature reserves of Africa, but even here lions are under threat as human numbers increase and the need for farmland becomes greater.

HYENAS

A snapping, snarling, cackling pack of Spotted hyenas is a nightmarish sight. These animals lope through the darkness in search of young or weakened animals. They use their strong jaws to pull their prey to the ground, where it is killed within seconds. Hyenas are not just humble scavengers but efficient killers.

Hyenas are dog-like mammals living in Africa and parts of Asia. They have a short, shaggy mane and a bushy tail. The tail is held upright when the animal is hunting, but down between the legs when it is running away from an enemy such as a lion. Male and female hyenas look the same, though the females are slightly larger. Hyenas have sloping backs, which gives them a lop-sided appearance. The neck and shoulder muscles are very strong, enabling hyenas to pull much larger animals to the ground.

Hyenas hunt mainly in the dark, so they have very good night vision. They can run at speeds of up to 60kph for several kilometres. A hyena can catch and eat a small animal in a matter of seconds. In order to catch larger and

▼Hyenas communicate by scent-marking from the anal pouch, as in this Brown hyena (1), or, as in these Striped hyenas, by raising their shoulder crests in greeting (2) or sniffing each other (3).

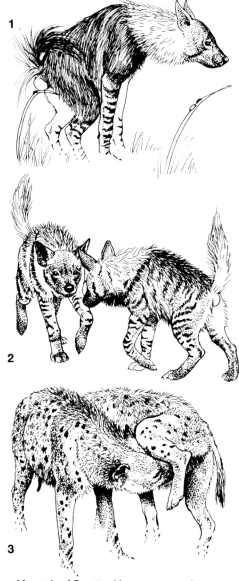

HYENAS Hyaenidae (*4 species*)

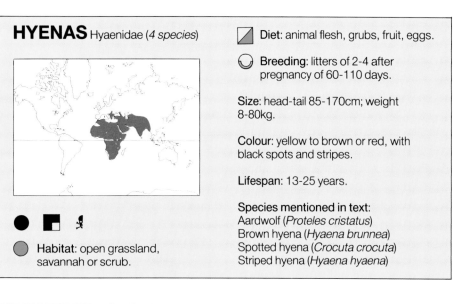

● ■ ⌇

● Habitat: open grassland, savannah or scrub.

▨ Diet: animal flesh, grubs, fruit, eggs.

◡ Breeding: litters of 2-4 after pregnancy of 60-110 days.

Size: head-tail 85-170cm; weight 8-80kg.

Colour: yellow to brown or red, with black spots and stripes.

Lifespan: 13-25 years.

Species mentioned in text:
Aardwolf (*Proteles cristatus*)
Brown hyena (*Hyaena brunnea*)
Spotted hyena (*Crocuta crocuta*)
Striped hyena (*Hyaena hyaena*)

◄A pack of Spotted hyenas crowds round a carcass. One animal may eat 15kg of flesh in one meal.

▲A frustrated Spotted hyena tries to break open an ostrich egg.

more powerful animals, hyenas hunt in packs of between 10 and 20. They can eat a zebra carcass in 15 minutes. If there is too much food, uneaten parts of the animal may be dragged off and hidden in water-holes.

Spotted hyenas have very large cheek teeth for crushing bone and tearing through tough hide. They eat all parts of an animal except for the hoofs and hair. Undigested bone passes out as a white powder. Striped and Brown hyenas have smaller cheek teeth. They hunt smaller animals, but catch less of their own food, relying more on scavenging dead animals and the remains of other animals' meals. Sometimes a hyena pack will drive away a lion from its kill. Hyenas also eat birds' eggs, insects, fruit and vegetables.

A type of hyena known as the aardwolf feeds almost entirely on termites, which it detects by sound and scent. This shy and rarely-seen creature has a slender muzzle and pointed teeth. It licks up its termite prey with a long sticky tongue. The aardwolf is a solitary forager. It does not need the help of others to find food.

▶The types of hyena
A Striped hyena scavenging (1). Young Brown hyenas playing (2). An aardwolf hunting termites (3). Spotted hyenas hunt a zebra (4).

LIVING TOGETHER

Brown hyenas live in groups of 4 to 14 in areas where there is little food, so they need large territories in which to hunt. Spotted hyenas live where there is much more prey so they join up in groups of 30 to 80 in rather smaller areas. Hyenas communicate by calls and scents. The Spotted hyena is often called the "laughing hyena" because of the high-pitched cackle it makes.

Hyenas have a special pouch at the base of the tail which produces a black and white scented paste. They spread this on to grass stems to mark their home range. The paste from each individual has a unique smell. When animals of the same kind meet, they can tell whether they belong to the same group or not by sniffing each other's pouches.

RAISING YOUNG

Female hyenas raise their young without help from the males. Spotted hyenas usually give birth to twins. The newborn are well-developed and covered with hair. They live with their mother in an underground den shared by several females, where they are suckled for up to 18 months. Then the young leave the den to fend for themselves.

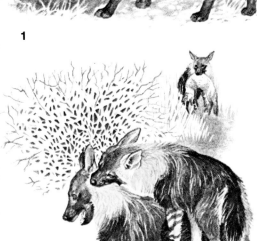

1

2

3

4

DOLPHINS

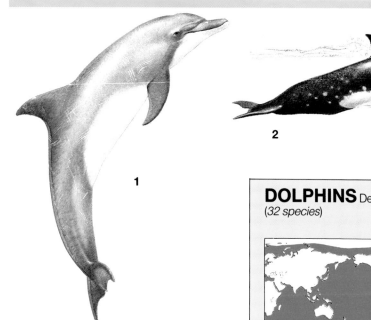

1

2

3

A group of dolphins have found a shoal of fish. They spread out round the edge of the shoal, leaping out of the water and diving back. They herd the fish into a tighter bunch. Now the dolphins feed well. They snap up fish one after the other. At last they are full. They begin to play, chasing, leaping and spinning.

DOLPHINS Delphinidae
(*32 species*)

○ ■

≈ **Habitat:** mostly coastal shallows, some open ocean.

■ **Diet:** fish, squid, other animals.

○ **Breeding:** 1 calf after pregnancy of 10-12 months.

Size: smallest (Heaviside's dolphin): head-tail 1.2m, weight 40kg; largest (Killer whale): head-tail 7m, weight 4.5 tonnes.

Colour: grey or black, often with white patches, sometimes with other patches of colour.

Lifespan: 20-50 years.

Species mentioned in text:
Bottle-nosed dolphin (*Tursiops truncatus*)
Dusky dolphin (*Lagenorhynchus obscurus*)
Heaviside's dolphin (*Cephalorhynchus heavisidii*)
Killer whale (*Orcinus orca*)

▲▶**Species of dolphin in common poses** Bottle-nosed dolphin **(1)**. Rough-toothed dolphin (*Steno bredanensis*) **(2)**. Atlantic white-sided dolphin (*Lagenorhynchus acutus*) **(3)**. Spotted dolphin (*Stenella plagiodon*) **(4)**. Common dolphin (*Delphinus delphis*) **(5)**. Northern right whale dolphin (*Lissodelphis borealis*) **(6)**. Dusky dolphin **(7)**. Atlantic humpbacked dolphin (*Sousa teuszii*) **(8)**. Melon-headed whale (*Peponocephala electra*) **(9)**. Commerson's dolphin (*Cephalorhynchus commersoni*) **(10)**. False killer whale (*Pseudorca crassidens*) **(11)**. Killer whale **(12)**. Risso's dolphin (*Grampus griseus*) **(13)**.

13

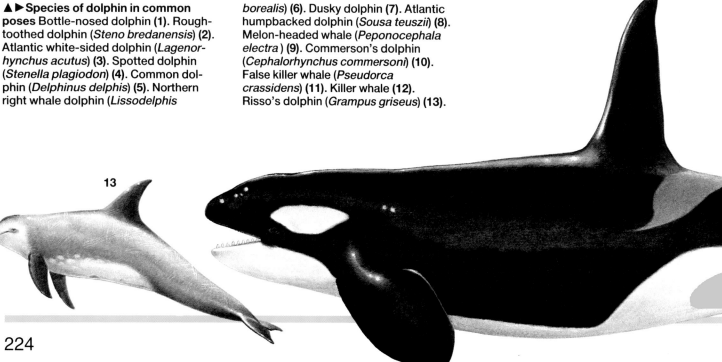

Dolphins are small whales. They are found in all the world's oceans. In most dolphins the jaws form a well-developed beak. Above this there is usually a "melon", a protruding rounded forehead. The nose is not on the beak. A dolphin breathes through a blowhole up on top of the head above the melon. Dolphins have a single dorsal fin which curves backwards.

Dolphins belong to the side of the whale family tree known as toothed whales. The description fits, because most have between 100 and 200 teeth in their jaws. Some have as many as 224. The teeth are all similar and sharply pointed. They are ideal for holding slippery prey.

Most dolphins feed on fish. Some prefer squid, and others will even eat shrimps. Many kinds of dolphin make use of shoals of fish swimming near the surface, but others will also dive deep for prey, or even pick fish from the sea bottom.

SOUND SENSE
Dolphins have good hearing and make many sounds themselves. Hearing is very important to them, both for keeping in touch with one another and for catching prey. Dolphins make some clicking sounds and whistles we can hear, and also other sounds which are much too high for the human ear. Some of the whistles are made when they are in particular moods or doing particular things. These can give information to other dolphins.

The very high sounds are used to beam out in front of the dolphin and produce echoes from objects. The dolphin hears the echoes and from them can tell what is around. Dolphins especially use this system to find prey. The melon on a dolphin's forehead helps to focus the sound. Although we cannot hear them, some high-pitched sounds produced by dolphins are very loud. They may frighten and confuse prey, and perhaps even stun them.

MERCILESS HUNTER
The biggest of all the dolphins is the Killer whale. It is long-lived and intelligent. It is also one of the fastest swimmers, able to travel at 38kph. The Killer whale is widespread but is commonest in cool seas where there is plenty of prey. It lives in groups called pods of up to 40 individuals which know one another and are able to co-operate in hunting.

The Killer whale eats squid and fish, including sharks. It also kills seals, walruses and porpoises and may even attack larger whales. One Killer whale is recorded as having the remains of 15 seals and 13 porpoises inside it. Killer whales have been seen tipping ice-floes to catch seals as they fell off. Although it is so strong, there is no

▲Dolphins can be inquisitive and playful. Here Bottle-nosed dolphins investigate two odd creatures at the edge of the sea.

record of a Killer whale making an unprovoked attack on a human.

GATHERING IN GROUPS

Killer whales stay together in their groups for life. In a group there is likely to be an adult male, three or four adult females and some younger whales of both sexes.

Other dolphins live in groups too, but they are often less fixed than those of Killer whales. The pair and calf, or mother and calf, keep together, but may join or leave bigger groups. Species that live inshore may form herds of 12 or so, and sometimes larger numbers come together where feeding is good. Some ocean dolphins form herds of 1,000 or even 2,000 at feeding areas. Dolphins are able to co-operate in hunting, driving the shoals of fish together.

Some dolphins live in small individual areas, such as the Bottle-nosed dolphin, which may keep within about 85sq km. The Dusky dolphin is very different – it may roam over 1,500sq km.

BORN BACKWARDS

Mating and birth can take place at any time of year, but in many species most births take place in summer. A baby dolphin is born underwater, tail first. As soon as the head is out, the baby must be got to the surface to take a breath and fill its lungs. The mother, and often other female dolphins, help the baby do this.

Once it is breathing, the youngster can swim, but the mother and "aunts" are very protective. Dolphin babies suckle underwater between breaths. The mother's milk is very fatty. She pumps it quickly into the baby.

BIG BRAINS

Dolphins have large brains compared to their body size. In animals this is usually a sign of intelligence. Dolphins can learn tricks readily, can remember complicated routines and can mimic some sounds and actions. It is doubtful, though, whether they are really much more intelligent than some other mammals such as dogs or elephants. Much of the large brain seems to be for dealing with the sounds that are so important to a dolphin.

DOLPHINS AND PEOPLE

Dolphins are curious, and sometimes are interested in humans. There have been several instances of "friendships" being struck up between wild dolphins and people.

People, though, are not always good for dolphins. Many dolphins have been killed by fishing boats using large nets. The animals get tangled and drown. Each year in the 1960s and 1970s about 110,000 dolphins were killed this way in the Eastern Pacific alone.

Now tuna fishermen can use special nets which reduce the threat to dolphins. The nets have a panel of fine mesh furthest from the boat. Fleeing dolphins do not get tangled in this and can escape over the net rim. Some countries, such as the United States, use human divers stationed in the nets to help trapped dolphins.

▶Killer whales have large dorsal fins. As well as eating fish, they feed on warm-blooded prey, including other dolphins.

PORPOISES

1

2

3

4

PORPOISES
Phocoenidae (*6 species*)

○ ■ ☠

Habitat: mainly coastal waters and estuaries.

Diet: fish, squid, prawns.

○ Breeding: 1 calf every 2-3 years after pregnancy of 11 months.

Size: length 120-225cm; weight 30-160kg.

Colour: black or grey with white belly.

Lifespan: 12-23 years.

Species mentioned in text:
Dall's porpoise (*Phocoenoides dalli*)
Finless porpoise(*Neophocoena phocoenoides*)
Gulf of California porpoise (*Phocoena sinus*)
Harbour porpoise (*P. phocoena*)

▲A Dall's porpoise ploughs through the sea. This species is the one most often attracted to boats.

6

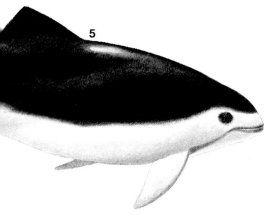

5

◄The six types of porpoise The Gulf of California porpoise (1), endangered by competition with fishermen. The little-known Burmeister's porpoise (*Phocoena spinipinnmis*) (2). The Finless porpoise (3) lacks a triangular back fin. The strikingly-colored Dall's porpoise (4). The black eye-rings give the Spectacled porpoise (*Phocoena dioptrica*) (5) its name. The Harbour porpoise (6) is the most frequently seen species, but its numbers are in decline.

Drifting out on the north Pacific Ocean, some fishermen on a small boat are startled by the sudden appearance of a Dall's porpoise, which swims boisterously around them. They glimpse at the blunt "smiling" face, and hear a loud snorting. Then, with a flick of its tail, the porpoise speeds away through the waves.

Porpoises are streamlined, fish-shaped mammals related to whales and dolphins. Unlike dolphins, they do not have a long snout, but, like all whales, they breathe through a blow-hole behind the blunt head. They swim at great speed, using the flat tail for power and flippers for steering.

Porpoises usually live alone, mainly in warmer coastal waters and estuaries. During the breeding season, though, porpoises form small groups called schools. After mating, the male and female pairs split up and each female rears her young (calves) without the help of the male. The common Harbour porpoise begins breeding at the age of 5 or 6 years. Dall's porpoise matures later, at around 7 years. A female Harbour porpoise suckles her calf for about 8 months, while Dall's porpoise may produce milk for up to 2 years. The calf may stay with its mother for a year or two after weaning, until the mother becomes pregnant again. Young Finless porpoises often hitch a ride on their mothers' backs by holding on to a series of small ridges.

Females and calves may form small groups of four to six, sometimes with additional young males. The young males may eventually form their own small, all-male groups.

USING SOUNDS
Porpoises communicate with each other using a wide range of sounds, including clicks, squeaks and grunts.

They hunt fish using keen eyesight and echolocation. They make high-pitched sounds which bounce back off squid or small shoals of fish and which the porpoises hear. An adult Harbour porpoise needs 3 to 5kg of food per day, while the larger Dall's porpoise eats 10 to 12kg daily. The Finless porpoise probably finds much of its food by digging about with its snout in the sandy or muddy bottoms of estuaries.

Harbour porpoises eat mostly herring, sardine and mackerel, while Gulf of California porpoises eat fish called grunts or croakers. The other species of porpoise probably live on mullet, anchovies and squid. All porpoises usually swallow their prey whole.

PORPOISE PROTECTION
Although porpoises are often seen in coastal waters and estuaries, little is actually known about their way of life. This makes their steady fall in numbers particularly worrying. We do not know how best to protect them. Porpoises, like whales, often "beach" themselves on shallow coastlines. It is possible then to examine the stomach contents of animals which die in this way to see precisely what they eat.

Fishermen also depend on the prey caught by porpoises, and many feel themselves to be in competition with these animals. Many porpoises become trapped in fishing nets because they cannot detect the fine mesh with their echolocation. They just follow the shoal of fish into the trap. They can be released unharmed if they are handled with care, but many are deliberately killed.

Some scientists would like to see all nets "labelled" with a device which makes a sound to warn off porpoises, but this would be very expensive. Chemical pollution of the seas also kills porpoises, and here the solution is simple and obvious. Only the will to do something about it seems lacking.

SPERM WHALES

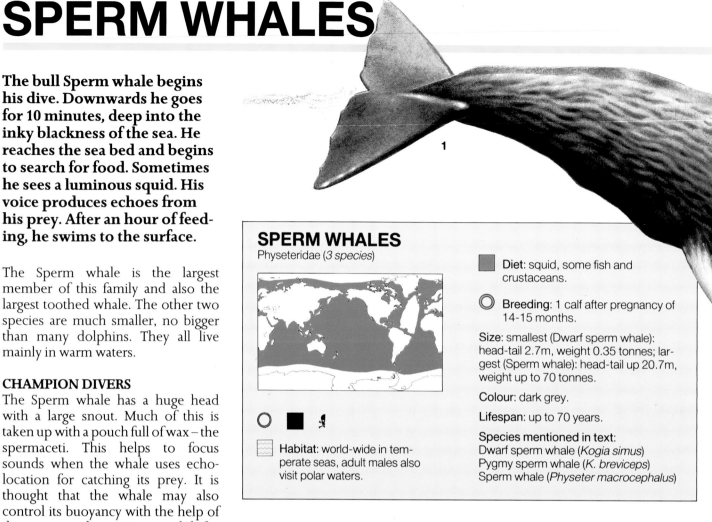

1

The bull Sperm whale begins his dive. Downwards he goes for 10 minutes, deep into the inky blackness of the sea. He reaches the sea bed and begins to search for food. Sometimes he sees a luminous squid. His voice produces echoes from his prey. After an hour of feeding, he swims to the surface.

The Sperm whale is the largest member of this family and also the largest toothed whale. The other two species are much smaller, no bigger than many dolphins. They all live mainly in warm waters.

CHAMPION DIVERS

The Sperm whale has a huge head with a large snout. Much of this is taken up with a pouch full of wax – the spermaceti. This helps to focus sounds when the whale uses echo-location for catching its prey. It is thought that the whale may also control its buoyancy with the help of the wax, cooling it to a solid for sinking, and warming it to liquid for rising.

Sperm whales make the deepest dives of all mammals. They have been picked up on sonar at 1,200m depth. They have been found to have eaten bottom-living sharks in an area where the sea bed was 3,200m down. Females can dive for an hour. The bulls, which are on average 4m longer and twice as heavy, can dive for longer.

HUNGRY FOR SQUID

Sperm whales eat many things, but much of their food is squid. Most of their prey are about 1m long, although some are smaller. One Sperm whale was found with 28,000 small squid inside it. Sperm whales sometimes also catch Giant squid, which are over 10m long, although then they may be scarred by bites or sucker marks.

SPERM WHALES
Physeteridae (*3 species*)

Diet: squid, some fish and crustaceans.

Breeding: 1 calf after pregnancy of 14-15 months.

Size: smallest (Dwarf sperm whale): head-tail 2.7m, weight 0.35 tonnes; largest (Sperm whale): head-tail up 20.7m, weight up to 70 tonnes.

Colour: dark grey.

Lifespan: up to 70 years.

Species mentioned in text:
Dwarf sperm whale (*Kogia simus*)
Pygmy sperm whale (*K. breviceps*)
Sperm whale (*Physeter macrocephalus*)

○ ■ ☠

Habitat: world-wide in temperate seas, adult males also visit polar waters.

▼A pod (small herd) of Sperm whales rise to the surface to breathe. The blow-holes are on the left of the heads.

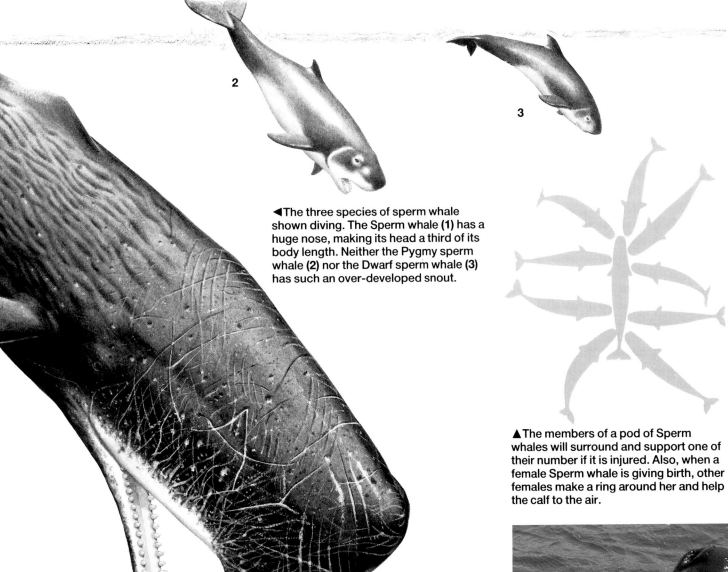

◄The three species of sperm whale shown diving. The Sperm whale **(1)** has a huge nose, making its head a third of its body length. Neither the Pygmy sperm whale **(2)** nor the Dwarf sperm whale **(3)** has such an over-developed snout.

▲The members of a pod of Sperm whales will surround and support one of their number if it is injured. Also, when a female Sperm whale is giving birth, other females make a ring around her and help the calf to the air.

TRAVELLING THE OCEANS

Sperm whales are commonest where ocean currents meet or water rises from the deep. Here there is plenty of food. The female Sperm whale lives in groups, and so do young males. Big bulls live alone except during the breeding season. Then they may fight for a harem.

Mating and birth take place near the equator. Afterwards the Sperm whale herds move to cooler water. The big males go much farther than others, as much as 8,000km to the cold waters near the North and South poles. Then all move back for the next breeding season.

About one-third of the weight of a Sperm whale is blubber that helps it keep warm in water. Blubber is a unique source of some lubricating oils, as is spermaceti. For these products, and for its meat to eat, the animal has been hunted relentlessly.

►A Sperm whale calf breaks the surface, showing the dark wrinkled skin of this species.

SEA LIONS AND FUR SEALS

Brown shadows weave in and out of the pounding surf, riding the waves and diving back underneath them. California sea lions are playing where the foamy sea meets the land. Beyond the breakers, more sea lions are exploring the sea bed for lobsters and octopus, trailing streams of bubbles behind them. Bull sea lions bark as they argue over ownership of their watery domains.

Sea lions and fur seals are sometimes called eared seals because, unlike the true seals, they have external ear-flaps. The males have thick manes of fur around their necks – the reason for the name sea lions. Fur seals have much thicker fur than sea lions.

SEA LIONS AND FUR SEALS Otariidae (14 species)

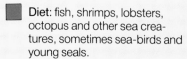

Habitat: offshore rocks and islands.

Diet: fish, shrimps, lobsters, octopus and other sea creatures, sometimes sea-birds and young seals.

○ Breeding: 1 young after pregnancy of 12 months.

Size: smallest (Galapagos fur seal): head-tail 120cm male, weight 27kg; largest (Steller sea lion) head-tail 287cm male, weight 1,000kg (males larger than females).

Colour: shades of brown, grey and tan, males often darker than females, juvenile coat often paler.

Lifespan: up to 25 years.

Species mentioned in text:
Antarctic fur seal (*Arctocephalus gazella*)
Australian sea lion (*Neophoca cinerea*)
California sea lion (*Zalophus californianus*)
Galapagos fur seal (*Arctocephalus galapagoensis*)
Northern fur seal (*Callorhinus ursinus*)
Steller sea lion (*Eumetopias jubatus*)

ACROBATS OF LAND AND SEA

Sea lions are popular performing animals because they are at home on land and in water. They can chase fish underwater or romp around the rocks, tossing fish in the air and catching them in their mouths.

To walk, a sea lion lifts its body off the ground, using its long foreflippers, and swings its hind flippers forwards under its body. When a sea lion wants to go faster over land, it gallops, putting both foreflippers down together, then the hind flippers, then the foreflippers again, and so on. A large fur seal can run faster than a fully grown man.

In the water, sea lions and fur seals are very agile swimmers, but they cannot hold their breath as well as true seals. They rarely dive for more

◀Bull sea lions paddle with their foreflippers as they patrol their water territories.

▼Species of sea lion and fur seal
Males are larger and usually darker than females. Often males have a large mane of thicker fur. Sea lions (**1-4**) have broader snouts than fur seals (**5, 6**), which have thicker coats. Male California sea lion (**1**). Female Steller sea lion (**2**).

Female South American sea lion (*Otaria avescens*) (**3**). Male New Zealand sea lion (*Phocarctos hookeri*) (**4**). Female South American fur seal (*Arctocephalus australis*) (**5**). Male Northern fur seal (**6**).

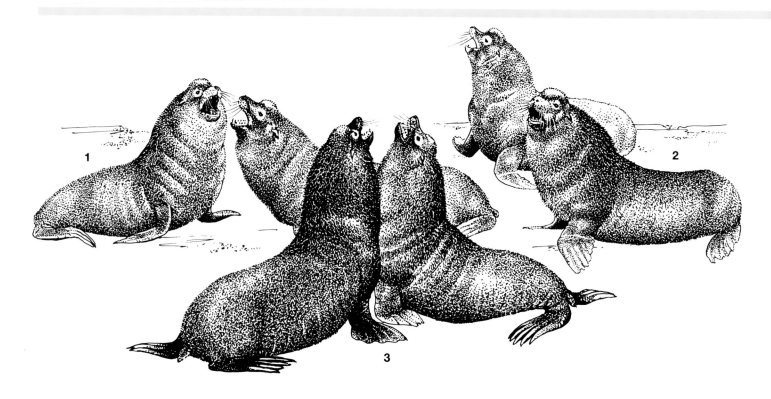

▲Male California sea lions use ritual threats to argue over territory boundaries on the beach. By using gestures instead of fighting, they have more energy left for mating. Head-shaking and barking as the males approach the boundary (1). Bulls look sideways at each other and make lunges (2). More head-shaking and barking (3). During the lunges, males try to keep their foreflippers away from each other's mouths. The thick skin on their chests softens the blows.

than 5 minutes. Unlike true seals, they use their foreflippers for swimming, flexing their hindquarters for extra power.

BATTLES ON THE BEACHES
In spring and early summer large numbers of sea lions and fur seals gather on their favourite breeding beaches to give birth and mate. The females are heavily pregnant when they arrive and soon give birth. About a week after giving birth, they are ready to mate.

Each male (bull) tries to mate with several females. To compete with other bulls for the females, he tries to defend a section of beach and the females in it. If every dispute led to a fight, the bulls would soon become too exhausted to mate. Instead, they make threatening displays and gestures, from which they can usually judge which animal is the stronger.

For a bull to defend his territory throughout the breeding season, he must stay on his patch. So most bulls do not feed at all during this time. Sometimes they may fast for 70 days. They can do this because they live off their fat (blubber). The biggest bulls have the most fat, so they are usually the most successful in holding a territory. The weather is usually warm at this time, and the seals get very hot on the beach. So the most prized territories are those nearest the water.

◄This Australian sea lion pup will soon shed his two-colour coat for a dark-brown adult one.

WELL-FED PUPS

Mother sea lions and fur seals stay with their pups for the first week of their lives, suckling them frequently. The pups need to be protected from the bulls, which can easily trample them during a fight.

As each pup grows bigger, its mother spends longer at sea feeding, returning from time to time to suckle her young. She finds her pup by calling to it and listening for its answering call. Many pups do not leave their mother until the next pup arrives 1 to 3 years later.

The Northern fur seal migrates hundreds of kilometres to different feeding areas in summer and winter. Its pups stop suckling when the migration starts. Female pups reach maturity at about 4 years old and male pups at 5 to 8 years of age.

PROTECTED POPULATIONS

Instead of having mainly long coarse hairs with just a few shorter ones, like the sea lions, the fur seals have a dense layer of woolly underfur. Glands among the hairs keep the animals coated with waterproof oil.

The thick fur causes problems in summer, when fur seals suffer badly from the heat. The only part of their bodies that can lose heat is the flippers. The animals often wave their flippers in the air to cool themselves.

But the fur seals' coats have caused them bigger problems than this. They have been much sought by hunters. By the end of the nineteenth century so many fur seals had been killed that some species were almost extinct. Laws were later passed to prevent the slaughter. Exploitation continues, but under strict international controls.

During the twentieth century fur seals have made a strong recovery. The Antarctic fur seal, whose population was reduced to probably fewer than 50 animals, now numbers around a million, and the population is increasing. Scientists think that this is partly because so many whales have been killed. The whales used to compete with the seals for one of their favourite foods, the tiny shrimp-like krill.

The Australian sea lion is the best example of the improved relationship between seals and people. In places, it is so accustomed to human visitors that tourists can mingle with the seals on the beach.

▼ An Antarctic fur seal with a plastic packing band cutting into its neck. Harmful waste kills many seals.

INDEX

PICTURE CREDITS